Philip's City

From Bethsaida to Julias

Fred Strickert

A Michael Glazier Book

LITURGICAL PRESS

Collegeville, Minnesota

www.litpress.org

A Michael Glazier Book published by Liturgical Press

Cover design by David Manahan, OSB. Photo courtesy of Mr. Rami Arav, chief archaeologist of the Bethsaida Excavations Project.

Portions of this work were previously published under the title *Bethsaida: Home of the Apostles* (Collegeville, MN: Liturgical Press, 1998).

Unless otherwise noted, all photographs are from the author or the Bethsaida Excavation Project.

1   2   3   4   5   6   7   8   9

Library of Congress Cataloging-in-Publication Data

Strickert, Frederick M.
　　Philip's city : from Bethsaida to Julias / Fred Strickert.
　　　　p.　　cm.
　　Includes bibliographical references and index.
　　ISBN 978-0-8146-5752-2 — ISBN 978-0-8146-8008-7 (e-book)
　　1. Bethsaida (Extinct city)—History.　2. Philip, the Tetrarch, d. 34.　3. Bible. N.T.—Criticism, interpretation, etc.　4. Bethsaida (Extinct city)—Antiquities. I. Title.

BR133.I753B488　　2010
　933—dc22
2010031063

Contents

Illustrations, Photographs, and Maps

Chapter 10

Chapter 11

Chapter 12

Chapter 13

Introduction

In 1995, I first decided to write an introduction to the city of Bethsaida, known best from the first century CE descriptions in the gospels as a place frequented by Jesus and his disciples. This monograph was published in 1998 by Liturgical Press under the title *Bethsaida: Home of the Apostles.* My intended audience included several groups:

- The many dig volunteers—like my own students—who needed a basic introduction to the site;
- Tourists and other visitors who would spend an hour or two walking around the ruins at the newly opened Israeli tourist site and who subsequently wanted to dig deeper from their armchairs;
- Pastors, educators, bible study leaders who were looking for a resource that might lay a foundation for their background study of the gospels;
- And scholars who wanted a synthesis of the growing body of reports and articles about Bethsaida.

The time seemed right. It had been seven years since I and a handful of students had first met Israeli archaeologist Rami Arav in May 1988 to begin turning the soil of et-Tell in quest of what some considered a lost city.[1]

By 1995 significant progress had been made at the site uncovering structures like the Iron Age Bit Hilani and Hellenistic courtyard houses that the tourist authority had dubbed the "Fisherman's House" and the "Winemaker's House." Under the administrative direction of Richard Freund a consortium of colleges and universities had bonded together to form the Bethsaida

---

1. The first excavations had actually begun with test probes in 1987 and a one-week excavation by students of Waterloo University in Canada in January 1988.

Et-Tell in 1988

Excavations Project, based at the University of Nebraska at Omaha. The number of dig volunteers was increasing each season and progress at et-Tell was phenomenal. The project also had found a home at Kibbutz Ginnosar where volunteers felt welcome and where the basement of its Yigal Alon Museum provided a storeroom and laboratory for artifacts.

Associated scholars had begun the process of reflection, interpretation, and publication in journals and presentations at national and international conferences. The first volume of official reports and interpretive articles came out in 1995 published by Truman State University Press in Kirksville, Missouri. In 1995 the Israeli Tourist Authority had opened the site for an influx of visitors, after providing a much needed infrastructure including access road, marked paths around the Tell, interpretive signs, and bathrooms with running water—all which benefitted the excavators as much as it did the tourists. So the time was right in 1995 to write a monograph on Bethsaida.

I quickly learned that writing such a summative introduction was a risky endeavor. Before the ink was dry the book was already out of date. Archaeology tends to do that, especially when new finds continue to be uncovered and when scholars continue in the research process. A case in point: no less than six months after I mailed off the completed manuscript to the publisher, several of my students in May 1996 had the audacity to make finds that would turn the dig in totally new directions. First, Michael Stadtmueller discovered a bronze incense shovel that led Rami Arav and others to dig further in nearby squares opened years earlier and to see structures quite differently—to expose what he believes is a first-century temple of the imperial cult.[2] A more dramatic shift came that same month when Leigh Yeakey and Kristen Oliver began a probe in Area A adjacent to three large stones that just peaked over the surface—we had been trampling these stones repeatedly since our discard pile was nearby on the side of the Tell—to find a wall continuing four courses deep. I shouldn't have been surprised when the email arrived at the end of July from Rami, "We found the city gate!" Those stones were the top of the seven-foot tall interior wall of chamber four of what would soon be revealed as one of the best preserved city gates in the southern Levant. For the next decade, the primary focus at et-Tell would be to uncover the massive gateway complex. So the initial attention on Bethsaida as a New Testament city was somewhat eclipsed by the Iron Age site that evoked images of King David himself and then the Assyrian Tiglath Pileser 3. In the meantime, the concentrated effort on the gateway area yielded abundant data on the later city.

Discovery of Incense Shovel in 1996

2. The find of the incense shovel also provided a bit of a detour to the Cave of Letters where Yigal Yadin had discovered a similar shovel. Yet it was there that we discovered new tools for archaeology such as ground penetrating radar which would assist us at et-Tell and also in demonstrating that nearby el-Araj was a later Byzantine site.

Archaeology also has a humbling effect, especially when one is proven wrong. For example, I was clearly wrong about my interpretation dealing with the destruction of Bethsaida. In those early days of excavation, one of our major questions dealt with the demise of the city since Roman and Hellenistic finds appeared near the surface in residential areas and among them only a handful of 2ⁿᵈ-3ʳᵈ century CE coins. When four early Trajan coins (ruled 96-117 CE) appeared during the 1994 season, things fell in place nicely with our geological reports to project the well-documented earthquake of 115 CE for the city's end. Yet subsequent seasons have yielded no less than fifty coins from the second and third centuries CE—ironically these coins came from Area A at the southern end of the Tell where exploration of the gate complex had extended back into the city—not far from where we began two decades earlier. It became clear that Bethsaida was still occupied following the 115 CE earthquake. So yes, there are times when theories must be refined, revised, and discarded.

One of the biggest compliments in publication is to have one's work critiqued. So I must offer a word of appreciation to those who have taken the time to criticize both my own work and that related to the Bethsaida Excavations Project in general. In some cases, that means realizing error. More often it means that our arguments have not been as clear as they should be and that they must be refined and restated. Sometimes it means that we will all have to wait to see what further excavations turn up. Disagreement is not all bad, and it sometimes occurs also among those of us who work together year after year in the Bethsaida excavations. That's why the University of Nebraska at Omaha holds the Batchelder Archaeology Conference each fall so that members of the project can test out theories on each other. This is also why our head archaeologist and other members of the team regularly present papers at regional, national, and international conferences.

The Bethsaida Excavation Project has taken the approach of timely and ample publication. This contrasts with some digs where publication is restricted to the director or a chosen few and where constant delays result in a good deal of knowledge going with him or her to the grave. Already four volumes of 1,450 pages, written by 34 scholars have been published by Truman State University Press in Kirksville, Missouri under the title *Bethsaida: A City by the North Shore of the Sea of Galilee.* Numerous articles have appeared in journals all over the world. Since the publication of my earlier book, *Bethsaida: Home of the Apostles* (Collegeville, MN: Liturgical Press, 1998), three monographs have been published on particular aspects of the dig:

- Monika Bernett and Othmar Keel, *Mond, Stier, und Kult am Stadttor:Die stele von Betsaida (et-Tell),* Orbis Biblicus et Orientalis 161 (Freiburg, Switzerland: Universitätsverlag, 1998).
- Ilona Skupínska-Løvset, *The Temple Area of Bethsaida. Polish Excavations on et-Tell in the Years 1998-2000* (Lodz, Poland: Lodz University Press, 2006).
- Carl Savage, *Bethsaida: A Study of the First Century CE in the Galilee* (Lanham, MD: Lexington Books, 2010).

In addition *four important dissertations have* appeared:

- Toni Gayle Fisher, *A Zooarchaeological Analysis of Change in Animal Utilization at Bethsaida from Iron Age II through the Early Roman Period.* Ph.D. Dissertation (Knoxville: University of Tennessee, 2005).
- Sandra Fortner, *Der Keramik und Kleinfunde von Bethsaida-Iulias am See Genezareth, Israel,* (München: Ludwig-Maximilians-Universität, 2008).
- Carl Savage, *Et-Tell/Bethsaida: A Study of the First Century CE in the Galilee,* Ph.D. Dissertation (Madison, New Jersey: Drew University, 2007).
- Patrick Scott Geyer, *Bethsaida/Julia and the Politics, Religion and Economics of Roman Syro-Palestine (BCE-33/34 CE),* Master's Thesis (Tempe, Arizona: Arizona State University, 1998).

Geologists, botanists, zoologists, anthropologists, and specialists in various aspects of archaeology have joined together with historians and biblical scholars to provide a multidisciplinary approach to understanding this ancient city. The works of these many scholars continue to be a primary resource for those who wish to understand fully and explore more deeply. The current book is meant to expand on my earlier work and to be a summation to make this work accessible to a wider audience.

Consortium members now include:

The University of Nebraska at Omaha
The University of Hartford
The University of Munich
Michigan State University
Truman State University
Rocky Mountain College

Creighton University
Wartburg College
College of Idaho
West Virginia State University
St. Francis Theological College of Brisbane, Australia

I remain indebted to Rami Arav and Richard Freund for their leadership, to the many scholars and colleagues who have taught me much, and to the thousands of volunteers who year after year find themselves covered in dirt, in a hot and filthy environment with minimal sleep, while digging into their own pocketbooks to share in the joy of discovery.

March 29, 2010
Waverly, Iowa

Chapter 1

Sources

Bethsaida is one of the more prominent towns in the gospels. Only Jerusalem, Capernaum, Nazareth, and Bethany are mentioned more often.[1] However, the importance of this city in the New Testament era is attested by its frequent mention among other first century authors, both Christian and secular. It occurs both in the local Hebrew designation "Bethsaida" and in the Roman name "Julias" given by the first century ruler Philip, son of Herod. Thus the subtitle of this book: *From Bethsaida to Julias*.

Josephus and Roman literary sources

Julias can appropriately be called Philip's city, because he is the one who named it. Only a few years following the writing of the first Gospel Mark, Josephus wrote his first work, *The Jewish War* (75 CE), in which he mentioned several cities founded by the tetrarchs Herod Antipas in Galilee and Perea and Philip in the territory northeast of the Sea of Galilee.

> On the death of Augustus, who had directed the state for fifty-seven years, six months, and two days, the empire of the Romans passed to Tiberius, son of Julia. On his accession, Herod Antipas and Philip continued to hold their tetrarchies and respectively founded cities: Philip built Caesarea, near the sources of the Jordan in the district of Paneas, and Julias in lower Gaulanitis; Herod built Tiberias in Galilee and a city which also took the name Julia in Peraea (Josephus, *War* 2.168).[2]

1. Jerusalem occurs 65 times, Capernaum 16 times, Nazareth and Bethany 12 times. The name Bethsaida occurs eight times in most textual traditions as well as in variant readings for John 5:2.

2. Josephus texts are taken from the ten volumes in the Loeb classical series translated by H. St. J. Thackeray, Ralph Marcus, Allen Wikgren, and L. H. Feldman. Josephus, *The*

1

With Philip giving his own name to his capital Caesarea-Philippi in the northern part of his territory, Julias to the south seems to have been Philip's second city.

Several decades later in *Jewish Antiquities,* Josephus provides a parallel report with additional details:

> Philip too made improvements at Paneas, the city near the sources of the Jordan, and called it Caesarea. He also raised the village Bethsaida on the Lake Gennesaritis to the status of city by adding residents and strengthening the fortifications. He named it after Julia, the emperor's daughter (Josephus, *Ant.* 18.28).

This is the only text that clearly connects the city Julias with the village of the gospels named Bethsaida. The gospels never use the name Julias; Josephus elsewhere never uses the name Bethsaida. This is more than a matter of a name change. Josephus is clear that the addition of new residents and the improvement in fortifications led to an elevation in status from village to city.

There is an irony in that Philip's capital Caesarea is only mentioned in one gospel episode: the confession of Peter (Mark 8:27; Matt 16:13),[3] while numerous events occur in Bethsaida. However, Josephus characterizes Philip's reputation as the most moderate of all the Herodian rulers, traveling exclusively and consistently throughout his own territory:

> In his conduct of the government he showed a moderate and easy-going disposition. Indeed, he spent all his time in the territory subject to him. When he went on circuit he had only a few select companions. The throne on which he sat when he gave judgement accompanied him wherever he went. And so, whenever anyone appealed to him for redress along the route, at once without a moment's delay the throne was set up wherever it might be. He took his seat and gave the case a hearing. He fixed penalties for those who were convicted and released those who had been unjustly accused (Josephus, *Ant.* 18:107).

Not confined to his first city, Caesarea Philippi, Philip's attention later turned to Bethsaida-Julias, where he seems to have spent the last years of his life. It is significant that the passage above is sandwiched between two statements about Philip's death in 34 CE:

Life, Against Apion, Jewish Antiquities, Jewish War, Loeb Classical Series (Cambridge, MA: Harvard University Press, 1926-65).

3. The gospels do not mention that Jesus even entered the city of Caesarea Philippi. Mark mentions the villages of Caesarea Philippi and Matthew mentions travel in the district of Caesarea Philippi. Luke 9:18 does not mention a specific location.

Now it was at this time that Philip, Herod's brother, died in the twentieth year of Tiberius' reign and after thirty-seven years of his own rule over Trachonitis and Gaulanitis, as well as over the tribe called the Bataneans . . . He died in Julias. His body was carried to the tomb that he himself had erected before he died and there was a costly funeral (Josephus, *Ant.* 18:106, 108).

After a short interim when Philip's territory fell under the authority of Syria, it passed to Agrippa 1. In noting the extent of this region, Josephus mentions the location of the city Julias at the southern extremity:

That kingdom beginning at Mount Libanus and the sources of the Jordan, extends in breadth to the Lake of Tiberias, and in length from a village called Arpha to Julias; it contains a mixed population of Jews and Syrians (Josephus, *War* 3.57).

Similarly in several other passages, the location of Julias on the northeast side of the Sea of Galilee near the point where the northern Jordan River entered the sea serves as a geographical reference point.

After issuing from this grotto at Paneas, the Jordan River, whose course is now visible, intersects the marshes and lagoons of Lake Semechonitis, then traverses another 120 furlongs, and below the town of Julias enters the Lake of Gennesar (Josephus, *War* 3.515).

Opposite to it and flanking the Jordan lies a second range, which beginning at Julias in the north, stretches . . . to Petra in Arabia (Josephus, *War* 4.454).

The fact that Julias can be mentioned in passing as a landmark confirms its stature in the first century. Likewise, such literary references add confidence to the modern identification of the ancient site.

Josephus' knowledge of this city is especially significant because it is based on his own experience in this region. In fact, he notes that during his days as commander of the Galilean forces in the Jewish revolt of 67 CE, he fought a battle outside the city to the west:

After this time reinforcements arrived from the king, both horse and foot, under the command of Sulla, the captain of his bodyguard. He pitched his camp at a distance of five furlongs from Julias, and put out pickets on the roads leading to the fortress of Gamla to prevent the inhabitants of Julias from obtaining supplies from Galilee. On receiving intelligence of this, I dispatched a force of 2,000 men under the command of Jeremiah, who entrenched themselves a furlong away from Julias close to the River Jordan, but took no action beyond skirmishing until I joined them with supports, 3,000 strong. The next day, after laying an ambuscade in a ravine not far from their earthworks, I offered battle to the royal troops, directing my division to retire until they had lured the enemy forward; as actually happened. Sulla, supposing that our men were really fleeing, advanced and was on the point of following in pursuit, when the others emerging from their ambush, took him in the rear and threw his whole force into the utmost disorder. Instantly wheeling the main body about, I charged and routed the royalists; and my success on that day would have been complete, had I not been thwarted by some evil genius. The horse on which I went into action stumbled on a marshy spot and brought me with him to the ground. Having fractured some bones in the wrist, I was carried to a village called Cepharnocus. My men, hearing of this, and fearing that a worse fate had befallen me, desisted from further pursuit and returned in deepest anxiety on my account . . . Sulla and his troops, learning of my accident again took heart. . . they did not follow up their success; for on hearing that reinforcements shipped at Tarichaeae had reached Julias, they retired in alarm (Josephus, *Life* 398-406).

This occasion was fixed in his memory because he was injured when his horse stumbled, at which point the tide turned in favor of Agrippa's troops. His description of this battle includes a number of details about geography which are critical for identifying the presently excavated et-Tell with the city described in literature as Bethsaida-Julias.

Following the Jewish revolt of 66-70 CE, few specifics are mentioned concerning the city. In geographic reports of this region, Pliny the Elder in 77 CE notes simply the prominence of this city:

There are four lovely cities on the Sea of Galilee: Julias and Hippos in the east and Tarichaeae and Tiberias in the west (Pliny, *Natural History* 5.15.71).

The second-century geographer Claudius Ptolemy likewise includes a short report:

The four main cities of Galilee are Sepphoris, Capernaum, Tiberias, and Julias (Ptolemy, *Geographia* 5.16.4).

Although large numbers of Jews migrated to Galilee and Golan during the next centuries, Bethsaida-Julias is not mentioned by later secular writers.

Early Christian sources

Although the name Julias is absent from early Christian literature, the name Bethsaida occurs eight times in the gospels. It is significant that it occurs in various strata of the gospels from the early sayings source Q to the late Gospel according to John. The earliest reference to the city Bethsaida is the Q saying of Jesus recorded in both Matthew 11:20-24 and Luke 10:13-15:

> Then he began to reproach the cities in which most of his deeds of power had been done, because they did not repent. "Woe to you, Chorazin! Woe to you, Bethsaida! For if the deeds of power done in you had been done in Tyre and Sidon, they would have repented long ago in sackcloth and ashes. But I tell you, on the day of judgment it will be more tolerable for Tyre and Sidon than for you. And you, Capernaum,
> > will you be exalted to heaven?
> > No, you will be brought down to Hades.
> For if the deeds of power done in you had been done in Sodom, it would have remained until this day. But I tell you that on the day of judgment it will be more tolerable for the land of Sodom than for you" (Matt 11:20-24).

> "Woe to you, Chorazin! Woe to you Bethsaida! For if the deeds of power done in you had been done in Tyre and Sidon, they would have repented long ago, sitting in sackcloth and ashes. But at the judgment it will be more tolerable for Tyre and Sidon than for you. And for you, Capernaum,
> > will you be exalted to heaven?
> > No, you will be brought down to Hades" (Luke 10:13-15).

Although this saying of woe places Bethsaida in a negative light, it points to the centrality of the town in the ministry of Jesus—along with Capernaum and Chorazin—since most of his miracles were done there. As the only Galilean cities mentioned in Q, this points to the area around the north shore of the Sea of Galilee, known as "the evangelical triangle," as the center of Jesus' ministry.

The two references in Mark likewise point to miracle activity. In one of the few episodes included only in Mark, Jesus heals a blind man outside Bethsaida:

> They came to Bethsaida. Some people brought a blind man to him and begged him to touch him. He took the blind man by the hand and led him out of the village; and when he had put saliva on his eyes and laid his hands on him, he asked him, "Can you see anything?" And the man looked up and said, "I can see people, but they look like trees, walking." Then Jesus laid his hands on his eyes again; and he looked intently and his sight was restored, and he saw everything clearly. Then he sent him away to his home, saying, "Do not even go into the village" (Mark 8:22-26).

In Mark 6:45, the name Bethsaida is cited in the transitional verse between the miracles of the feeding of the 5,000 and the walking on the water:

> Immediately he made his disciples get into the boat and go on ahead to the other side, to Bethsaida, while he dismissed the crowd (Mark 6:45).

Luke, who omits the episode of the walking on water, does not include this reference to Bethsaida at the end of the feeding story. Instead Bethsaida is introduced at the beginning of the feeding:

> On their return the apostles told Jesus all that they had done. He took them with him and withdrew privately to a city called Bethsaida. When the crowds found out about it, they followed him; and he welcomed them, and spoke to them about the kingdom of God, and healed those who needed to be cured (Luke 9:10-11).

This creates something of a problem since the two accounts portray Jesus going in opposite directions. Matthew does not mention Bethsaida in connection with the feeding episode.

The Gospel according to John differs from the synoptic tradition in that citations to Bethsaida are not directly related to Jesus' miracle activity. Rather Bethsaida is mentioned as the home of a number of the apostles. In the call narrative of the disciples in John 1:43-44, Philip is introduced as a disciple from the city of Bethsaida, the home of Andrew and Peter:

> The next day Jesus decided to go to Galilee. He found Philip and said to him, "Follow me." Now Philip was from Bethsaida, the city of Andrew and Peter (John 1:43-44).

Likewise, in John 12:21, the importance of this location is emphasized as the reader is reminded once again that Philip originated from Bethsaida:

> Now among those who went up to worship at the festival were some Greeks. They came to Philip, who was from Bethsaida in Galilee, and said to him, "Sir, we wish to see Jesus." Philip went and told Andrew; then Andrew and Philip went and told Jesus (John 12:20-23).

The connection of Bethsaida to the miracle tradition is only indirect since both Philip and Andrew are main characters in the feeding miracle of chapter 6. A later scribe has also linked this site with the miracle story of the healing of the lame man in chapter 5 by changing the place name Bethzatha to Bethsaida:

> Now in Jerusalem by the Sheep Gate there is a pool, called in Hebrew Bethsaida, having five porches (John 5:2 – variant reading).

The focus in the Book of Acts on the city of Jerusalem as the center of post-Easter activity of the disciples results in the absence of attention to the Galilean church and thus the mention of Bethsaida—as also other cities of the gospels such as Capernaum, Chorazin, and Nazareth—is missing. The name never occurs in the rest of the New Testament.

In second century Christian literature, however, interest in Bethsaida continues. In the Jewish-Christian Gospel of the Nazareans, the woe saying from Q is expanded to note that the miracles worked by Jesus in that city were 53 in number. On the other hand, 2 Esdras 1:11—written shortly after the Bar Kokhba revolt in 132-5 CE—mentions the fulfillment of that woe saying, citing the destruction of Bethsaida as one more in a series of mighty works of God:

> Did I not destroy the city of Bethsaida because of you, and to the south burn two cities, Tyre and Sidon? (2 Esdras 1:11, Spanish Recension).

However, even this important reference to the fate of the city is not without complication since one family of manuscripts does not include reference to this New Testament city.

In later centuries, Bethsaida continues to be mentioned by interpreters of the gospel traditions and by pilgrims who visited the site. Among the more significant references is the report of the sixth-century visitor Theodosius:

> From Seven Springs [Tabgha] it is two miles to Capernaum. From Capernaum it is six miles to Bethsaida, where the Apostles Peter, Andrew, Philip, and the sons of Zebedee were born. From Bethsaida it is fifty miles to Panias, that is the place where the Jordan rises from the two places Ior and Dan.[4]

Two centuries later Willibald wrote:

> From there [Capernaum], they went to Bethsaida, the city of Peter and Andrew; there is now a church there in the place where originally their house stood.[5]

In some cases one must allow for the possible preservation of authentic independent traditions, yet the tendency to speculative elaboration is often evident.

---

4. John Wilkinson, *Jerusalem Pilgrims Before the Crusades* (Westminster: Aris and Phillips, Ltd., 1977), 63. P. Donatus Baldi, *Enchirdion Locum Sanctorum* (Jerusalem, 1982), Section 381, 266.

5. Wilkinson, *Jerusalem Pilgrims Before the Crusades*, 128.

Rabbinic literature

The names Bethsaida and Julias do not occur in rabbinic literature. However, there are a number of references to a place called Tzaidan, which have resulted in considerable debate. There are a number of issues to be dealt with. First of all, one is faced with the relatively late date of these sources even though they refer to figures from as early as the first century. Second, one is faced with a different name for this site, Tzaidan. Just as Christian sources preferred Bethsaida, and secular sources used Julias, it may be that rabbinic sources provide simply a variation in name. Third, there is confusion with the name Sidon on the Phoenician coast. Many older studies have assumed that location for the majority of texts. In some cases, one can judge from context which city is more likely, but, more often than not, that remains a difficult task.[6]

A number of significant readings are included which identify names of prominent rabbis. Among the earliest is one referring to Rabbi Yehudah ben Batayrah, a contemporary of Akiba at the very beginning of the second century:

> And it happened Rabbi Eleazar ben Shamoa and Rabbi Yohanan HaSandlar were going to Netzivim to study Torah with Rabbi Yehudah Ben Batayrah. They arrived in Tzaidan and remembered the Land of Israel. Their eyes opened and filled with tears and they ripped their clothes . . . They returned to their original place and said that living in the Land of Israel outweighs all the commandments in the Torah (Sifrei Devarim, Reeh 80:4.80).

The location of Bethsaida just to the east of the upper Jordan River is a fitting setting for this episode.

One of the names most frequently connected with Tzaidan is the important second century Rabbi Simeon ben Gamaliel 2. Among the more significant passages relating his name is one that deals with fish:

> Rabbi Simeon ben Gamaliel said, "It happened that I went to Tzaidan, and they put before me more than three hundred kinds of fish in a single dish" (PT Sheqalim 6.2,50c).

---

6. These issues are thoroughly discussed by Richard Freund, "The Search for Bethsaida in Rabbinic Literature," *Bethsaida: A City on the North Shore of the Sea of Galilee,* eds. Rami Arav and Freund (Kirksville, MO: Thomas Jefferson University Press, 1995), 267-311. See also Dan Urman, "Jews in the Golan," *Ancient Synagogues: Historical Analysis and Archaeological Discovery,* eds. Urman and Paul V. M. Flesher (Leiden: E.J. Brill, 1995), 2:378-385.

Others describe legal concerns:

> If a man says this is your Get on condition that you give me two hundred
> Zuzim, she is divorced thereby and she has to give . . . Rabbi Simeon ben
> Gamaliel said: "It happened in Tzaidan that a man said to his wife, 'This is
> your Get on condition that you give me my robe,' and his robe was lost, and the
> Sages said that she should give him its value in money" (Mishnah Gittin 7:5).

> Rabbah bar Hanah said in the name of Rabbi Yohanan: "Wherever Rabbi
> Simeon be Gamaliel gives a ruling in our Mishnah, the Halachah follows
> him, save in the matters of Surety, and Tzaidan, and of a later proof" (BT
> Gittin 75a).

Several passages refer to Rabbi Simeon ben Yohai, a student of Akiba
and contemporary of Simeon ben Gamaliel:

> What is an Asherah? Any tree under which is located an idol. Rabbi Simeon
> says: "Any that people worship." It happened in Tzaidan, there was a tree
> that people worshipped, and they found a pile of stones underneath it. Rabbi
> Simeon said to them, "Investigate the type of pile of stones." They did inves-
> tigate it and found an image in it. He said to them, "Since they are worship-
> ping the image, let us permit them to make use of the tree" (Mishnah Avodah
> Zarah 3:7).

A later commentary provides yet a further incident from Tzaidan:

> It happened that there was a non-Jew in Tzaidan who used to write scrolls of
> the Law and the incident came before the Sages and they said it was permitted
> to buy from him (Tosefta Avodah Zarah 3:7).

Both incidents seem to point to settings with mixed population appropriate
for Bethsaida. Another passage refers to a couple unable to have children
and ends with a miraculous answer to prayer:

> If one has married a woman and lived with her for ten years and not produced
> offspring, he has not got the right to stop trying. Said Rabbi Idi, "It happened
> in Tzaidan that one who married a woman and stayed with her ten years and
> they did not produce offspring. They came before Rabbi Simeon ben Yohai
> and wanted to be parted from one another. He said to them, 'By your lives!
> Just as you were joined to one another with eating and drinking, so you will
> be separated from one another only with eating and drinking.' They followed
> his counsel and made a festival and made a great banquet and drank too much.
> When his mind was at ease, he said to her, 'My daughter, see anything good
> that I have in the house! Take it and go to your father's house.' What did she

do? After he fell asleep, she made gestures to her servants and serving women and said to them, 'Take him in the bed and pick him up and bring him to my father's house.' Around midnight he woke up from his sleep. When the wine wore off, he said to her, 'My daughter, where am I now?' She said to him, 'In my father's house.' He said to her, 'What am I doing in your father's house? But I have nothing in the world as good as you!' They went to Rabbi Simeon ben Yohai and he stood and prayed for them and they were answered (and given offspring)" (Song of Songs Rabbah 1. 4:89).

This passage and others above are characterized by the formula "It happened in Tzaidan." In Hebrew this construction includes the single letter ב to denote the preposition, thus resulting in the reading "BeTzaidan," extremely similar in pronunciation to Bethsaida.

A final passage mentions a figure who spent most of his life in the Golan region, Rabbi Judah ha-Nasi, the son of Simeon ben Gamaliel 2:

> Rabbi Hanina said: "An incident in one wagon of the house of Rabbi that went more than four miles. The incident was brought before the sages and they permitted the use of that wine. They said, 'The incident took place on the highway of Tzaidan and it was completely of Israel'" (PT Avodah Zarah 5:5. 44d).

With good reason, some argue that the city of the apostles became the city of prominent rabbis. It may be that a conclusion will be possible only through further archaeological research.

Material sources

Interest in the material remains of Bethsaida began as early as 1838 CE when the American explorer Edward Robinson[7] first visited the site of et-Tell, located 500 meters east of the Jordan River and 2.5 to 3.0 kilometers north of the Sea of Galilee. Although Robinson saw no problem in designating this site as the biblical city, a number of later explorers and surveyors, such as Gottlieb Schumacher[8] and Dan Urman,[9] preferred a location on the modern shore line at either el-Araj or el-Mesadiye. Renewed interest

---

7. Edward Robinson, *Biblical Researches in Palestine and Adjacent Regions: A Journal of Travels in the Years 1838 & 1852* (2nd ed,; 3 vols.; London: Murray, 1856).

8. Gottlieb Schumacher, *The Jaulan* (London: R. Bentley, 1888).

9. Dan Urman, *The Golan: A Profile of a Region during the Roman and Byzantine Periods* (BAR International Series 269; Oxford: B.A.R., 1985).

in et-Tell came about primarily through the careful analysis of Benedictine Father Bargil Pixner[10] in the 1980s.

Aerial Photo of et-Tell from the west

Because of geographic and political complexities, scientific stratified archaeological excavation began at et-Tell only in 1987. Nearly a quarter of a century of research has now been completed under the direction of Dr. Rami Arav. Their findings are now being published in a series of volumes by Truman State University Press (formerly Thomas Jefferson University Press) under the title *Bethsaida: A City by the North Shore of the Sea of Galilee.*[11]

Archaeology today involves a number of different disciplines to recover information about ancient sites like Bethsaida. Geological study is extremely important to this particular location because it is located on the major Jordan

10. Bargil Pixner, "Searching for the New Testament Site of Bethsaida," *BA* 48 (Dec. 1985), 207-216.

11. Rami Arav and Richard Freund, eds., *Bethsaida: A City by the North Shore of the Sea of Galilee, volume 1* (Kirksville, MO: Thomas Jefferson University Press, 1995); Rami Arav and Richard Freund, eds., *Bethsaida: A City by the North Shore of the Sea of Galilee, volume 2* (Kirksville, MO: Truman State University Press, 1999); Rami Arav and Richard Freund, eds., *Bethsaida: A City by the North Shore of the Sea of Galilee, volume 3* (Kirksville, MO: Truman State University Press, 2003); and Rami Arav and Richard Freund, eds., *Bethsaida: A City by the North Shore of the Sea of Galilee, volume 4* (Kirksville, MO: Truman State University Press, 2009).

River rift where there is both gradual shifting of continental plates and where dramatic earthquake activity has brought about changes throughout history. This is of special significance since the present geography of the site can be misleading with the remains of the fishing village located 2.5 to 3.0 kilometers from the coastline of the sea.

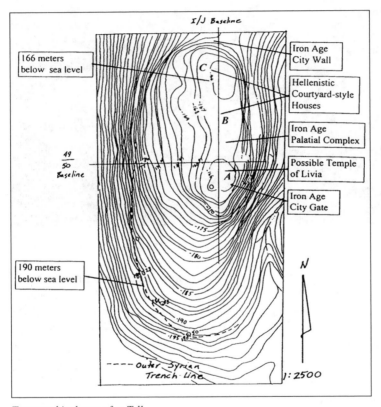

Topographical map of et-Tell

Archaeological excavation reveals much about the first-century city including information about city planning, the construction of houses, daily labor, lifestyle, diet, and trading patterns. Artifacts such as pottery shards, coins, implements of work and war, ornaments of dress, building stones, bones, and a few figurines provide a wealth of information about these inhabitants when analyzed carefully.

Unfortunately, there have been no significant inscriptions uncovered from this first-century site. Coin finds are always helpful sources of information concerning contact with other regions. This is even more significant during the first four decades of the first century when the ruler of this particular area, Philip, minted his own coins.

While literary and archaeological sources are very different in nature and often lead to variant conclusions—even, at times, contradictions—it is crucial that our search for understanding ancient Bethsaida be carried out with a book in one hand and a trowel in the other.

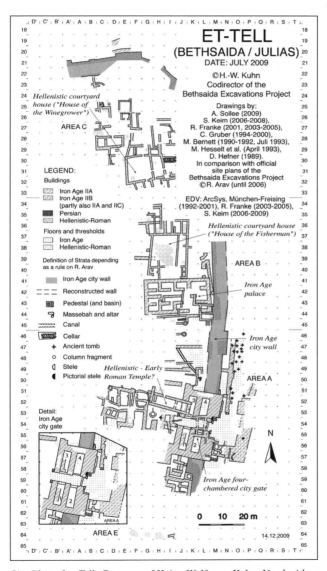

Site Plan of et-Tell. Courtesy of Heinz-Wolfgang Kuhn. Used with permission.

Chapter 2

The Iron Age City of Tzer

The name Bethsaida occurs for the first time in first-century-CE literary sources; yet its roots extend much deeper in the soil of et-Tell. Josephus makes this clear when he credits Philip, son of Herod, as the founder of the city. Previously Bethsaida had been simply a village that Philip expanded through additional settlers and fortifications (Josephus, *Ant.* 18:2.1.28). The usual connotations associated with that word village had to be placed aside almost from the moment that the trowel began to turn the soil. Remains from earlier occupations of the Tell presented evidence of an impressive city with a rich and long history.

Remnants in an Old Testament name

As with many Hebrew place names, the commonly used *Beth* means "house" or "dwelling place," while the syllables that follow provide a distinguishing characteristic of that location. So Bethsaida is the "house of the fisherman" or "house of the hunter." The Anglicized *Saida* perhaps would be written better as *Tzaida.* In the list of cities within the territory of Naphtali in Joshua 19:35, two names are significant: *Ziddim* as a plural form might be used to introduce four fishing towns around the Sea of Kinneret (Galilee) which are named in a clockwise direction around the lake. The leading name *Tzer* fits both in terms of location at the north of the lake and possible description as a fisherman's city. Because of similarity in the formation of letters *resh* and *dalet,* it is not difficult to see how Tzer in the Biblical manuscripts was originally Tzed—a name linguistically similar to Bethsaida.[1]

---

1. Rami Arav, "Bethsaida, Tzer, and the Fortified Cities of Naphtali," in *Bethsaida* (1995), 193-202.

Bronze-Age settlement

The site of et-Tell offered two basic characteristics looked for in building ancient settlements. It was located on a hill—presently situated about forty meters above the surrounding plain—and it had two fresh water springs, one at the southwest base of the hill and another on the eastern side. In addition, it was accessible to the Lake Kinneret (Sea of Galilee) with its resources for fishing and travel by boat. The Jordan River was situated about five hundred meters to the west. An abundance of basalt stone for building is strewn throughout the area from earlier volcanic activity. The Tell itself was relatively large comprising an area of nearly twenty acres with an acropolis sloping toward the plain in the south.

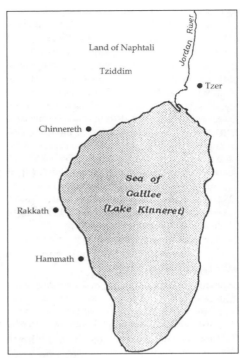

Sea of Kinneret with fishing towns

The first settlement at Bethsaida likely comes from the early bronze age (3050-2700 BCE) when the Golan experienced an increase in population. However, the evidence from et-Tell is less than clear. Numerous Bronze I and Bronze II pottery shards have been found, yet always in a context mixed with Iron-age pottery. It would seem that any significant early structures were destroyed by later occupations.

The Geshurite capital

The second settlement occurs during Iron Age 2 (1,000-586 CE) or roughly the time of the Israelite monarchy in the Old Testament. Rami Arav has proposed that at its height this city—including the largest and best preserved gate of the region—served as capital of the Geshurite kingdom. The Geshurite history is known from limited literary sources as early as the Amarna Letters in 1400 BCE.[2] From their names the Geshurites may have been a non-Semitic people (possibly related to the Hurrians of northern Mesopotamia) who spoke

---

2. Benjamin Mazar suggests that the name Gari was a scribal mistake for Gashuri. Richard Hess, "'Geshurite' Onomastica of the Bronze and Iron Age," in *Bethsaida* (2004), 49-62.

a form of Aramaic and who at that time made up a kingdom comparable to the size of the Kingdom of Judah on the east side of the Sea of Galilee and upper Jordan River from the Yarmuk River north to Mount Hermon. Perhaps the name Geshur reflects its role as a land-bridge between peoples.

Their first mention in the Bible occurs at the time of David with the significant information that the Geshurite King Talmai offered his daughter Maacah to David in marriage (2 Sam 3:3). Following the pattern of political marriages, this implies that David, as king of a weaker kingdom Judah, was seeking a stronger alliance. Such an arrangement assisted in David's consolidation of power. It would also explain the situation of Absalom (David and Maacah's son) in murdering David's heir Amnon and leading the rebellion against his father (2 Sam 13-15). For three years, Absalom returned to the home of King Talmai to use Geshur as his base. When he finally did return south, Absalom exclaimed, "Why have I come from Geshur? It would be better for me to be there still." (2 Sam 14:32). Absalom, of course, died in the rebellion. Yet he left a daughter named Maacah, like his Geshurite mother.

One might think that Absalom's legacy would be minimal with the ascendancy of Solomon. However, Absalom's daughter, Maacah, played a significant role in the later monarchy of Israel. She married Solomon's son Rehoboam, who succeeded him in Jerusalem following the split into the two kingdoms and, according to 2 Chronicles 11:21, "he loved her more than all his wives and concubines." Later she served as the Queen Mother for King Abijam (1 Kings 15:3) and (grand)mother for King Asa (1 Kings 15:10). The biblical record is quite critical of her role in introducing Asherah worship to Jerusalem (1 Kings 15:13). However, it would seem that Maacah's significance was linked to her role in the continuation of the Geshurite alliance as a check against the growth of the Northern Kingdom of Israel.

The archaeological record at et-Tell shows the marks of a significant capital city that reached its zenith over several centuries from the mid-tenth century to the last third of the eighth century BCE. The evidence centers around a magnificent four-chamber gate complex and the *Bit Hilani* style palace. Thus far remains of residential areas are minimal with rebuilding in later eras.

How well do the literary record and the archaeological record come together? There are really two separate questions:

1. Was the iron-age city at et-Tell the Geshurite capital?
2. Was this the city of King Talmai and his daughter Maacah? In other words, is it likely that King David visited this site? Is this the location where Absalom would have retreated to begin his rebellion against his father?

There are, of course, no inscriptions that might lead to an absolute identification. The answer to the first question is derived primarily by way of comparison to other sites northeast of the Sea of Galilee (Kinneret). Already in the 1980s, archaeologists began surveying sites in the Golan region in what was known as the "Land of Geshur Project." Sites such as Hadar (2.5 acres) and Soreg (1 acre) were no match for et-Tell's twenty acres and certainly fell short in comparison when it came to the architectural remains.[3] So it is highly likely that this was the Geshurite capital.

The second question is a bit more complicated. The Geshurite city at et-Tell in some ways parallels the development of early Jerusalem. In the case of the latter, we are reminded that David ruled first from Hebron, and only later moved his capital to Jerusalem. While David was responsible for transformations in this Jebusite village, it was Solomon and later rulers responsible for development into a major city. So when we are faced with a rough date of "middle tenth century BCE" for the construction of the walls and early gate of Bethsaida, how does that fit with the chronology of Talmai and his daughter Maacah? Rami Arav conjectures that Talmai (his name followed by a question mark) may have been responsible for the gate in Stratum VI at Bethsaida.[4] Yet if David had married Maacah by 980 BCE, then such a suggestion is less certain. What we know of Talmai's city—assuming he was at et-Tell—would point to a more humble capital city prior to the major building campaign.

The Geshurite palace

The Assyrian-Aramaen-style *Bit Hilani* structure[5] is a rectangular building laid out east to west from the city wall extending 27.7 meters with a breadth of 15 meters. It was constructed with huge boulders so that the walls have a width of 1.4 meters. As a result the building was reused in later phases of occupation and is well preserved yet today reaching as high as one and a half meters. Higher courses of wall were built with red mud brick.

Eight rooms surround a main hall (19.7 m. by 4.5 meters) that would have served as the throne room. The floor was covered with crushed limestone. Among the impressive finds in this main hall was a jar handle with the three

3. M. Kochavi, T. Renner, I. Spar, and E. Yadin, "Rediscovered! The Land of Geshur," *BAR* (July/ August, 1992), 31-44, 84-5.

4. Rami Arav, "Towards a Comprehensive History of Geshur," in *Bethsaida* (2004), 1-48, especially 18.

5. Rami Arav and Monika Bernett, "The Bit Hilani at Bethsaida: Its Place in Aramaean/ Neo-Hittite and Israelite Palace Architecture in the Iron Age II," *Israel Exploration Journal* 50 (2000), 47-81.

Walls of Bit Hilani

Hebrew letters MKY and a fine Egyptian *Pataekos* figurine in faïence.[6] This latter find points to Egyptian connections as do several other Bethsaida figurines—cruder figures resembling the goddess Hathor. Another figurine from the palace complex is characterized by an *atef* headdress, similar to that described in 2 Samuel 12:30 of the Ammonite *Malkam*. A ninth-century Phoenician-style bulla (used to seal letters), reflects influence of Phoenician culture and connections with Samaria, the capital of the Northern Kingdom of Israel.[7] Such finds demonstrate the extent of connections of the local ruler.

On the domestic side, clay loom weights (discovered in a line likely from their actual use for weaving), and extensive pottery including cooking pots, jars, and juglets, offer a glimpse of palace life. Bethsaida's staff zooarchaeologist Toni Fisher, in analyzing all the bone fragments from the *Bit Hilani*, found a wide range of animals eaten: cattle, sheep, goats, catfish, and pigs.[8] Since pigs were not found in other iron-age samples on the tell, but comprise 10% of the remains in the palace, Fisher suggests that they are likely wild

6. Rami Arav, "An Iron Age Amulet from the Galilee," *BAR* (Jan/ Feb, 1995), 44.

7. Baruch Brandl, "An Israelite Bulla in Phoenician Style from Bethsaida (et-Tell)," in *Bethsaida* (1995), 141-64.

8. Toni Fisher, *A Zooarchaeological Analysis of Change in Animal Utilization at Bethsaida from Iron Age II through the Early Roman Period*. Ph.D. Dissertation (Knoxville, TN: The University of Tennessee, 2005), 34-75.

pigs captured in the hunt and brought as gifts to the king. Other wild game include deer and gazelles. When all the bone finds in iron-age loci were examined together (from the *Bit Hilani* and the city gate), cattle bones appear in a high percentage (38%), typical of more urban settings. Examination of the cattle bones suggests that they were consumed in an adult age, which would mean that they were raised for other purposes than meat, most likely for milk and as draft animals for plowing fields. It would appear, however, that sheep and goats (with twice as many goats as sheep) were raised primarily for meat since they are slaughtered as young adults.

Seven clay figurines

Iron-age oil lamps

With the evidence of cattle usage and the finds of grain storage at the gate it would appear that Bethsaida was primarily an agricultural settlement. Fishing did supply a small amount of fish, but it does not appear that this was a major industry during this period.

The city gate

While palaces reflect the life of the royal family, the city gate reflects the life of the city. Among the best known images are Boaz meeting the elders at the gate of Bethlehem to discuss his marriage with Ruth (Ruth 4:1); David sitting at the gate of Jerusalem to hear from his generals about the fate of Absalom's rebellion (2 Sam 19:8); Samuel encountering Saul for the first time (1 Sam 9:14); and King Ahab and King Jehoshaphat together listening to the Prophet Micaiah concerning the prospects of war (1 Kings 22:1). The city gate functioned as the place for meeting, a center of business, a setting for court, a place for religious rituals, and, of course, as the protection for the city.

The city gate complex was constructed on the east side of the tell with several terraces providing a platform to the highest point of the tell with a drop off of forty meters to the fields below.[9] An approaching roadway has

---

9. Rami Arav, "Final Report on Area A, Stratum V: The City Gate," in *Bethsaida* (2009), 4:1-122.

From plaza looking into the gateway. Courtesy of Dr. Walter Bouzard.

been traced a hundred meters northeast of the tell. As it makes its gradual ascent to the gateway a four-meter wide cobblestone road provides a majestic approach for the final fifty meters.

The city wall itself has been exposed on both the eastern and northern sides of the city, comprised of both an inner wall and a shorter outer wall where a paved walkway intervenes. The width of the inner wall is about six meters and the height of preserved sections reaches at places to three meters. Periodic offsets extend out another meter. The black basalt boulders were covered with plaster and whitewash, presenting an impressive site to all approaching.

An outer gateway provides an approach from the road to the north before it merges into a paved plaza that enters the inner gateway in a westerly direction. The intervening plaza covers nearly 200 square meters, a space which could accommodate a gathering of several hundred people. The inner gateway was flanked by two towers, measuring 12.5 by 5.6 meters each and preserved up to 3 meters. It is projected that two additional stories reached to an impressive height. The threshold of the gateway remains intact for a four meter wide passageway. On both sides the door pivots remain, just inside the threshold lies a piece of carbonized oak wood from the door itself.

The Bethsaida gate is a typical four-chamber gateway, paralleling sites such as Dan, Megiddo, Dor, Beer Sheba, and Ashdod. However, Bethsaida is the largest and the best preserved. Each chamber measures 3.5 meters by 10 meters. Three of the chambers show evidence from several

Gate chamber used for grain storage

layers of wheat and barley that they were used as granaries, where farmers deposited their crops from near-by fields.[10] To the south of the gate was a 11.5 meter by 9.5 meter storage house filled with large storage jars that have been reconstructed. It is likely that olive oil and wine were also stored in this complex.

Restored pottery vessels from Chamber 4

The religion of the Geshurite city

While there is no evidence of an iron-age temple in the city, the gate complex shows extensive evidence of religious practice. On the right side, just before entering the inner gate, stood a stepped high place where an iconic stele was positioned above a large dressed basalt basin. Visitors would climb the two steps to the 90 centimeter high platform (2.17 meters by 1.7 meters) where they would present their gifts to the god of the city, represented on the 1.35 meter tall stele. The bull-head figure with long horns and with a dagger

10. Patrick Scott Geyer, "Pollen Analysis at et-Tell, 1996-2006: Laboratory Report on the Iron Age Gate," in *Bethsaida* (2009), 4:180-92.

Stepped High Place

Stele with Bull Figure

Three-legged cup

through his belt has been identified by Monika Bernett and Othmar Keel as the moon god of Haran.[11] They identify two parallel steles at Tell el-Aŝ ʿsri and ʿAwas found a short distance away in southern Syria.

Two three-legged perforated cups were discovered in the basin of the high place.[12] Among possible functions for these cups, the following have been proposed:

- incense burners;
- libation cups;
- vessels holding herbs and spices to enhance the aroma of meal offerings.[13]

More recently during the 2010 season a bull-shaped figurine vessed was discovered, likely used to sprinkle water.

11. Monika Bernett and Othmar Keel, *Mond, Stier und Kult am Stadttor: Die Stele von Bet-saida (et-Tell),* Orbis Biblicus et Orientalis 161 (Freiburg, Switzerland: Universitätsverlag, 1998). Osnat Misch-Brandt presents an alternative interpretation of Hadad the Aramaen weather god.

12. Rami Arav, "Final Report," 84-8.

13. Nicolae Roddy, "Perforated Tripodal Vessels at Iron II Bethsaida-Tzer," *Biblische Notizen* 141 (2009), 91-100.

Directly inside the gate in the northeast chamber, remains from numerous vessels were stored that likely had been offered on the high place, including several additional three-legged cups. A large jug included an inscription with the Hebrew letters representing LESHEM and an ankh-like symbol (LESHEM♀). The letters mean "to the name of" or "on behalf of the name of" and the ankh-like symbol likely represents the moon god.[14]

LESHEM♀ Marking on Pottery

On the left side of the gate was a direct access high place. Rami Arav suggests that this reflects the prohibition of Exodus 20:26 of not climbing onto the high place and "showing one's nakedness." Seemingly the parallel high places demonstrate the coexistence of several religious traditions. In addition to the iconic bull-head stele, six other "aniconic" steles were positioned in pairs throughout the gateway area. Each stele, measuring over a meter in height, was carefully dressed with a curved top and a flat façade.

14. Carl Savage, "The *Leshem* Inscription," in *Bethsaida* (2009), 4:125-35.

Sacrificial high place

Inside the four-chamber gateway, there was a paved sacrificial high place (measuring 3.8 meters by 4.5 meters) approached by a ramp. On the high place there were bones and a broken basalt basin. Nearby there was large boulder with a crouching bull figure etched into one side. In a pit to the north of the high place were ashes and bones deposited from sacrifices. Among the bones identified were cows, sheep, and goats—typical of Israelite sacrifices—but also fallow deer that had been hunted—an animal not acceptable for Israelite sacrifices.

The building of the gateway

The excavations of the city gate show several periods of destruction and present evidence for a reconstruction of the history of et-Tell over a period of several centuries during the Israelite monarchy. While remains of an earlier gate and wall are yet evasive, a major gate structure was constructed in the middle of the tenth century BCE. Rami Arav suggests that this could have been carried out under King Talmai, or at least one of his immediate successors.

Two waves of destruction over the next century point to a period in which the Geshurite kingdom was coming under the sway of Aram Damascus whose kings Ben Hadad 1 and Ben Hadad 2 were engaged in conflict with the Israelite Kingdom. The rule of Hazael in the latter half of the ninth century (842-814 BCE) corresponded with the rise of the Assyrian threat under Shalmaneser 3, who attacked Damascus and possibly also et-Tell. This is the period when Bethsaida's leaders can be credited with reinforcing the city walls, rebuilding the gateway under the four-chamber gate plan, and leading Bethsaida into a period of prosperity.

There is evidence that Bethsaida may have developed its closest relations with the Israelite kingdom during the middle-eighth century when Jeroboam

2 (786-746 BCE) carried out a campaign against Damascus. It is during this latter period that "Samarian ware" bowls appear. Three complete examples of this red slip and burnished shallow bowl were reconstructed from the northeast chamber of the gate and other examples were found in the Bit Hilani. The most intriguing piece of evidence for Samarian connections comes from a jar handle impression with the name "ZKRYW" or Zekaryau—one with an almost identical parallel discovered in Dan. Baruch Brandl has suggested that the seal refers to Zechariah, the son of Jeroboam 2 who ruled the northern kingdom for six months in 746 BCE (2 Kings 14:29).[15]

The Iron Age city of Bethsaida eventually met its end during the campaign of Assyria's Tiglath-pileser 3 in 734-732 BCE, which, according to his annals, were launched against Hanun, the king of Gaza, and "the house of Hazael" (King Rezin) in Damascus. Along the way major cities were destroyed, including Dan, Hazor, Kinneret, Ein Gev, Beth Shean, Megiddo, and also Bethsaida.

The destruction by Tiglath Pileser III

The attack upon Bethsaida would seem to have included a long siege— only one fourth of the grain capacity in the gate complex was full—and a major assault from the east upon the gate. No evidence of destruction was uncovered at the northern wall. [16] Sixty-five arrowheads and spear heads from the Assyrian attack were discovered in the northeast chamber of the gateway—some bent from impact against the walls. Others were found in the passageway.

After the city was conquered and the citizens removed, the Assyrian army undertook a systematic demolition of the gateway. All of the steles were "beheaded"—the tops broken off. The bull-head iconic stele, however, was broken into five pieces and carefully laid upside down upon the high place. Inside the northeast chamber of the gate, the many storage vessels and votive offerings were smashed into bits

Arrowheads from Assyrian destruction

---

15. Baruch Brandl, "An Israelite Administrative Jar Handle Impression from Bethsaida," in *Bethsaida* (2009), 4:136-146.

16. John T. Greene, "Tiglath-pileser III's War Against the City of Tzer," in *Bethsaida* (2004), 3:63-82.

and spread across the floor. Then the gate was set on fire with a fire so hot that many of the bricks from the upper stories were turned to clinkers. Even the hinges of the gate door were melted and iron arrowheads were found fused to pottery. The plaster from the walls was petrified upon the basalt boulders. Rubble from the gate, towers, and wall was accumulated to a height of several meters so that rebuilding was impossible.

The End of the Iron Age City

The campaigns of Tiglath-pileser 3 resulted in a total disruption of life in the southern Levant. Within a decade Shalmaneser had conquered Samaria and dismantled the Northern Kingdom of Israel (2 Kings 17). The deportation of residents, as described in the biblical record, is supported by archaeological surveys which show a large decrease in population throughout the entire region.[17] Bethsaida, destroyed and deserted, remained in ruin for nearly three centuries.

Stele discovered broken in pieces

Broken pottery in chamber 4

17. Zvi Gal, *The Lower Galilee during the Iron Age* (Winona Lake, IN: Eisenbrauns, 1992).

Chapter 3

Resettlement in the Hellenistic Age

Among the finds of the 1994 season of excavation at Bethsaida were two cylinder seals that may provide symbolic bookends between the Iron-age destruction of the city and its resurgence several centuries later during the Persian period. These are the kind of seals made in the administrative workshops from Assyria and Persia and used to seal official documents. They provide certain evidence for the presence of Assyrians and Persians at et-Tell.

The first of these, partially broken, includes a human headed genie figure in combat with a winged sphinx with a star and crescent in the sky above. Baruch Brandl dates this seal to the Neo-Assyrian period, approximately the time of Tiglath-pileser 3.[1] The significance of this seal is that it represents

Drawing of Assyrian seal impression

1. Baruch Brandl, "Two First-Millennium Cylinder Seals," in *Bethsaida* (1999), 2:225-230.

the kind that might be used by Tiglath-pileser's troops in reporting on the status of Bethsaida's destruction or perhaps the later status of the site in ruins.

The second seal, Baruch Brandl dates between 540 and 400 BCE at the heart of the Persian Period. Unlike the previous example, this seal is divided into two separate registers. In the upper register is depicted a walking winged bull and in the lower register a bearded fish-man holding a staff.[2] While the former motif is Persian, the latter is Phoenician. Brandl suggests that the quality of the seal demonstrates that it was made in a central workshop of the Achaemenian Empire. The question for archaeologists is how much to make of it? Does its presence

Drawing of Persian seal impression

at Bethsaida signify that Persian emissaries saw a role for the ruined city rising from the ashes? What was that role? Or is it just an anomaly that cannot be explained?

Bethsaida reestablished

There is no question that a major gap exists between the devastation of Bethsaida by the Assyrians and its refounding centuries later. In a survey of Galilean sites, Zvi Gal found that this whole area was virtually unoccupied in the 7th and 6th centuries BCE.[3] This is significant because it means that there were no remnants of the former Israelite population who provided some continuity.[4] The situation was not a resurgence of an old culture at Bethsaida, but the establishment of a new settlement by newcomers to the area. The major questions are who were they, when did they come, and why did they come?

With the rise of monetary currency during this period, coin evidence is often cited to demonstration settlement patterns. The difficulty with this

---

2. Among other seals Brandl identifies a Phoenecian bulla from the 9th century BCE and an Assyrian cylinder seal from the time of Tiglath-pileser 3. Baruch Brandl, "An Israelite Bulla in Phoenician Style from Bethsaida (et-Tell)," in *Bethsaida* (1995), 141-164.

3. Zvi Gal, *Lower Galilee during the Iron Age* (Winona Lake: Eisenbrauns, 1992).

4. Jonathan L. Reed, *Archaeology and the Galilean Jesus,* (Harrisburg, PA: Trinity Press, 2000), 23-43. Contra Richard A. Horsley, *Archaeology, History, and Society in Galilee* (Harrisburg, PA: Trinity Press, 1996), 15-28.

approach is that coins were durable and often reused for several centuries. However, they can provide a starting point that can be cross-checked by other evidence. A comparison of coin finds for Bethsaida by century (out of 480 coins[5]):

Fifth Century BCE—3 coins
Fourth Century BCE– 8 coins
Third Century BCE– 52 coins
Second Century BCE– 109 coins
First Century BCE—51 coins

It should not be surprising, then, that contrasting cases have been made by different persons for the resettlement of Bethsaida under Ptolemy 2 in the early 3rd century, for the later Ptolemaic period of the late 3rd century, and also for the end of the Persian era in the 4th century BCE.

The resettlement of Bethsaida must be understood in the context of the political and economic development for this whole region during this period. The coastal cities of Sidon, Tyre, Acco, and Dor all had interest in developing inland territory. Tyre, in particular, seems to have made inroads toward Bethsaida as is evidenced by the numerous coins minted in that city.[6] This is the case across Upper Galilee to Dan and Baneas and down through the Huleh Valley. A minor settlement in Dan existed already in the Persian period along with eight very small settlements around the Huleh Valley.[7] As more and more communities arose during the Hellenistic Period, the main road ran south from Dan to Tel Anafa and to Bethsaida, continuing on to new cities of Hippos and Gadara. This marked a change from the Iron Age when the primary road followed the west side of the Jordan River from Kinneret through Hazor to Dan.

The main purpose of these settlements was to manage the "Royal Farms" controlled by the ruling powers. In some ways this was similar to the role the Bethsaida had in the Iron Age, when grain was collected in the city from the local farmers, except now the beneficiary was not the Geshurite King, but

---

5. Bethsaida coins accumulated from 1988 through 2008 seasons of excavation.

6. Richard Simon Hanson, *Tyrian Influence in Upper Galilee* (Cambridge, MA: Harvard University Press, 1980). D. Barag, "Tyrian Currency in Galilee," *Israel Numismatic Journal* 6-7 (1982-3), 13.

7. Wolfgang Zwickel, "The Huleh Valley from the Iron Age to the Muslim Period," in ed. Jürgen Zangenberg, Harold W. Attridge, and Dale B. Martin, *Religion, Ethnicity, and Identity in Ancient Galilee: A Region in Transition* (Tübingen: Mohr Siebeck, 2007), 163-85, especially 176.

a distant ruler. Evidence for the way these Royal Farms operated is found in the Zenon Papyri which describes an official working for Ptolemy 2 who visited a number of these sites on the eastern side of the Jordan River passing north (perhaps along the route of Bethsaida) to Kedesh in Upper Galilee and ending up in Acco on the coast.[8] Zenon describes his visit to a half a dozen settlements along the way, including one called Beth Anath where a local official named Apollonius showed him the vineyards and fields of grain that were marked for export to Egypt. Bethsaida is not mentioned in the Zenon Papyri, but one is faced with the difficulty that most of the place names are unknown. Yet this is the kind of situation that Bethsaida represented during this period of resettlement.

The Persian Period

There is some evidence that Bethsaida may have had a role in grain collection already during the late Persian era. While pottery finds have been rather meager for the period, there is one type that stands out. Sandra Fortner has identified several different types of mortaria dating from the fifth to the fourth century BCE.[9] The primary use of these bowls was for measuring grain according to the Mesopotamian measurement standard.[10] Since the Mesopotamian system was discontinued for this region following the time of Alexander, these bowls are critical for the chronological record. Since fifteen different morataria have been recorded in the Bethsaida catalogue, it would seem that Bethsaida had been established as a minor administrative center for grain collection. This would explain the presence of a Persian era cylinder seal at Bethsaida.

The coin finds from this period are minor. However, for the most part they were excavated in the same context in the northern section of Area C, which is the most accessible part of the tell. In fact, several coins—all minted in Tyre—were discovered just inside the remains of the northern city wall, where the Assyrians had not bothered to carry out their destruction devices. However, no evidence remains of any new permanent building structures. Rather remains of Iron Age structures were put to use, such as the south wall of the building that later became the winemaker's house in Area C. A fourth

8. Andrea Berlin, "Between Large Forces in the Hellenistic Period," *BA* 60:1 (1997), 14.

9. Fortner includes a catalogue of fifteen examples at et-Tell. Sandra Fortner, "Persian Period Mortaria at Bethsaida-Julias," in *Bethsaida* (2009), 4:147-171.

10. A secondary use for such bowls was as grinding bowls, so this must be considered as a possible alternative. Yet the number of finds suggests otherwise.

to fifth-century BCE figurine of a bearded man in Greek-archaic style[11] was discovered next to this reused wall. This figurine (see page 20, upper right of photo) demonstrates Phoenecian connections since the closest parallel has been found at Tel Amrit along the North Phoenician coast.

It would seem that the debris in the Iron Age gateway was simply avoided. The cylinder seal was found in the area south of the gateway, as was also a beautiful silver stater minted in Athens dating about 450 BCE. A piece of opaque-white glass with zigzag bands of white and yellow, the base of a core-formed juglet complements this picture. Andrea Rottloff has identified this fragment as imported ware, possibly from Rhodes, that dates to the middle of the sixth to the early fourth century BCE.[12] When combined with coin and pottery evidence, this points to a minor occupation of Bethsaida in the Persian Period.

Bethsaida under the Ptolemies

When Alexander the Great led his troops south from Cilicia toward Egypt in 332 BCE, he brought about change that affected all of Palestine. To begin with he brought an end to Persian rule and the network of cities along the Mediterranean Coast. In some ways that brought new beginnings as cities like Tyre and Acco made even greater inroads into the hinterland in their efforts to reassert themselves in the economics of the Mediterranean. Alexander also left Palestine in a precarious position between two competing powers—with Bethsaida positioned right on the fault line— the Ptolemies of Egypt and the Seleucids of Syria, who struggled for nearly two centuries for the upper hand. The Battle of Ipsus in 301 BCE—the first of five major Ptolemy-Syrian wars—ended with Ptolemy 1 defeating Antigonus and resulting in a century-long control over Palestine.

Ptolemaic coin

11. The clay sculpted figure is 74 mm. tall although it is broken and may have originally been part of a sculpture group. Rami Arav, "Bethsaida, Preliminary Report, 1994-1996," in *Bethsaida* (1999), 2:104-105.

12. Andrea Rottloff, "Pre-Roman, Roman, and Islamic Glass," in *Bethsaida* (2009), 4:204-251, especially 205.

There is no doubt that Bethsaida was fully established by the time of Ptolemy 2 Philadelphus (285-246 BCE). Of the 52 Ptolemaic coins, 27 were minted by Ptolemy 2. This is typical of both Judean and Galilean sites as Ptolemaic coinage was used to consolidate power. The Tyrian mint and the Seleucids had followed the Attic monetary standard with the silver drachma weighing 4.3 grams. However, the Ptolemies introduced a different standard of 3.8 grams. The result was that 100 Ptolemy drachmas were equal to only 80 Attic drachmas or 80 Seleucid drachmas. Allowing the latter to coexist in Ptolemaic territory was out of the question. In order to supplement the mint in Alexandria, Tyre was incorporated as a Ptolemaic mint, then in 261 BCE, Ptolemy 2 established mints in Acco—which he renamed Ptolemais—Joppa, and Gaza. In spite of geographic proximity to Ptolemais-Acco, not a single coin from Bethsaida originated there under the Ptolemies. Tyre remained as the main source of Bethsaida coins.

The Ptolemy 2 coins signal another shift in the resettlement of Bethsaida. The two Ptolemy 1 coins followed the earlier pattern, found in the northern part of the tell. However, twenty of the 27 Ptolemy 2 coins were found in the gateway area, suggesting an effort to clean up the debris left behind from the Assyria destruction. This pattern fol-lows throughout the remainder of the 3rd century BCE although this period marks the beginning of residential sections in Areas B and C.

The most significant evidence of wider trade for this period comes from the large number of pieces of Rhodian Amphorae. These amphorae have a dis-tinctive character with a sandy hue and shards made from material that seems indestructible. Beginning in the 4th Cen-tury BCE the island of Rhodes became involved in the wine export business and it soon became such a popular commod-ity that archaeological sites throughout the Mediterranean display their share of Rhodian ware. The Rhodian amphorae are distinguished in another way. Begin-ning in the third century BCE, handles were stamped with the name of a licensed manufacturer and the name of an annu-

Rhodian Wine Amphora

Area A Sq 155
L352 B5131
22/06/99
DR# 99-34

0   5 cm

Stamped Rhodian amphora handle

ally appointed official. As a result of comparative analysis, the stamped handles have taken their place alongside coins for establishing the chronology of a site.

Donald Ariel has now catalogued thirteen Rhodian stamped handles at Bethsaida.[13] Nine are dated to the last third of the 3rd century BCE, and the other four from the beginning of the 2nd century BCE. What is striking about this distribution is that the presence at Bethsaida of Rhodian amphorae phases out at the very time that the Rhodian wine export business increases fourfold as it continues over the next two centuries. There is a definite correlation with Ptolemy rule. Over 100,000 Rhodian stamped handles are stored in the Alexandria Museum. So this may point to the presence of Ptolemaic government officials stationed at Bethsaida.

Another possibility is that Bethsaida was used for some military purpose by the Ptolemies. During the Ptolemaic period there were five Syrian wars (280-279; 276-2; 242-1; 219-17; 198 BCE). For most of the period the Ptolemy line of defense was the Litani River from near Mount Hermon on the east to just north of Tyre where it empties into the Mediterranean. In 217 BCE, Antiochus 3 was defeated by Ptolemy 4 at Raphia along the southern Mediterranean coast. However, Gerald Finkelsztejn has observed that the number of Rhodian amphora in Ptolemais (Akko) increased dramatically following 217 BCE until the defeat of the Ptolemies at Baneas in 198 BCE when the numbers drop off again. He suggests that the Ptolemies were building up their military strength against further attacks. Syon and Yavor 2001 have proposed something similar for Gamla on the basis of evidence there and Ma'oz (1983) has suggested that all of the Golan was strengthened at this time. It is critical to think of Bethsaida's position in relation to the final battle between Seleucids and the Ptolemies at Baneas in 198 BCE.[14]

13. Donald T. Ariel, "Stamped Amphora Handles from Bethsaida," in *Bethsaida* (2009), 4:267-92.

14. IBID, 270.

Bethsaida under the Seleucids

Following the Battle of Baneas, Antiochus 3 turned his attention to battles in Asia Minor eventually confronting Rome. This left Palestine with room for growth. Likewise Antiochus 3 released these lands to the south from taxation leading to new ventures in economic development. As with many other sites, former soldiers were given land to settle. This may explain the growth of Bethsaida. Thirty-three Antiochus 3 coins have been found for the first decade following the Battle of Baneas in 198 BCE. A large concentration of these coins in Area B show that former walls of the *Bit Hilani* and the city wall to its east were incorporated into new dwelling places. However, the center pieces of Hellenistic construction were the two large courtyard houses: "The Fisherman's House" in Area B and "The Winemaker's House" in Area C.

Seleucid Coin

Aerial photo of residential sections of Area B and C

"The Winemaker's House" stands out in particular because of the discovery of a sealed wine cellar to the rear of the house with four large jars *in situ* and three bronze pruning hooks discovered in the courtyard. Marks of Hellenistic culture were present with a strigilis as well as a delicate gold filigree earring. While the court yard was surrounded by bedrooms and a triclinium to the north, its larger kitchen on the east was an impressive room. Iron nails and a key lay where a wooden door once stood. An oven, several grinding stones of various types, and numerous examples of broken kitchen ware, including some examples of Eastern Terra Sigillata, discovered broken along the south wall. Along the west of the court yard, a winding paved lane makes its way amidst numerous smaller houses of this residential section.

Clearly the largest number of coins found at Bethsaida come from this period—109 Seleucid coins—scattered over the entire top of the tell and signifying perhaps the largest extent of the city's expansion. The situation at Bethsaida is reflected by a period of general

Gold earring

growth in Galilee and the Golan, especially in the later part of the 2nd century BCE. One survey suggested that the number of settlements increased three-fold with most across Upper Galilee and into the Huleh Valley[15] within the sphere of influence of Tyre which had been granted independence in 135 BCE.

Fine ware pottery

15. Eric Meyers, James Strange, and Dennis Groh, "The Meiron Excavations Project. Archaeological Survey in the Galilee and Golan," *BASOR* 230 (1976), 1-24.

Especially significant for the story of Bethsaida are two neighboring settlements. To the east, the village of Gamla was established as a completely new settlement. To the north at Tel Anafa, where a minor Ptolemaic settlement on a mound had been abandoned, a new settlement appeared with rather luxurious trappings including a bath house and a large stucco building with Greek masonry. While the three towns would later experience quite different fates, all three of them exhibit similar characteristics during the last quarter of the 2nd century BCE including Tyrian coinage and pottery styles. One particular type of fine table ware that is found in all three sites is called Eastern Sigilatta A, a Phoenician pottery form with a red slip that developed in Phoenicia in the latter 2nd century BCE.[16] According to Andrea Berlin, "The popularity of the new ESA tableware was such that it appeared at almost every later 2nd century BCE site to which Phoenician merchants had access."[17] While ESA appeared in Palestinian coastal sites and along the northern network of settlements, it is significantly absent from Judea and Samaria before the Roman Period. Other particularly common Hellenistic forms during this period include the molded relief-decorated Megarian Bowl[18] and plates with palmette stamps at the bottom.

Black Athenian pottery with palmette pattern

16. Sandra Fortner, "Hellenistic and Roman Fineware from Bethsaida," in *Bethsaida* (1995), 116, IX. 37.xi.3.

17. Berlin, "Between Large Forces" (1997), 25.

18. Sandra Fortner, *Der Keramik und Kleinfunde von Bethsaida-Iulias am See Genezareth, Israel,* (München: Ludwig-Maximilians-Universität, 2008), 17-19 and catalogue # 120-153.

While these luxury items did appear, Bethsaida finds also include a simpler form of pottery known as "spattered wash ware," so called because the lower portions of the vessels are spattered lightly with paint. Manufactured at Tel Anafa this type of popular ware is common during this period within the Huleh Valley, but nowhere else. The exception is Bethsaida[19] where numerous shards show evidence of a close connection between Bethsaida and Tel Anafa.

One further similarity between Tel Anafa, Bethsaida, and Gamla is that they all were generally Gentile towns. Up until this time at the end of the 2nd century BCE, there is no evidence of Jewish activity in the Golan, neither migration from Jerusalem nor return from exile.

A Hellenistic style temple

During the Iron Age, the gate complex offered sacred space to the residents of the city. This included the various steles positioned throughout the gateway, the stepped altar with a basin for offerings, a second "no-access" altar in the paved external courtyard, and a sacrificial altar on the interior. During the Hellenistic period, the new residents continued this sacred awareness by constructing a temple at the highest part of the acropolis, upon the ruins of the northwest chamber of the four-chamber gate and in the area directly west and to the north. A single column on the east rests upon the burned remains from Assyrian destruction.

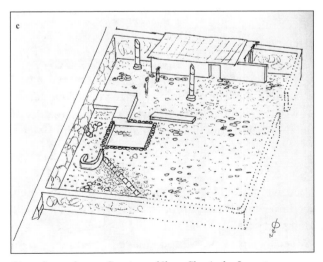

Plan of sacred area. Courtesy of Ilona Skupinska-Lovset.

19. Fortner, *Die Keramik* (2008), 21, catalogue # 209-253.

Ilona Skupińska-Løvset with a Polish team of archaeologists delineated an area of about 25 meters by 25 meters for this sanctuary with a large open paved area.[20] From the number of animal bones documented by zooarchaeologist Toni Fisher, the Polish team proposes that communal meals were a regular part of the ritual observance. A paved canal carried water to a large 5 meter by 5 meter basin on the eastern side of the complex where priests likely slaughtered the animals behind a stone barrier on an altar. There were also benches where participants sat. At the southern end of the complex is located a typical Phoenecian broadhouse-style temple with the main door on the north. The walls were well constructed, 110 cm. in width. The north and south walls extend about 20 meters. Shorter north-south walls (about five meters long) divided the structure into several internal rooms. The bases of a number of pillars were positioned around the temple structure.

Reconstruction of Seleucid Temple. Courtesy of Ilona Skupinska-Lovset.

Four fragments of pregnant women figurines with hand on belly. Courtesy of Hanan Shafir, photographer, BEP.

A number of figurines from the Hellenistic era have been found throughout the tell. However, recent seasons of excavation just to the south of the temple complex have yielded numerous figurines of pregnant women, typical of Hellenistic Phoenician cults of Astarte. It is likely that this sacred complex was related to fertility rituals.

Hasmonean Era

Prior to the Hasmonean era, residents of the new Bethsaida likely knew little or nothing about Jerusalem. Five Antiochus 4 Epiphanes (175-164 BCE) coins found at Bethsaida are a reminder that the conflict in Jerusalem that gave rise to the Maccabean revolt, went unnoticed in these northern

20. Ilona Skupińska-Løvset, *The Temple Area of Bethsaida: Polish Excavations on et-Tell in the Years 1998-2000* (Lódź, Poland: Lódź University Press, 2006).

areas. The Seleucid coins continue through the rule of Antiochus 7 Sidetes (139-129 BCE), who made one last, but unsuccessful effort to wrest control from the Maccabees before John Hyrcanus broke the siege on Jerusalem and went on the offensive to begin expanding Jewish territory. John Hyrcanus (130-104 BCE) never made it to Galilee or the Golan, but his coins symbolize a major change for Bethsaida. The presence of Hasmonean coins mark a disruption in the dominance of Tyrian coins at Bethsaida and a shift from the influence of Tyre in the north to Jerusalem in the south.

Although Hyranus' son Aristobulus ruled only one year (104-103 BCE), he expanded Jewish territory to include much of Galilee. According to Josephus, "Aristobulus made war against Iturea, and added a great part of it to Judea, and compelled the inhabitants, if they would continue in that country, to be circumcised, and to live according to the Jewish laws" (Josephus, *Antiquities* 13. 318). Alexander Janneaus (103-76 BCE) followed up in ways that seemed designed to improve the economic situation of the Jewish state. His campaigns included coastal cities north to, but not Ptolemais-Acco, and independent cities east of the Jordan River including Gerasa, Gadara, Abila, and Hippos. Josephus reports that by 80 BCE, Jannaeus had ventured also into the Golan, capturing the towns of Gamla and Seleucia (Josephus, *Antiquities* 13. 395-7).

However, Josephus' report has been widely criticized. Richard Horsley says, "It would be unrealistic to imagine that the extension of Hasmonean rule over Galilee resulted in a sudden or thorough conformation of social life in Galilee to 'the laws and customs of the Judeans.'"[21] It is true that since the latter part of the 2nd century BCE Itureans had been expanding south from their home in the mountains of Lebanon around Chalcis. From their distinctive brownish-pink "Golan ware" pottery, it is possible to trace their expansion to some sixty sites south of Mount Hermon. In fact, a small number of shards show some influence as far as Bethsaida. However, Itureans never occupied Galilee, as Josephus would suggest, and there is no evidence of conflict at any Iturean sites.[22] As Peter Richardson suggests, Josephus is showing his bias, as has come to him from Strabo that "All Ituraeans and Arabs are robbers" (Strabo, *Geography* 16. 2. 18).[23] While the historical record does show evidence of brigandage in the rugged areas around Mount Hermon, the archaeological record shows expansion with small, agrarian settlements

21. Richard Horsley, *Galilee: History, Politics, People* (Valley Forge, PA: Trinity Press, 1995), 51.

22. Berlin, "Between Large Forces" (1997).

23. Peter Richardson, *Herod: King of the Jews and Friend of the Romans* (Minneapolis: Fortress Press, 1999), 71.

in the northern Golan.[24] Josephus' report idealizes Aristobulus' militaristic
campaigns as a pacification of the Galilee, simply reechoing his description of
John Hyrcanus' policies with the Idumeans in the south.

Hasmonean coin

There is no question that most of
Galilee and parts of Golan underwent
a major change both with an influx of
population and a transformation of culture. In a study of coins from archaeological sites across Galilee and Golan,
Danny Syon recorded 5,632 Hasmo-
nean coins, by far the largest group.[25] He concluded that this signals a dramatic change which considerably reduced the demand for bronze coinage
of cities like Tyre and Ptolemais-Acco. As a result, it is common to draw a
line across northern Galilee on the basis of the presence Hasmonean coins.[26]
So at Tel Anafa, where there was a continuous history of 185 Tyrian coins
in the 1st century BCE, only three Hasmonean coins appear. Yet at Gamla
over 3,900 Hasmonean coins appear, 62% of all coins from that site. The
conclusion is obvious, Gamla totally succumbed to Hasmonean rule while
Tel Anafa remained independent. On the basis of ethnic markers such as
Mikvaoth (ritual baths), a synagogue, and stone vessels, it is clear that Gamla
became a Jewish town. In stark contrast, Tel Anafa displays no such evidence
of Jewish piety or purity concerns. Mark Chancey has demonstrated that
Galilee was primarily Jewish by the first century, but what about Bethsaida?[27]

The name Bethsaida is significantly missing from Josephus' report about
Jannaeus' activity in the Golan. Some would argue that the thirty Hasmonean coins found at Bethsaida demonstrate that Bethsaida was now a Jewish

24. Berlin, "Between Large Forces" (1997).

25. Danny Syon, *Tyre and Gamla: A Study in the Monetary Influences of Southern Phoenecia on Galilee and the Golan in the Hellenistic and Roman Periods,* Dissertation [Hebrew]
(Jerusalem: Hebrew University, 2004). Summary of data is available in English in Morten
Horning Jensen, *Herod Antipas in Galilee: The Literary and Archaeological Sources* (Tübingen: Mohr-Siebeck, 2006), 175-77 & 213-15.

26. Mordechai Aviam, "Distribution Maps of Archaeological Data from the Galilee: An
Attempt to Establish Zones Indicative of Ethnicity and Religious Affiliation," in *Religion,
Ethnicity, and Identity* (2007), 115-132, especially 117-8.

27. Mark A. Chancey, *The Myth of a Gentile Galilee* (Cambridge: Cambridge University
Press, 2004).

village. Accordingly, its gentile residents would have converted to Judaism while those who refused would have been forced to leave to make room for immigrants from an overcrowded Judea. Bethsaida was clearly affected by the Hasmonean conquest of these northern regions. However, the thirty Hasmonean coins at Bethsaida pale in comparison to the enormous number at Gamla. They also represent only one third of the number of Seleucid coins from the previous century, they are just over half of the number of Ptolemaic coins in the century prior to that. More importantly, there is no dramatic halt in Tyrian coins. Rather, twenty first-century BCE city coins of Tyre stand in tandem with the Hasmonean coins. The situation at Bethsaida then appears quite different from Tel Anafa on one side or Gamla on the other.

During the 2005 to 2007 seasons, a house was excavated that sheds light on the situation at Bethsaida during the Hasmonean era. Located along a winding paved walkway at the far north section of the tell in Area C, the nine meter by four meter courtyard and surrounding rooms yielded two Hasmonean coins, yet also two Tyrian city coins. Finds include a Hellenistic juglet, Eastern Sigilatta fine dinner ware, a complete spattered wash ware fish plate, and a complete Erotes lamp. The two Hasmonean coins certainly do not prove Jewishness, and, in fact, one would be inclined to assume that the inhabitants were Gentile. However, what is most interesting is that the excavators stated that it appeared the residents had "left in a hurry." In addition to the complete vessels mentioned above, the house included a wine cellar covered by flat basalt stone slabs with seventeen jars and juglets left inside. There is no evidence of a later occupation for this house.

The picture of this newly excavated house is reflected elsewhere in the residential section Area C. As has been seen throughout this chapter, this residential section had played a central role in the resettlement of the village going back as early as the Persian period. The coin record has shown evidence of extensive activity: Seven fourth-century Tyrian City coins, twelve Ptolemaic coins, and thirty-three Seleucid coins. In the Hasmonean era, the coin count falls to a total of five, three Hasmonean coins and two Tyrian city coins—that is, one coin of John Hyrcanus I (130-104 BCE) in addition to the four in the newly excavated house. This is followed by a gap of over six centuries until a coin of Justinian 2 (571 CE). There are no early Roman, middle Roman, or later Roman era coins. It would seem that the residential section in Area C was abandoned sometime in the first century BCE with no rebuilding except for maybe a couple smaller houses. It is significant that Herodian lamps—clear first-century CE markers—are almost absent from Area C.

In many ways, the newly excavated house at the north of Area C reflects the residential center-piece called "The Winemaker's House." Both are courtyard houses, both have a covered wine cellar, and both show signs of sudden desertion. In the cellar of the Winemaker's House the complete storage jars and a casserole had been left in place. Flat roofing stones had collapsed in a pile in the southeast corner of the courtyard and a lintel lay fallen next to the doorway of the *triclinium* on the north side of the courtyard. The western courtyard wall appeared in places twisted from some kind of violent activity. In the kitchen, hundreds of shards of kitchen ware lay in piles along the southern wall as if a shelf had collapsed. Most importantly the key to the kitchen door had been found on the floor inside the eastern doorway, suggesting an unexpected, sudden departure.

This is the house that had suggested a comfortable, perhaps even luxurious, lifestyle, with a coin record including a fifth-century Tyrian silver obol, four Ptolemaic coins, fourteen Seleucid coins, and then only one John Hyrcanus coin from the end of the second century BCE. Then not a single coin occurs until one of Justinian 2 in the late sixth-century CE, found in a large pit dug in the courtyard. This gap points to a dramatic change. So when exactly did the residents leave the Winemaker's House?

When looking at the pottery record archaeologists look for two things, one the general pattern within a locus, and two the shard with the latest date. The pottery record, as would be expected, is primarily Hellenistic for all sections of the house. In her analysis of Bethsaida ceramics, Sandra Fortner dates the jars from the wine cellar from the third to first centuries BCE and the two casseroles, one from 50 BCE to 100 CE and the other from 25 BCE to 25 CE.[28] Other jar fragments are overwhelmingly Hellenistic. Similarly loci from the courtyard and kitchen reveal Hellenistic, but not early Roman pottery. A strong case can be made that both the large and small courtyard houses and much of Area C was abandoned sometime in the first century BCE.

Not that far away to the south, "The Fisherman's House" in Area B continued to be occupied into the early Roman era—with one of the Philip coins discovered in the courtyard. In Toni Fisher's analysis of bone finds, the Fisherman's House is the only location that shows a complete absence of pig bones.[29] Similarly there are only several catfish bones while in other

---

28. Fortner, *Die Keramik* (2008). In the preliminary reports, Rami Arav noted that "The jars and the casserole [in the wine cellar] date from the end of the second to the early first century BCE." Rami Arav, "Bethsaida, Preliminary Report, 1994-1996," in *Bethsaida* (1999), 2:99. In Strickert, *Bethsaida: Home of the Apostles* (1998), 150-1, I dated the jars from 100 BCE to 70 CE and the casserole to the first century CE. I chose the later part of the range.

29. Toni Fisher, *A Zooarchaeological Analysis of Change in Animal Utilization at Bethsaida from Iron Age II through the Early Roman Period.* Ph. D. Dissertation (Knoxville, TN: The

parts of the tell catfish are quite common through all eras.[30] In other locations pigs generally comprised between 3-5% of bone totals.[31] Is this the first sign of Judaism at Bethsaida? There were no first-century BCE Tyrian city coins found in the Fisherman's House, though there were five Hasmonean coins.

With regard to coin evidence during the Hasmonean era, a word of caution is in order. Most of the coin finds were not in the residential sections of Areas B and C, but in Area A, particularly in the vicinity of the city gate—namely 19 Hasmonean coins and 12 city coins from Tyre. This is not a picture of exclusivism. Also from Syon's study of the distribution, it is obvious that the Hasmoneans flooded the markets of Galilee and Golan with bronze coins. While it is always the case that coins were reused in later generations, Syon concludes that the surplus of Hasmonean coins resulted in their frequent use well into the Roman era. So the situation at Bethsaida is clearly different from either Tel Anafa, that remained independent, or Gamla, that was transformed to a Jewish town. It may well be that Bethsaida became a city mixed between Jew and Gentile. It may also be that change was gradual at Bethsaida during the first century BCE or that there were several changes.

If anything, Gaulanitis as well as neighboring Galilee was not stable during this period. The activity of the Hasmoneans during the first decades of the century was followed by the Roman conquest under Pompey in 63 BCE. To the south of Bethsaida, in 53-52 BCE, thousands of people were enslaved at Magdala (Josephus, *Ant,* 14.120). At the Arbela caves brigands organized in revolt (*Ant.* 14. 415), and to the north on the Syrian frontier, the brigand chief Ezekias mobilized his own army and raised havoc (*Ant.* 14. 159). Finally, when the Romans appointed Herod over Galilee, he brought a strong-armed approach to rule with heavy taxation (*Ant.* 14. 168-171). The uprising that occurred at the time of Herod's death in 4 BCE demonstrates the increased dissatisfaction during the last decades of the century.

Through all this turmoil, it would appear that Bethsaida diminished in size with Area C all but abandoned. Perhaps it is best simply to present several scenarios that might explain the changes at Bethsaida in the northern residential section:

1. The inhabitants of these houses may have been forced to leave because they refused to follow Jewish laws, as Josephus suggests.

University of Tennessee, 2005), 107.

30. IBID, 109.

31. Unfortunately due do an administration error, Fisher's study does not extend to Area C.

2. The inhabitants may have fled in fear of approaching Hasmonean troops and never returned.

3. The inhabitants may have voluntarily left because they did not accept Hasmonean rule.

4. The inhabitants may have left because they had been part of trade networks with Tyre that were now diminished.

5. The inhabitants may have left because of catastrophes unrelated to political, religious, or economic concerns, such as the earthquake that hit the rift valley in 31 BCE.

Whatever the cause, one third of the acropolis at Bethsaida was no longer utilized. With Bethsaida's political connections now pointing south, it is likely that the settlement pattern also began to move to the southern slopes of the tell toward the lake. As Philip undertook to expand the city in the first century, it makes sense that future excavation will focus on those lower portions of the tell.

Chapter 4

Home of the Apostles

Bethsaida, more than any other New Testament town, can rightly be called the home of the apostles. Specific references in the Gospels link three disciples of Jesus to Bethsaida, namely Simon Peter, Andrew, and Philip. Later traditions also connect James and John, as well as another disciple James, to Bethsaida. No other location can make such a claim about the disciples.

The Synoptics and the Apostles

From the beginning Jesus was identified in terms of his childhood home: Jesus of Nazareth. However, the Synoptic Gospels show absolutely no interest in identifying the places of origin of the disciples. A possible exception is Judas Iscariot since the Hebrew *Ish* (= man) could possibly connect Judas with the town of Kerioth in Judea. At least as well accepted is the theory that the name Iscariot characterizes Judas as a "man of the dagger" (*sicarius*) or "man of red hair" (*seqar*) or "man of lies" (*seqarya*). This fits more the pattern of the Synoptic writers (Mark 3:16-19; Matt 10:2-4; Luke 6:14-16) who describe Simon as the rock or foundation (Peter); James and John as "sons of thunder" (Boanerges); and the other Simon as Zealot (= *Qanana* in Aramaic). Elsewhere the Synoptics give patronymics such as "sons of Zebedee" for James and John; "Bar-Jonah" (Matt 16:17) for Simon Peter; and "son of Alphaeus" for James (Mark 3:18) and also for Levi (Mark 2:14). In no case do the Synoptics connect these disciples with particular towns or regions.

The Fourth Gospel and the Apostles

The fourth Gospel, in contrast, identifies the places of origin of four disciples. In the later appendix, Nathanael is identified as coming from Cana, presumably located near Nazareth in Galilee (John 21:2)—this in spite of no such identification when Nathanael was first introduced in the opening chapter (John 1:45). In John 1:44, the writer identifies three disciples with the city of Bethsaida: "Now Philip was from Bethsaida, the city of Andrew and Peter."

This identification of Bethsaida as the home of three disciples is interesting for several reasons.[1]

- It elevates to prominence Philip, a disciple who does not really play a major role in the Synoptic reports.
- It mentions Andrew and Peter as if it were already common knowledge that Bethsaida was the home of these two brothers.
- It is surprising to find Peter mentioned last since the name of Andrew usually follows that of Peter with the notation "brother of Simon Peter."
- The information in this verse is later repeated in the same Gospel: "They came to Philip, who was from Bethsaida in Galilee" (John 12:21).

The fourth evangelist is clearly presenting a different tradition from the Synoptics. Nevertheless, it need not be treated as a late tradition. John 1:44 is usually attributed to an early signs source which focused on the deeds of Jesus as signs of his messianic role.[2] The information passed on may well have developed in the context of an early Jewish-Christian community in the same area as that of Jesus' ministry.[3]

The Character of the Bethsaida disciples

The association of these three disciples with Bethsaida is consistent with our knowledge of this community. Philip's name is quite appropriate since the region around Bethsaida was governed by the rather popular son of Herod, also named Philip. The names of all three of these disciples, in fact, are Greek in contrast to all the other disciples who have Semitic names. Although Simeon

---

1. Mark Appold, "The Mighty Works of Bethsaida: Witness of the New Testament and Related Traditions," in *Bethsaida* (1995), 229-42. Mark Appold, "Jesus' Bethsaida Disciples: A Study in Johannine Origins" in Paul N. Anderson, Felix Just, and Tom Thatcher, ed., *John, Jesus, and History, volume 2: Aspects of Historicity in the Fourth Gospel* (Atlanta: SBL, 2009).

2. Robert Fortna, *The Fourth Gospel and Its Predecessor: From Narrative Source to Present Gospel* (Philadelphia: Fortress Press, 1988).

3. K. Wengst, *Bedrängte Gemeinde und verherrlichter Christus* (Neukirchen-Vluyn: Neukirchener, 1983).

was a popular Hebrew name, Simon was the Greek form of that name. This is consistent with the description by Josephus that this area contained "a mixed population of Jews and Syrians" (Josephus, *War* 3.57). As a border town, residents would likely speak several languages.[4] Thus it is not surprising that when Greeks wished to see Jesus, they approached Philip and Andrew as intermediaries (John 12:20-24). It is difficult to imagine the success of Simon's missionary journeys to Antioch, Corinth, and Rome without some knowledge of the Greek language. Even the attribution of the name "Peter" by Jesus implies some knowledge of Greek. The connection with the Greek term πετρός meaning "rocky" is appropriate, not just in terms of Simon's subsequent leadership role, but also because the area around Bethsaida is characterized by the rocky soil with volcanic basalt rock scattered everywhere. The connection of Philip, Andrew, and Peter with Bethsaida is thus quite fitting.

Bethsaida in Galilee

The expression "Bethsaida of Galilee" (John 12:21) has been a concern for some since the location of et-Tell was not included in the political realm of Galilee governed by Antipas during the time of Jesus. It has been suggested that this demonstrates a lack of precise geographical knowledge or that it points to the existence of two Bethsaidas, one in Galilee and the other in the Golan.[5] However, one must understand that the expression is used in a Jerusalem context and merely designates the general area in the north away from Jerusalem. In the same way, the Easter directive for the disciples to go to Galilee where they will see Jesus (Mark 16:7) points to a return to the area frequented by Jesus during his ministry along the northern shores of the Sea of Galilee, including both the Galilee and the Golan. In the latter part of the first century, both the Golan and Galilee were connected under the rule of Agrippa 2. Thus it was not unusual for later texts to speak of Bethsaida-Julias as a city of Galilee.[6]

The call narratives of the disciples

Another difficulty with this statement about Bethsaida as home of the disciples is that it occurs in the midst of a call narrative quite different from

4. Markus Bockmuehl, "Simon Peter and Bethsaida," *Supplements to Novum Testamentum* 115 (2005), 53-91.

5. Bargil Pixner, "The Search for the Lost City of Bethsaida," *BA* (December, 1985), 207-16.

6. Ptolemy, *Geographia* 5.16.4; Pliny, *Natural History* 5.15.71.

the more familiar Synoptic accounts. The well-known picture is that of Jesus passing along the western shore of the Sea of Galilee where he meets two pairs of brothers fishing and he calls them to leave their nets to follow him. The Johannine picture also presents Jesus encountering four individuals (John 1:35-51). The names Peter and Andrew are the same, but here are found Philip and Nathanael rather than James and John. There is no motif of fishing and it is through the intervention of Andrew and Philip that Peter and Nathanael are called. Most significant is that the calling takes place before Jesus arrives in Galilee (John 1:43).

On closer analysis, the Synoptic picture is not so fixed as the traditional view assumes. Place names on the western side of the sea are not included in the call episodes. The early Markan account mentions only that "Jesus passed along the Sea of Galilee" (Mark 1:16). It is not until verse 21 that Capernaum is first mentioned. The Matthean and Lukan call narratives (Matt 4:18-22 and Luke 5:1-11) likewise are not in themselves tied to any particular geographic location on the sea. However, these later accounts make the connection by implication since they have already mentioned Jesus' ministry in Capernaum (Matt 4:13 and Luke 4:31). Matthew is even stronger in creating that impression since Jesus has established his home in this town on the western shore.

A more realistic picture may be that presented by Q (Matt 11:20-21 = Luke 10:13-15) in which Jesus travels about within the evangelical triangle of Chorazin, Bethsaida, and Capernaum "without a place to lay his head" (Matt 8:20 = Luke 9:58).

Excursus: "The House of Peter" at Capernaum

Modern visitors to Capernaum are shown the remains of what is called "The House of St. Peter"—somewhat in conflict with the reports connecting Peter with Bethsaida. Archaeological reports about this house demonstrate that early Christians clearly believed that this house had some significance for the life of Jesus and the church.[7] This has been long established by the presence of a fifth-century octagonal structure, which corresponds in style to other church buildings erected during this period to commemorate places and events important in the life of Jesus. This is corroborated by the report

---

7. Virgilio Corbo, "The Church of the House of St. Peter at Capernaum," *Ancient Churches Revealed,* ed. Yoram Tsafrir (Jerusalem: Israel Exploration Society, 1993), 71-6. James F. Strange and Herschel Shanks, "Has the House Where Jesus Stayed in Capernaum Been Found?" *BAR* (Nov/ Dec 1982), 26-37.

of the Spanish pilgrim Egeria who visited this area in the late fourth century and writes: "In Capernaum a house-church was made out of the home of the prince of the apostles, whose walls still stand today as they were."[8] These words actually point to a building already existing prior to the octagonal church and found underneath later structures.

When archaeologists dug below these structures they discovered a regular domestic dwelling which was first inhabited in the middle of the first century BCE. The structure was built around a central courtyard with smaller rooms both to the north and to the south. There was a second courtyard to the south of the house. The main entrance to the house was on the east which opened to a large (7 meters by 7.5 meters) room that had doorways leading to both courtyards. Its floor was composed of unworked basalt stone. This particular house was larger than most that were found in Capernaum, but there was nothing extraordinary during this early stage of occupation. A typical assortment of domestic pottery was found throughout the house.

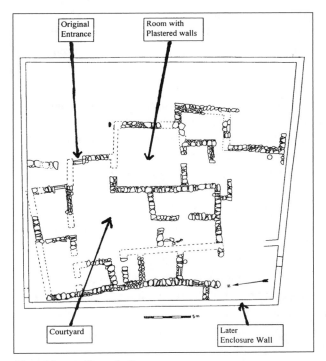

Plan of Peter's House in Capernaum

8. John Wilkinson, *Jerusalem Pilgrims Before the Crusades* (Warminster, England: Aris & Phillips Ltd., 2002), 94.

Later in the second half of the first century CE, a major change took place. The east room was plastered, which is without parallel for structures at Capernaum. There was also a significant change in the pottery found from this time on. Instead of regular domestic pottery, only lamps and storage jars were found. This suggests that this structure was now restricted for public gatherings. While this in itself could be interpreted in various ways, the continuing development of this site clearly suggests that the early inhabitants associated the structure with the life of Jesus.

During the following centuries, this main room was replastered and various graffiti were etched on the walls including crosses and boats with the words "Christ" and "Lord." The inscriptions were primarily Greek although a few were in Semitic languages and one in Latin. Some have interpreted roughly etched inscriptions also to include the name of Peter, but this is questionable.[9] In the fourth century, the entire house was walled off from the rest of the compound and an atrium 9 meters by 9.5 meters was constructed on the east side. Within the plastered room, two pilasters were erected on the north and south apparently to support an arch for a new roof. It would be assumed that this is the structure visited by Egeria, which was then replaced a century later by the more elaborate octagonal church. Today a modern church structure is suspended above the archaeological remains.

Although this structure has been labeled as the house of Peter, one must be careful not to make hasty conclusions. There are stories of Peter and Jesus in Capernaum. Yet there is no hard evidence from the first century linking Peter to this particular building. The finds do present a convincing case that this structure was viewed by early Christians as having importance in the life of Jesus. Normally early churches were established over places long considered sacred including sites of theophanies, but they are not usually erected over domestic dwellings. Is it possible that this structure simply represented a typical house church with no memorial significance? Perhaps one of the wealthier Christians from Capernaum made it available for gatherings because it was one of the larger structures in this community.

If, however, it also had a commemorative purpose, can one be certain it accurately reflects a particular event in the life of Jesus?[10] It was not until the mid-first century that this structure was set apart. Can we be sure that they had accurate knowledge of events taking place a generation earlier? Is it possible that the site commemorated the general work in Capernaum rather

---

9. Strange and Shanks, "Has the House Where Jesus Stayed in Capernaum been Found?"

10. Jonathan L. Reed, *Archaeology and the Galilean Jesus: A Re-examination of the Evidence* (Harrisburg, PA: Trinity Press, 2000), 157-60.

than a single event? If it represents one particular event, then which event? These questions are not meant to say that this building is without importance. It does represent an early gathering place for the church—perhaps one of the earliest that can be established. Yet one can only speculate from that point on.

The conclusion that this house once belonged to Simon Peter is based on a single episode in the Synoptics. Upon Jesus' first visit to Capernaum, after visiting the synagogue on the Sabbath, he was called upon to heal Peter's mother-in-law who was suffering from a fever. A comparison of the Synoptic texts follows:

Matthew 8:14-15	*Mark 1:29-31*	*Luke 4:38-39*
When Jesus entered Peter's house,	As soon as they left the synagogue, they entered the house of Simon and Andrew, with James and John. Now Simon's mother-	After leaving the synagogue he entered Simon's house.
he saw his mother-in-law lying in bed with a fever;	in-law was in bed with a fever, and they told him about her at once. He	Now Simon's mother-in-law was suffering from a high fever, and they asked him about her. Then he
he touched her hand,	came and took her by the hand and lifted her up.	stood over her and rebuked the fever,
and the fever left her,	Then the fever left her,	and it left her.
and she got up	and she	Immediately she got up
and began to serve him.	began to serve them.	and began to serve them.

The focus of this account is on Peter's mother-in-law, not on Peter himself. Many have seen this as a way to avoid the discrepancy with Peter's Bethsaida connection. They would argue that Peter merely married into a family from Capernaum. Possibly, because of fishing connections, he relocated to this particular city or he considered Capernaum a second home and visited there often. Still this solution leaves a number of questions unanswered.

The Markan account notes that Jesus' visit to the house occurred as soon as he left the Capernaum synagogue. This has been advanced as an argument for the authenticity of the house church because of its proximity to the synagogue—assuming a first-century synagogue is represented by the black basalt foundation beneath the impressive third- century limestone structure. Yet Mark uses the word εὐθύς (immediately, as soon as) some 41 times to convey a sense of urgency for the entire Gospel. As is frequently the case both Matthew and Luke have omitted it. So its occurrence at the beginning of this account need not be used to determine the location of the house.

This also raises several questions. Would Peter have possessed a house in such a prominent location? Would it be likely that such a house be more than substantial in size? The excavated house church comprises about 400 square meters and includes two courtyards. This stands in contrast to the smaller houses in the insula between the house church and the synagogue. In his book on comparative dwellings from this period, Hirschfeld includes as the best example of a courtyard house from Capernaum one which has an area less than half the size (180 square meters).[11] On the other hand, "the house of Peter" at Capernaum is roughly the size of the two excavated courtyard houses at Bethsaida (the "Fisherman's House" in area B is 450 square meters and the "Winemaker's House" in area C is about 280 square meters)—homes exhibiting a rather comfortable lifestyle. The excavated house at Capernaum, therefore, is out of character with what we know about and expect of Peter.

There is also a question of why the early Christians plastered the walls in only one room of this structure setting it apart from the rest of the house. It would seem that they wished to designate it as the place where something significant had taken place. In this particular account, the memorable event is the healing of Peter's mother-in-law of a fever. Yet the healing apparently does not take place in the central part of the house. In the early Markan version, "they told him about her," which suggests that she was reclining in one of the side bedrooms. Thus there seems to be no direct connection between the plastered room and this particular miracle of Jesus.

Finally, one might ask whether Peter even owned a house at Capernaum. The point of the call narrative in Mark 1:16-20 is that the disciples have left behind their occupations, families, and possessions. Later Peter proclaims, "Look, we have left everything and followed you" (Mark 10:28). The actual miracle of the healing of Peter's mother-in-law was probably an independent unit (Mark 1: 30-31) that was later combined with other materials to present a typical day in the life of Jesus. The introductory verse 29, which ties this episode to Capernaum, appears to be the work of the evangelist Mark. The sentence itself is quite awkward as it provides continuity with the earlier call episode naming again not only Simon, but also Andrew, James, and John. The description that it was the house of both Simon and Andrew creates something of an unusual situation with the presence also of Peter's mother-in-law. The changes in both Matthew and Luke demonstrate that they also see the difficulties of Mark's introduction. They omit reference to the other disciples, James and John, and they describe the house as belonging

---

11. Yizhar Hirschfeld, *The Palestinian Dwelling in the Roman-Byzantine Period* (Jerusalem: Franciscan Printing Press, 1995), 68-69. See also comparative charts on pages 100-1.

only to Peter. A more likely scenario is that the house belonged to Peter's mother-in-law and that Peter was merely visiting. The tradition that Peter owned a house at Capernaum, therefore, is suspect. If he does have a link to Capernaum, it is possibly through marriage.

What then is the significance of the house church at Capernaum? The Gospels relate a number of other events which take place in houses at Capernaum. According to Synoptic reports Jesus himself may have had a house at Capernaum. Mark 2:1 reports that when Jesus returned to Capernaum he was ἐν οἴκῳ. This can be translated as "in a house" or "at home." The Matthean tradition is stronger stating that Jesus "made his home in Capernaum" (Matt 4:13). It is here apparently that he taught the crowds so that on one occasion some had to make a hole in the thatched roof (characteristic of Capernaum buildings) to let down a paralytic before Jesus (Mark 2:1-12). On another occasion, this is the setting for further teaching with the crowds when Jesus' family came down from Nazareth and sought to control him (Mark 3:19-35). Is it possible that the Capernaum house church commemorated this teaching activity? Yet again one wonders if this larger house is really fitting for the character of Jesus.

The Gospels, however, do report about two individuals who would be quite at home in such a large house in this prominent location in Capernaum. One is a centurion stationed in Capernaum who sought Jesus' help to heal his slave (Luke 7:1-10). The other is Jairus who sought Jesus' help to save his daughter from the point of death (Mark 5:21-43). In the case of the centurion, Luke writes that "he loves our people, and it is he who built our synagogue for us."[12] In the case of Jairus, all three Synoptic writers describe him as the "leader of the synagogue" (Mark 5:22; Matt 9:18-26; Luke 8:41-56). The excavated house church would be appropriate for either of these men.

The story of Jairus is especially appealing because Jesus actually came to his house and raised his daughter from death. The courtyard setting and the large eastern room provide a proper context for a wake. Thus Mark notes that Jesus "came to the house" and "saw a commotion, people weeping and wailing loudly" (Mark 5:38). Then "he put them all outside, and took the child's father and mother and those who were with him, and went in where the child was" (Mark 5:40). The room where they gathered, therefore, becomes the scene of one of the most dramatic of Jesus' miracles, bringing the child from death to life. Not only does the setting of the excavated

12. The parallel account in Matthew 8:5-13 does not include this detail. A variant account in John 4:46-54 raises questions about historical details.

house fit the details of the miracle account, but one can easily imagine the possibility that a grateful Jairus later would have made his house available for the gathering of the early Christian community in Capernaum and that the actual room would have been eventually marked off in commemoration.

This discussion has attempted to show that there are difficulties with Father Corbo's identification of the Capernaum house church as "The House of St. Peter" and that a number of alternative explanations are just as attractive. There is no way to prove the ownership of this house for the time of Jesus' ministry in Capernaum, whether it belonged to Peter, Jairus, or anyone else. What can be established is that a generation or so later, this building was set apart for a special purpose, probably as a gathering place for the Christian community. The designation of this site as "the house of Peter" did not come about until the fourth century—after the gospel reports had established a connection between Peter and the town of Capernaum. Since these written reports derive from a single problematical verse in Mark, one must treat them with some degree of skepticism.[13] They do not necessarily challenge the Johannine report that Bethsaida was the home of Peter and Andrew.

Later traditions: Bethsaida and other disciples

As the era of pilgrimage began, European Christians found interest in establishing the places of the apostles.[14] Constantine allowed a certain Jewish-Christian named Josephos from Tiberias to build churches at Sepphoris, Nazareth, Tiberias, and Capernaum. In the fifth century, the elaborate octagonal church singled out Capernaum for special attention. Just as Egeira reported on the connection of Peter to the house church at Capernaum, so others were attracted to Bethsaida.

In 530 CE, Theodosius demonstrated that the Bethsaida tradition for Peter and Andrew had not subsided, but that it continued alongside the Capernaum tradition. The account of Theodosius is especially noteworthy because he establishes geographical information for the sites. He writes about the northern Sea of Galilee area as follows:

> From Seven Springs [Tabgha] it is two miles to Capernaum. From Capernaum it is six miles to Bethsaida, where the Apostles Peter, Andrew, Philip, and the

---

13. *Contra* Jerome Murphy O'Connor, "Fishers of Fish, Fishers of Men," *Bible Review* 15 (June 1999) 22-27, 48-49.

14. Elizabeth McNamer, "Medieval Pilgrim Accounts of Bethsaida and the Bethsaida Controversy," in *Bethsaida* (1999), 2:397-411.

sons of Zebedee were born. From Bethsaida it is fifty miles to Panias, that is the place where the Jordan rises from the two places Ior and Dan.[15]

The six-mile distance between Bethsaida and Capernaum may seem at first too long to the modern traveler crossing from Capernaum to Bethsaida via the modern Aphik Bridge. In reality, it denotes authenticity for the ancient traveler who naturally followed the ancient Roman road via Chorazin. The traditions reported, therefore, seem to be gathered from an on-site visitation.

Theodosius reports that five apostles were born in Bethsaida. The first three names correspond to the Johannine list although Philip is no longer prominent. Peter, possibly because of his reputation, is now mentioned first. By referring to those "born" in Bethsaida, Theodosius seems to reflect knowledge of the complexity of the traditions. Yet the addition of the two sons of Zebedee, James and John, naturally follows because of the fishing partnership between the four disciples as well as the connection by friendship as the inner circle among disciples of Jesus. It is impossible to know whether this information is derived from independent sources or from a process of deduction using the gospel texts. This report, however, elevates the status of Bethsaida as the home of five disciples. What is striking is that these names occur at the top of all lists of the twelve disciples underscoring their importance (Mark 3:16-19; Matt 10:2-4; Luke 6:14-16; Acts 1:13).

Two centuries later in 725 CE, Willibald, later the first bishop of Eichstätt in Bavaria, also visited the site and left his report:

> From there [Capernaum], they went to Bethsaida, the city of Peter and Andrew; there is now a church there in the place where originally their house stood.[16]

Here the place of Peter and Andrew has been elevated so that Philip has dropped out of the picture. However, the mention of the church may point to confusion with a visit to Capernaum. There is no archaeological evidence for such a structure at Bethsaida.

The ninth-century Saxon gospel, known as *The Heliand,* does not mention Bethsaida by name. However, it provides an intriguing version of the call of the disciples:

---

15. John Wilkinson, *Jerusalem Pilgrims before the Crusades*, 63. P. Donatus Baldi, *Enchiridion Locum Sanctorum*, Section 381, 266.

16. Wilkinson, *Jerusalem Pilgrims before the Crusades*, 128.

He walked along the shore of a body of water where the Jordan has created a sea on the border of Galileeland. There He found the brothers, Andrew and Peter, sitting by the stream at the place where they worked hard setting out their nets on the wide waters as they fished in the current . . . . He told them that He would give them so much of God's kingdom. "Just as you catch fish here in the Jordan river, you will be hauling in the sons of men hand over hand . . . ." As they came farther along the seashore, they came across an old man and his two sons, James and John, young men, sitting by the sea. The father and his sons were sitting up on a sand dune. They were hard at work with both hands repairing and reweaving the nets that they had torn the night before on the water.[17]

While there is no question that *The Heliand* includes much elaboration to relate the gospel tradition to a Germanic audience,[18] this episode includes several details which point to the possibility of an independent tradition.

- The name Andrew is given prominence over Peter.
- There is no mention of the town of Capernaum.
- The linking of this event with the Jordan River is unique since the Gospels never even mention the upper Jordan.
- The geographical description of the mouth of the upper Jordan River opening into the Sea of Galilee is quite accurate in our understanding of first century geography.
- The account correctly characterizes the upper Jordan as the eastern boundary of Galilee at the time of Jesus.

It is impossible to know whether such details originate in an early tradition or whether they came from the reports of pilgrims such as Willibald. However, they point to the fishing activity of disciples nearby Bethsaida.

Later the Syrian author Simon of Basra mentions a prayer house erected by the apostle Philip.[19] One would tend to give some credibility to such a report because it gives focus to Philip rather than Peter and Andrew. Still, it is not substantiated by other documentation.

One also is faced with the problem in the Middle Ages that the site of Bethsaida became lost and alternative sites were proposed. Maps frequently positioned the city of Bethsaida on the west side of the Jordan near Caper-

17. G. Ronald Murphy, trans., *The Heliand: The Saxon Gospel* (New York: Oxford University Press, 1992), 40-41.

18. G. Ronald Murphy, *The Saxon Savior: The Germanic Transformation of the Gospel in the Ninth-Century Heliand* (New York: Oxford, 1989), 58-61.

19. F. M. Abel, *Geographie de la Palestine* (Paris: Librarie Lecoffre, 1967), 2:195.

naum. This resulted in a confusion of information rather than solutions. During this period further speculation linked Bethsaida with other disciples including James, son of Alphaeus, and Bartholomew.[20] Clearly Bethsaida had the reputation as "City of the Apostles."

20. The name Bartholomew is usually thought to be derived from "Son of Ptolemy." However, it is possible that the actual meaning comes from "Son of Talmai," which could be a distant connection with the Geshurite king, grandfather of Absalom. Bartholomew has often been identified with Nathanael, mentioned only in the fourth Gospel. John 1 clearly links Nathanael with Philip from Bethsaida and it is only the later appendix in John 21 which connects Nathanael with the town of Cana.

Chapter 5

Across the Sea . . . to Bethsaida

Bethsaida-Julias is consistently depicted in ancient literature as a city by the sea. Pliny notes that Julias was one of four prominent seaside cities and that it was located on the eastern shore: "There are four lovely cities on the Sea of Galilee: Julias and Hippos in the east and Tarichaeae and Tiberias in the west (Pliny, *Natural History* 5.15.71). Josephus notes that it is located "in lower Gaulanitis" (Josephus, *War* 2.168) and that the Jordan River entered the lake just "below the town" (Josephus, *War* 3.515). In his own eyewitness report of the battle that took place outside Bethsaida in 67 CE between Josephus' Galilean forces and Agrippa's army under Sulla, a number of details corroborate the location (Josephus, *Life* 398-406):

- the position of the Jordan River just to the west;
- the arrival of supporting troops by boat from Tarichaeae (Magdala);
- his own evacuation by boat from Julias (Bethsaida) to Cepharnocus (Capernaum) when injured as his horse stumbled in marshy ground.

Clearly Bethsaida is located on the northeast shore of the Sea of Galilee.

General gospel references

In the gospel accounts, one is struck by the frequent reports of Jesus and his disciples traveling by boat over the northern part of the sea with Bethsaida often included in the itinerary. One interesting sidelight to these reports is that the evangelists often describe the trips to or from Bethsaida as *across the sea.* In Mark 8:13, prior to the healing of a blind man at Bethsaida, Jesus

61

got into a boat and "went across to the other side." In this case Mark makes clear the points of departure and arrival as Dalmanutha (Magadan in Matt 15:39 = Magdala or Tarichaeae), half-way down the western coast (Mark 8:10), and Bethsaida on the northeast (Mark 8:22). In contrast, in describing a boat trip between two locations on the western shore (Capernaum and Dalmanutha), the evangelist merely reports that Jesus "went by boat" (Mark 8:10; Matt 15:39) with no suggestion of crossing.

Josephus and cities around the lake

The feeding of the 5,000

Likewise the expressions "they went across" and "to the other side" occur in connection with the miracles of the feeding of the 5,000 and the walking on the water. In this context, Bethsaida is mentioned explicitly both in Mark 6:44 and Luke 9:10—the travel descriptions are as follows:

Before the feeding

> Mark 6:32—They went away *in the boat* to a deserted place by themselves.
>
> Matt 14:13—He withdrew from there *in a boat* to a deserted place by himself.
>
> Luke 9:10—He took them with him and withdrew privately to a city called Bethsaida.
>
> John 6:1—Jesus went *to the other side* of the Sea of Galilee.

After the feeding

> Mark 6:45—He made his disciples get *into the boat* and go on ahead *to the other side,* to Bethsaida.
>
> Matt 14:22—He made his disciples get *into the boat* and go on ahead *to the other side.*
>
> John 6:16-17—His disciples went down to the sea, got *into a boat*, and started *across the sea* to Capernaum.

Upon return to land

Mark 6:53—When they had *crossed over*, they came to land at Gennesaret.

Matt 14:34—When they had *crossed over*, they came to land at Gennesaret.

John 6:21—The boat *reached the land* toward which they were going.

At the beginning of our analysis it is important to make two points. First, Luke contains only a description of the departure because he omits the Markan material between the two feeding narratives and proceeds directly to the confession episode at Caesarea Philippi (Luke 9:18-22). Second, there is good reason to question the accuracy of geographical details redacted by Mark. Mark 7:31 betrays a similar confusion in directing Jesus from Tyre to the Sea of Galilee by way of Sidon (to the north) and the Decapolis (to the southeast). A number of scholars, therefore, have suggested that Mark accidentally substituted *Sidon* for *Bethsaidan* in that verse—a reading that would make more sense.[1] The direction of travel in Mark 6:45 "to Bethsaida" contradicts the subsequent report of arrival in Gennesaret in Mark 6:53.[2] By reading "from Bethsaida" in Mark 6:45, the Markan picture is clarified so that the four Gospels paint a consistent picture with the disciples traveling from the western shore to Bethsaida and returning to the western shore in the direction of Capernaum, but ending up at Gennesaret.

What is most significant is that Bethsaida is consistently described as "on the other side" or "across the sea" from the

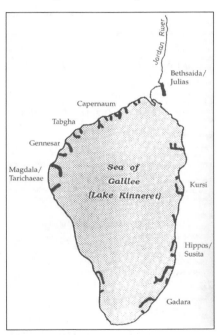

Harbors on the Sea of Galilee

---

1. Julius Wellhausen, *Das Evangelium Marci* (Berlin: 1909), 58; W. C. Allen, *The Gospel According to Saint Mark* (London: 1915), 110; Vincent Taylor, *The Gospel According to St. Mark* (New York: St. Martin's Press, 1957), 353.

2. Variant readings in the manuscript tradition of Mark 6:45 demonstrate a perceived difficulty. *Ms* D includes εἰς Βησσαιδάν rather than πρὸς Βηθσαιδάν. *Mss P*45 and W omit εἰς τὸ πέραν.

various cities on the western shore. Travel to Bethsaida is expressed in terms of "withdrawing" from the crowds and heading towards a deserted place where they could be by themselves. In many ways the picture is more like that of a trip to the far side of the lake as is the case, in fact, in one Synoptic episode: the healing of the demoniac in the territory of the Gerasenes/ Gadarenes identified today with Kursi on the eastern shore (Mark 4:35; 5:1, 21; Matt 8:18; 9:1; Luke 8:22, 26, 40). Apparently travel straight across the lake was common and the expression "as from Tiberias to Susita"—a distance of about eight or nine miles—became a common metaphor for speed.[3] Yet in the case of Bethsaida, the distance from Capernaum is only a few miles. Nevertheless, there was a great chasm separating these two cities frequented by Jesus.

Bethsaida outside the land of Israel

In one respect the separation was psychological. Bethsaida was not located in Galilee, but in Gaulanitis (the modern Golan). It was under the rule, not of Antipas, but of Herod's other son Philip. To some, it was not considered *eretz Israel*, but the beginning of the diaspora. Although it comes from a later period, one such rabbinic text illustrates this well:

> And it happened Rabbi Eleazar ben Shamoa and Rabbi Yohanan ha-Sandlar were going to Netzivim to study Torah with Rabbi Yehudah ben Batayrah. They arrived at Tzaidan and remembered the land of Israel. Their eyes opened and filled with tears and they ripped their clothes . . . . They returned to their original place and said that living in the Land of Israel outweighs all the commandments in the Torah.[4]

In contrast to the desire on the part of Jesus to withdraw to this place for temporary respite and solitude, such a withdrawal on the part of early second-century Rabbis Eleazar ben Shamoa and Yohanan ha-Sandlar to Tzaidan (quite possibly Bethsaida) was devastating. They were cut off from the land.

Geography

In order to understand properly the expression "across the sea," one must come to know the geography of the area. The Galilee and the Golan

---

3. Genesis Rabbah 31:13; 32:9.

4. Tannaitic Sifrei Devarim, Reeh 80:4.80. While I tend to agree that this passage refers to Bethsaida rather that Sidon on the Phoenician coast, one must consider the possibility that Tzaidan refers to the region around Bethsaida or even a later settlement somewhat to the north of et-Tell. Richard Freund discusses the basic issues in "The Search for Bethsaida in Rabbinic Literature," in *Bethsaida* (1995), 267-311.

are separated by the Jordan River which descends rapidly from the foothills of Mount Hermon to an elevation of 210 meters below sea level at the lake. The river cuts a gorge that rises quickly on both sides making fording nearly impossible. The only crossing points in the ancient world were the Daughters of Jacob Bridge near Kibbutz Gadot seven miles to the north and, in the Roman period, a bridge, or at least a ford, slightly north of Bethsaida that led to Chorazin to the west.

Today's visitor can easily be misled, as can those relying on common biblical maps, who see a natural land connection to Capernaum across a relatively tame Jordan River to the south. Yet the Q woe saying of Jesus does not connect Bethsaida with Capernaum, but rather with Chorazin to the west. Access between Bethsaida and Capernaum in the first century was, not by land, but by sea.

A Roman road

Until recently little has been known about the road system in the lower Golan. Most studies acknowledged that the *Via Maris* passed from Megiddo to the northeast, crossing at the Daughters of Jacob Bridge before continuing on to Damascus.[5] A second north-south road crossed the Jordan near Beth Shean (Scythopolis) and traveled up the eastern side of the Jordan River in the Golan. East-west roads connected Tyre on the coast with Caesarea Philippi and Acco (Ptolemais) with Tiberias and Hippos, crossing the Jordan to the south of the lake, and then continuing east from Hippos. Already in the Hellenistic era, Bethsaida was linked by a road north toward Caesarea Philippi.

However, with the excavations at Chorazin, new interest was aroused about further links in the road system. The discovery of an ancient section of road passing north of Chorazin led to a more comprehensive survey that has identified an east-west road linking Acco, Chorazin, and Bethsaida.[6] Ilan and Stepanski discovered a three-mile section of this road near Chorazin that measures from 4 meters to 6 meters in width and includes curbstones

5. Michael Avi-Yonah, "The Roman Road System," *The Holy Land: A Historical Geography* (Grand Rapids, MI.: Baker, 1966); Israel Roll, "The Roman Road System in Judaea," *The Jerusalem Cathedra,* vol. 3 (Detroit: Wayne State University Press, 1983), 136-61; Dan Urman, *The Golan: A Profile.*

6. Zeev Yeivin, "Chorazin," *The New Encyclopedia of Archaeological Excavations in the Holy Land,* vol. 1, ed. E. Stern (Jerusalem: Israel Exploration Society, 1993), 302; Zvi Ilan, "Eastern Galilee, Survey of Roman Roads," *Excavations and Surveys in Israel* (1989/ 90), 9:14-16. Yosi Stepanski, *Hadashot Arkheologiyot,* 104 (1995) 27-9.

and typical techniques of Roman road building. There were also several small bridges that leveled out low spots and provided waterflow through ravines. This confirms earlier reports of portions of the road discovered at Rama to the west and it establishes a junction with the north-south route at Gov Yosef. The survey reports on an extension south to Capernaum where a second-century milestone has been uncovered, though the precise route of this road is unclear. The critical point is that it links up with the east-west Chorazin road on the heights to the west of the Jordan River which then provides direct access to Bethsaida.

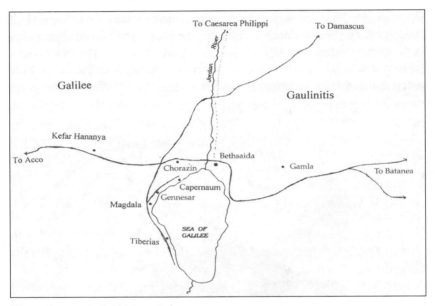

The road system in Rabbinic period

There are a number of uncertainties concerning the exact course of the road as it approaches Bethsaida. Near the ridge overlooking the Jordan River from the west, evidence of the ancient road appears at several places. However, sections of the ancient road appear to have been covered by a new road near Moshav Almagor. This road jogs in a northern direction as it makes its way down to the river at a point about a mile north of et-Tell. Because there are no easy points for crossing the Jordan and because the course of the river has been altered over the centuries, its exact crossing remains uncertain.

Ilan's rough map would erroneously suggest that this east-west road passed just to the south of Bethsaida. It is more likely that the road passed about a mile to the north. This would not be unusual since ancient cities were usually constructed a short distance away from the roads which would provide access for passing armies as well as robbers and thieves.[7]

Troop positions at the battle of Julias

Evidence for reconstructing the ancient route comes from Josephus' description of the battle of Bethsaida in 67 CE. In this confrontation, Josephus was present as the commander of the Galilean forces and thus presents first-hand information. Significantly, his opponent Sulla's camp was located five furlongs (= 1,100 meters) north of Bethsaida. Sulla's mission was not to besiege Bethsaida (which was quite possibly temporarily deserted), but to cut off the Galilean supply route to the rebellious cities of the Golan (Josephus, *Life* 398-400).

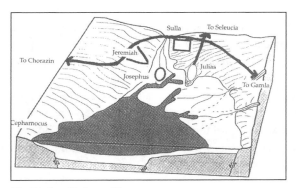

The Battle of Julias—67 CE

Sulla, therefore, posted guards on the roads leading to Seleucia and Gamla. This statement is very important for our understanding of the road system because it indicates roads in three directions:

- a road to Galilee in the west;
- a road to Seleucia in the north;
- a road to Gamla in the east.

If our assumptions about the location of this junction are correct, there would also be a short spur connecting Bethsaida to the south. Although Gamla lies directly to the east of Bethsaida, the course of the road would have been affected by the Wadi Daliot—continuing east before turning south. The course

---

7. Tosefta Erubin 4.5.

of the road to Seleucia is less clear since three different sites have been suggested for this city: Tell Seleucia, Khirbet Qusbiyye, and Dabura.[8] However, the existence of such a road confirms the connection between Bethsaida and Caesarea Philippi to the north. Avi-Yonah's discovery of a milestone in the area of Dabura, about three miles northeast of the Daughters of Jacob bridge points to the likelihood of a north-south route along the eastern side of the Jordan River gorge. This is consistent with the gospel reports of a stopover in Bethsaida on Jesus' way to Caesarea Philippi (Mark 8 and Luke 9).

There is one further complicating factor. Two Josephus manuscripts offer the reading of *Cana* instead of *Seleucia*. If this reading is correct it would point to the town in the plain of Asochis, about eight miles north of Sepphoris and not far from the Acco-Bethsaida road. Josephus himself spent some time there early in the war (Josephus, *Life* 86). Because it was located near Jotapata, a center for the Galilean forces, it would be a potential point for the origin of the supply route to rebel forces in Gamla. In other words, the statement about Sulla's forces guarding the road between Cana and Gamla would point to its importance as an east-west communications and trade route. It is interesting that Jesus' route from Bethany across the Jordan to Cana in Galilee likewise brought him to Bethsaida (John 1:28, 43-44; 2:1). During the war, this route served to transport military forces to the Golan. Not only was this the case with regard to Sulla's troops, but later following the defeat of Gamla, Titus passed this way with one thousand horsemen in route to Gischala in Galilee (Josephus, *War* 4.87-92).

East-West trade route

The role of this route in trade has been the topic of an important study by David Adan-Bayewitz.[9] Pottery manufactured at Kefar Hananya, west of Chorazin, has been traced to various sites in the Galilee as well as Gamla, Ein Nashut, and Kanaf. In addition, the influence of the Kefar Hananya market on Golan sites resulted in the local manufacture of Golan kitchenware with very similar forms as early as the second half of the first century BCE. However, this is not to say that access to the Golan was easy. These three Golan sites include only 10-20 percent Kefar Hananya ware among samples studied while Galilean sites at a similar distance included around 60 percent

---

8. Tell Seleucia is proposed by G. Schumacher, *The Jaulan*; Khirbet Qusbiyye is suggested by Urman, *The Golan: A Profile*; Dubura is suggested by Ilan.

9. David Adan-Bayewitz, *Common Pottery in Roman Galilee: A Study in Local Trade* (Tel Aviv: Bar Ilan University Press, 1993).

of this type of pottery. Especially significant is the contrast with Capernaum where there is a very high percentage of Kefar Hananya ware. Such a disparity in percentages from Capernaum to Golan sites can be attributable to difficulty in transporting Galilean goods to Golan sites. Subsequent studies demonstrate that Bethsaida kitchen ware exhibits a high degree of similarity to Kefar Hananya forms.[10]

Ilan also proposed that the Acco-Bethsaida road continued east to extend communications with Bashan and Hauran. It is only logical that the cities of Caesarea Philippi and Bethsaida would have been linked to these areas on the eastern edge of the territory of Philip. One only need turn to the conflict between King Aretas of Nabatea and Herod Antipas shortly after Philip's death to understand the significance of such a route. The discovery in this eastern area of Philip's tetrarchy of several inscriptions mentioning the *cohors Augusta* points to a military presence in the first century and the need for access to the west.[11] Interestingly, pottery from Si in the Hauran displays a striking similarity to Kefar Hananya ware[12] and points to the need for further study concerning this trade route.

There is one further piece of literary evidence from the second century CE concerning the Bethsaida road. In a passage referring to Rabbi Judah ha-Nasi there is a debate concerning the transportation of wine on the Sabbath. At the end it is noted that "the incident took place on the highway of Tzaidan and it was completely inhabited by Israel."[13] While the meaning of the expression "highway of Tzaidan" is not totally clear, it may well point to this same road passing to the north of Bethsaida. The settlement of Jews in this area following the New Testament era is supported by the location of the ed-Dikke synagogue from this period.[14]

There was some sort of a chasm, therefore, between the Golan and the lower Galilee so that Bethsaida was viewed as "across the sea." Primary access to Bethsaida from the western shore of the Sea of Galilee was by boat. However, an east-west road, passing about a mile to the north, connected Bethsaida with the northern Galilee via Chorazin and provided also a link to the east.

10. Toni Tessaro, "Hellenistic and Roman Ceramic Cooking Ware from Bethsaida," in *Bethsaida* (1995), 127-39. Sandra Fortner, *Der Keramik und Kleinfunde von Bethsaida-Iulias am See Genezareth, Israel,* (München: Ludwig-Maximilians-Universität, 2008).

11. Henry Innes MacAdam, *Studies in the History of the Roman Province of Arabia: The Northern Sector.* BAR International Series 295 (1986), 61-7.

12. Adan-Bayewitz, *Common Pottery in Roman Galilee,* 239.

13. PT, *Avodah Zarah* 5.5, 44d.

14. Heinrich Kohl and Carl Watzinger, *Antike Synagogen in Galilaea* (Leipzig: J .C. Hinrichs, 1916). Urman, *Ancient Synagogues*, 2: 503-9.

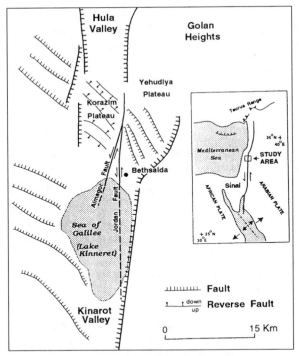

Geological fault lines in the northern Jordan valley

Thus the pairing of Bethsaida and Chorazin in Q is understandable. Access by road from Capernaum to Bethsaida via Chorazin would have been more difficult as is attested by the six-mile distance noted by the sixth-century pilgrim Theodosius. A north-south road linked Bethsaida with Caesarea Philippi.

Geological Findings

Today the visitor is surprised to find Bethsaida located 2.5 to 3.0 kilometers (approximately 1.5 to 1.8 miles) from the shore.[15] This was not the case in biblical times when Josephus measured the length of the Sea of Galilee as 140 stades or furlongs or about 28 kilometers (17 miles), while today it

15. Markus Bockmuehl suggests a uniform figure of 2.5 kilometers based on the 1994 Road Atlas approved by the Survey of Israel and the Mission of Tourism, "Simon Peter and Bethsaida," *Supplements to Novum Testamentum* 115 (2005), 53-91, especially 67, note 73. Past publications have used rough estimates ranging from 1.5 km. to twice that figure. The truth is that the northeast shoreline is in a constant state of flux having extended further south by significant distances several times during the two plus decades of excavations, most notably during the 2009 summer season.

is closer to 21 kilometers (13 miles) in length (Josephus, *War* 3.506). Two thousand years since the New Testament era have brought major changes. Then the sea reached the base of the small hill on which Bethsaida is located, and a much more dramatic gulf of water separated Bethsaida from the Galilean land to its west.

Geologists John F. Shroder Jr., and Moshe Inbar note that these dramatic shifts are due to three natural causes.[16]

- First, its location on the Jordan rift fault line led to a gradual passing of two continental plates so that Bethsaida has been moving to the north while the Galilee has been gradually shifting to the south.
- Second, the instability of the land on this fault line led to periodic earthquakes and to shifting and upward pushing of the land.
- Third, the natural flow of the Jordan River has carried tons of silt from the northern valley to be deposited in the Beteiha plain below.

Aerial photo of et-Tell and Beteiha Plains

16. John F. Shroder Jr. and Moshe Inbar, "Geologic and Geographic Background to the Bethsaida Excavations," in *Bethsaida* (1995), 65-98; John F. Shroder Jr., M. P. Bishop, K. J. Cornwell, and Moshe Inbar, "Catastrophic Geomorphic Processes and Bethsaida Archaeology, Israel," in *Bethsaida* (1999), 2:115-74. Recent studies independent of the Bethsaida Excavations Project provide further support to the proposals of Shroder and his team of geologists, S. Marco, A. Heimann, A. Agnon, T. Rockwell, and U. Frieslander, *Paleoseismicity of the Jordan Fault, the Beteiha Valley.* Geological Survey of Israel, Report-ES/ 55/ 97 (Jerusalem: Geological Survey of Israel, 1997).

This can be illustrated in modern times by the flood of 1969 when once-in-a-century rainstorms led to a peak discharge of nearly 6,000 cubic feet per second causing a change of shoreline no less than 1,500 feet. The combination of these last two causes brought about dramatic changes on several occasions when landslides caused by earthquake blocked the Jordan River so that an artificial lake was built up behind it. The subsequent dissolution of these landslide dams brought about such a massive force which carried boulders, mud, and debris into the mouth of the river below.

Flood gravels over black mud

The geologists have found evidence that the Beteiha plain below Bethsaida was once submerged below water. Boreholes dug in the plain paint an interesting history of change. Just twenty meters south of the base of et-Tell, there is a dramatic change in soil composition when one digs several feet into the ground. The upper level composed of flood gravel covers a black organic-rich mud characteristic of lakes and lagoons. Deposited in this mud were bones and shells, including ostracods that are found only in quiet waters. Carbon-14 dating of these organic deposits points to the existence of quiet waters below Bethsaida about 2,700 to 1,800 years ago. In other words, there is good reason to believe that Bethsaida had ready access to the sea, whether the shores of the lake itself reached the base of et-Tell or estuaries made their way out to the sea. The maps provided by Shroder and Inbar illustrate the development from the time when et-Tell was a peninsula sticking out

Pool at base of et-Tell and stone wall

into the lake—corresponding perhaps to the first habitation of this site—to an estuary model by the end of the New Testament era. The city of Bethsaida therefore was separated dramatically from the Galilean lands to the west, and access by boat was expressed in literary sources as *crossing to the other side.*

The remains of an ancient wall were found in a shallow pool presently filled by the nearby fresh-water spring which once served the inhabitants of Bethsaida. This yet-to-be-excavated wall may have served as a mooring point for sea-going vessels of Bethsaida. The fate of the city would easily have been connected to accessibility to the lake. When this passage was blocked by further silting and dramatic land uplifts, the role of Bethsaida as a port leading to the cities of Galilee would have come to an end.

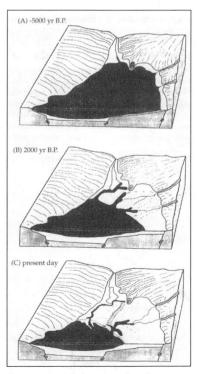

Progression of changing shoreline

The view of critics

Since the inception of the Bethsaida Excavations Project, skeptics have continued to question how a town identified by name for its relation to fishing can be located so far from the shore. Leading the way has been Mendel Nun, whose career as a Galilean fisherman has resulted in a personal interest in preserving knowledge about fishing practices over the centuries. Nun's dedication and efforts have led to an impressive "Mendel Nun" fishing museum at Ein Gev near ancient Hippos and several publications cataloging finds and demonstrating his theories about ancient fishing.[17] In one publication,[18] Nun identified sixteen harbors around the lake documenting the elevation for the promenade at Capernaum at 686.5 feet below sea level (- 209.25 meters) and the ports of Kursi and Tiberias at 686.4 feet below sea level (- 209.25 meters) and 683.4 feet below sea level (- 208.3 meters) respectively. Nun estimates the sea level in the late twentieth century at 690 feet below sea level (-210.5 meters), which he states is "about three feet higher than the ancient level" due to a dam on the southern end of the lake.[19] For the water to have reached et-Tell in the first century, according to Nun's reasoning, the higher level of the Sea of Galilee would have inundated all the lakeside villages and their ports. However, the geologists have never proposed higher water levels as a reason for the alteration of the northern shoreline. The shifting of plates, the uplifting of land segments, and the dramatic silting of the river's mouth do not require any change in water level. The change is no different than has occurred in two millennia at Ephesus where that former coastal city now finds itself miles from the Aegean Sea.

Mendel Nun has gathered a following of persons who are impressed with his "common sense" approach that a rising of the lake level would have drowned out the nearby villages. Most recently, Stephen Notley has followed Nun's argument uncritically in a full article on Bethsaida in the highly respected magazine *Near Eastern Archaeology* published by the

---

17. Mendel Nun, *The Sea of Galilee and its Fishermen in the New Testament* (Kibbutz Ein Gev, Israel: Kinnereth Sailing Co., 1989; *The Sea of Galilee: Water Levels, Past and Present* (Kibbutz Ein Gev, Israel: HaKibbutz Ein Gev, 1991); "Cast your Net upon the Water: Fish and Fishermen in Jesus' Time," *BAR* 19 (Nov/Dec, 1993), 46-56, 70.

18. Mendel Nun, *The Sea of Galilee: Newly Discovered Harbors from New Testament Days* (Kibbutz Ein Gev, Israel: Tourist Departement [sic] and Kinnereth Sailing Co., 1992).

19. Other current estimates of the surface elevation often use the figure of – 209.0 meters, though there have been dramatic fluctuations of the water level over the last decades. However, Nun's conclusion may be the result of some confusion in calculating figures below sea level.

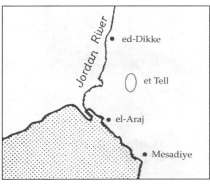

El-Araj

American Schools of Oriental Research.[20] In particular Notley points out that the current level of a proposed, yet still unexcavated, docking wall at the foot of Bethsaida is 669 feet below sea level (-204 meters) or some 22 feet above the current lake level. Notley argues, "If the BEP excavators are correct and the lake reached what they claimed was the docking facility of Bethsaida, then the lake would have inundated . . . every other known first-century settlement around the lake."[21]

This is quite true. However, the geologists have not argued that the lake would have reached up to this wall, rather seismic activity would have lifted the facility above its first-century level and removed from the lake. Such changes would have rendered the docking facility obsolete. As noted above, this wall has yet to be excavated and we will all wait with anticipation for that work to be done. However, subsequent geological samples from the immediate vicinity of the wall (potentially "the docking facility") yield two thousand-year-old black lake mud at an elevation of 205 meters below sea level.[22]

Sites in the Beteiha plain

The reluctance to accept geological studies about the origins of the Beteiha Plain have gone hand in hand with a defense of alternative sites for Bethsaida at el-Araj and el-Mesadiyeh. Already a century ago Schumacher had rejected Robinson's identification of et-Tell as Bethsaida because of its distance from the shore. Schumacher's conclusion that Bethsaida must have been located at el-Araj was based on his observation of Greco-Roman artifacts and remains of a road that he believed dated to the Roman period. From Schumacher's 1888 observations to Dan Urman's 1985 general survey of the Golan and continuing with other more recent visitors including

20. R. S. Notley, "Et-Tell is Not Bethsaida," *Near Eastern Archaeology* 70:4 (2007), 220-30.

21. IBID, 223.

22. John F. Shroder Jr., Harry D. Jol, and Philip P. Reeder, "El Araj as Bethsaida: Spatial and Temporal Improbabilities," in *Bethsaida* (2009) 4:293-309, especially 299-300.

Nun and Notley,[23] the one ines-
capable fact is that there are artifacts and architectural elements
that are Roman. In the words of
Markus Bockmuehl, "even with
the untrained eye I could easily
verify scattered surface remains
of large-scale public architecture
in both basalt and imported limestone, analogous to buildings in
nearby Capernaum that date back
to at least the early Byzantine
period."[24] The truth is that surveys and informal observations
are no substitute for methodical
excavation. Otherwise, the observations of remains at el-Araj
and el-Mesadiyeh are no more
conclusive that Bethsaida could
have been located there than at
Ein Gev where Nun has since
transported his finds or at Gin-

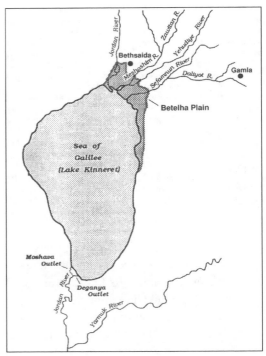

The Beteiha plain

nosar where Bethsaida Excavations Project artifacts are stored in a lab.

To date only one group has undertaken scientific research at el-Araj and
that is the Bethsaida Excavations Project under the direction of Rami Arav.
Three different kinds of studies have been undertaken:

- In 1987, Rami Arav excavated a four by four meter test probe that
  found Byzantine era pottery among the foundations for single-
  occupation buildings.[25]
- In 1999, Harry Jol made use of ground-penetrating radar to analyze
  a fifty-meter section around the el-Araj "tower" to a depth of ten

23. Mendel Nun, "Has Bethsaida finally been found?" *Jerusalem Perspective* (July/ Sept.,
1998), 12-31, 54; Anson F. Rainey and R.S. Notley, "The Search for Bethsaida," *The Sacred
Bridge: Carta's Atlas of the Biblical World* (Jerusalem: Carta, 2006), 256-9; S. Feldman, "The
Case for El Araj," *BAR* 26 (2000), 52.

24. Bockmuehl, "Simon Peter and Bethsaida," (2005), 77.

25. Rami Arav, "Et-Tell and El-Araj," *IEJ* 38 (1988), 187-8.

meters. The study showed no evidence of earlier layers or other structures other than stones randomly scattered by alluvial forces.[26]

- In 1999, geological fieldwork was carried out as a follow-up of 1993 and 1995 studies, extracting a total of twenty-six deep back-hoe trenches and two five-meter deep boreholes located throughout the Beteiha plain between et-Tell and el-Araj. Particularly significant was the discovery of pottery at various locations, though often turned "upside-down" with Iron Age pottery at higher levels than Roman era pottery—a not unexpected result when alluvial soils are washed out toward the lake.[27] This finding underscores the dubious role of coins or pottery as evidence when found in the alluvial plain, especially apart from a stratiographic context.

The geologists conclude that El-Araj is situated on a beach ridge between two channels, one about thirty meters wide formed at the mouth of the Jordan River, the other formed from the more erratic Meshoshim River and resulting in an estuary about two hundred meters wide extending a full kilometer inland. Between these two channels a series of beach ridges protrude into the lake as the periodic floods have moved the shoreline outward. The beach ridge identified as el-Araj covers a diameter of about sixty meters and contains four or five small mounds each about two or three meters high. Such an unstable setting would not have provided a favorable environment for a permanent settlement.[28]

There is no evidence that el-Araj was inhabited in the first century. The Jordan River channel, the Meshoshim estuary, and other likely estuaries and embayments provided access for fishermen from et-Tell to the lake. Sometime later, perhaps as a result of the well-documented earthquake of 363 CE, the harbor of Bethsaida was destroyed or blocked so that et-Tell no longer provided a practical base for fishermen. At that point et-Tell would have been abandoned by a significant portion of its population, if not all. Some would have moved north to the village of ed-Dikke near the road crossing at the Jordan, where an impressive synagogue provides testimony of significant habitation. Those engaged in fishing would have sought habitable space

---

26. Shroder Jr., Jol, and Reeder, "El-Araj as Bethsaida," (2009), 4:293-309, especially 297, 305.

27. Laura Banker, John F. Shroder Jr., and Moshe Inbar, "Sedimentologic and Paleogeomorphologic Character of the Bethsaida (Beteiha) Plain of the Sea of Galilee," in *Bethsaida* (2009), 4:310-25.

28. Shroder Jr., Jol, and Reeder, "El-Araj as Bethsaida," (2009), 4:302-4.

closer to the lake on beach ridges like el-Araj and el-Mesadiye. It may be that they migrated from one site to another over the years, building temporary housing and then more permanent structures. Since the alluvial plain lacked the large number of basalt stones needed for building, it would make good sense for builders to transport already dressed stones from et-Tell to el-Araj.

Chapter 6

Fishing Village

The name Bethsaida means "House of the Fisherman" or, as it might be called today, "Fishertown." In the New Testament it mainly occurs in the form βηθσαίδα although in Mark 8 it is written βηθσαίδαν. Technically, the former form should be translated "fishing," while the latter form means "fisherman" since the final "n" in Semitic languages denotes the person who carries out a particular activity. There is good reason to believe that the name originally was simply Tzaidan, mistakenly written by a scribe as Tzer (Josh 19:35).[1] As in the case of a number of towns, the prefix "Beth," which means "house," was added in the second-temple period. Later, the name Tzaidan appears to have resurfaced in the Rabbinic period.[2]

Hunting Traditions

Tzaidan can also mean "hunter." The same term could be used for both fishing and hunting because nets were employed in both ventures. In a sense both connotations were appropriate for Bethsaida because of the sparsely populated Golan region. In Toni Fisher's analysis of bone finds through various periods of time at et-Tell, the amount of wild game ranges from 8 to 12 percent. Most common among hunted animals are gazelle and deer. In addition, the pigs eaten at Bethsaida—usually about 3 to 5 percent—were

1. Rami Arav, "Bethsaida, Tzer, and the Fortified Cities of Naphtali," in *Bethsaida* (1995), 193-202.
2. Richard Freund, "The Search for Bethsaida in Rabbinic Literature," in *Bethsaida* (1995), 267-311.

likely wild.[3] When the Emperor Hadrian visited Palestine in 129 CE, he was fed with pheasants from Tzaidan.[4] Other than this example, however, the theme of hunting is less prominent in the literature about Bethsaida.

Fishing in the Old Testament era

From the beginning, Bethsaida, as a city on the sea, seems to have been known for its fishing. Reports about Israelite history, however, do not give much attention to Lake Kinneret (= Galilee) (Num 34:11; Deut 3:17; Josh 12:3; 13:27). The Tribe of Naphtali was given fishing rights. In the allotment of fortified cities in Joshua 19:35, four of them are designated as Tziddim, which may simply mean "fishing towns." The practice of fishing with nets is used by a number of writers for illustration (Eccl 9:12; Job 19:6; Hab 1:15; Ezek 26:5, 14; 32:2; 47:10). Other than these examples, there is little about the fishing industry in the Old Testament.

General picture from the gospels

The picture is quite different in the Gospels where the fishing motif dominates. At least one parable (Matt 13:47-50) and several miracles involve fishing (Matt 17:24-27; Luke 5:1-11; John 21:1-14). Jesus even teaches from a fishing boat (Mark 4:1). It is not surprising that among early symbols are the *ichthus*, representing an early Christian creed, and the anchor. Even among opponents of Christianity, it was noted that Jesus' associates included fishermen.[5] At least four of Jesus' disciples—associated with Bethsaida—were known as fishermen by trade: Peter, Andrew, James, and John. They were called while engaged in fishing and their calling is described in terms of fishing for people (Mark 1:16-20). These four formed an inner circle around Jesus according to the Synoptic reports. In addition, Levi's role as tax-collector (Mark 2:14) was probably that of a government agent who owned fishing rights on the lake. Following the death of Jesus, no less than seven disciples are described as returning to fishing (John 21).

---

3. Toni Gayle Fisher, *A Zooarchaeological Analysis of Change in Animal Utilization at Bethsaida from Iron Age II through the Early Roman Period*. Ph.D. Dissertation (Knoxville: University of Tennessee, 2005), 109.

4. Midrash Kohelet 2.8.

5. Origen, *Against Celsus* 62. "Jesus collected around him ten or eleven men, the most wicked tax-collectors and sailors, and with these fled hither and thither, collecting a means of livelihood in a disgraceful and importunate way."

Rabbis: fishing and Tzaidan

In Rabbinic literature there are several sayings about fish connected with Tzaidan. On the one hand, the fish are of high quality as the following tradition states:

> He taught that the fish which comes from Akko is as good a taste as the fish which comes up from Tzaidan and that those fish are not as good as the fish which comes from Paneas.[6]

On the other hand, the fish are plentiful and of various kinds:

> Rabban Simeon ben Gamaliel said, "It happened that I went to Tzaidan and they put before me more than three hundred kinds of fish in a single dish.[7]

One must be cautious in reading these texts since Tzaidan could refer to either Sidon, north of Tyre on the Mediterranean coast, or Bethsaida on the Sea of Galilee. In the former reading, one city is clearly coastal (Acco) and another inland (Paneas). However, there may well be a progression from salt water fish at Acco to lake fish at Tzaidan to fish caught in rivers and streams at Paneas. One must also be cautious because these written records are somewhat late. Yet the *maaseh* form—"it once happened . . ."—is used for the transmission of important traditions.[8] In this case, there were two persons named Rabban Simeon ben Gamaliel, one first century and the other second century CE. Thus the tradition about Bethsaida's reputation for good plentiful fish may be quite applicable to the New Testament era.

Fishing artifacts from Bethsaida

During the first decade of excavations at Bethsaida, well over one hundred fishing artifacts were uncovered at et-Tell.[9] These include stone anchors, both stone and lead net weights, fish hooks, and needles. This collection provides the best selection of fishing equipment from any one site around the Sea of Galilee. Mendel Nun, resident fisherman and expert on fishing practices, has previously published examples of ancient fishing implements.

6. Sifrei Devarim 4.39.

7. PT Sheqalim 6.2, 50a.

8. Richard Freund, "The Search for Bethsaida in Rabbinic Literature," 281.

9. Sandra Fortner, "The Fishing Implements and Maritime Activities of Bethsaida-Julias (et-Tell)," in *Bethsaida* (1999), 2:269-80; Sandra Fortner, *Der Keramik und Kleinfunde von Bethsaida-Iulias am See Genezareth, Israel,* (München: Ludwig-Maximilians-Universität, 2008), 47-55, tables 73-79, catalog numbers 1333-1413.

Large anchors and weights

However, his collection is an accumulation from various sites all around the lake and most have come from the surface.[10] The impressive collection from Bethsaida is extremely helpful in understanding ancient fishing practices and demonstrates conclusively that fishing played an important roll at et-Tell. Nun still criticized the number of fishing artifacts, noting that he would have expected a far larger number if Bethsaida were indeed a fishing town.[11] With regard to net weights, for example, he would have expected hundreds to accommodate all the nets from such a village.

Yet Nun's criticism needs to be turned on its head since it fails to recognize that only the acropolis of the town has thus far been excavated. Common sense will acknowledge that a much greater number would be expected when the excavations move down the southern slopes of et-Tell. The fact

---

10. Mendel Nun, *Ancient Stone Anchors and Net Sinkers from the Sea of Galilee* (Ein Gev: Kibbutz Ein Gev Tourist Department, 1993).

11. Mendel Nun, "Has Bethsaida finally been found?" *Jerusalem Perspective* (July/ Sept, 1998), 12-31, 54, especially 29-31.

that residents carried this many fishing implements the 40 meters to the top of the tell is striking—especially when one considers several of the heavier anchors. Fishing played a significant role in this community.

Fishing with nets

The discovery of a large number of net weights points to the preponderance of fishing by net in this region. Much is known about this type of fishing by comparison to modern practice with ancient drawings, especially from tombs in Egypt. In fact, an ancient fishing net complete with lead sinkers was found in an Egyptian tomb and a two thousand-year-old net is among the Bar Kokhba discoveries from caves near the Dead Sea.[12] It is likely that Bethsaida residents made their own nets—as will be discussed in the next chapter. Because of the climate at Bethsaida, one would not expect to find remains of nets, rope, and string. Yet the weights survive.

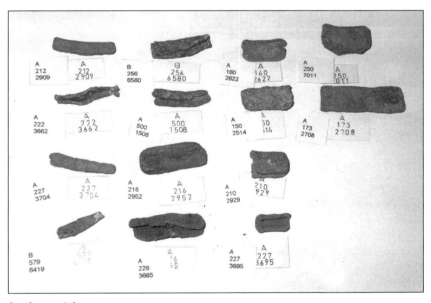

Lead net weights

In his description of fishing practices, Mendel Nun noted three different types of nets used on the Sea of Galilee:[13] The cast net is operated by a single

12. Nun, *Ancient Stone Anchors and Net Sinkers from the Sea of Galilee,* 35, 41.
13. IBID, 51-5.

fisherman and extends twenty to twenty-five feet in diameter. This is the type of net mentioned in the call narratives of the disciples (ἀμφίβληστρον). Simon and Andrew had been casting their nets in a circle around schools of fish when Jesus called them to cast their nets for people (Mark 1:16-20). Throughout the lake area small stones with bored holes were often used as weights to sink the net to the bottom. However, lead weights were also in use, attached every foot or so along the bottom.

Cast net. Courtesy of Jo Moore.

Over fifty lead weights have been collected at Bethsaida—coming from all areas of the tell. These were made when molten lead was poured into flat sheets and then cut into strips 3/4 inch by 2 1/4 inch. They were then folded over to create a gap for the string usually measuring less than 1/4 inch. The discovery of one unfolded lead strip suggests that these weights were made in Bethsaida itself. Only a few other examples of the folded-lead weight have been found elsewhere, near Capernaum and Magdala. In contrast, about one hundred ring-shaped lead weights were discovered in the ancient harbor at Kursi.[14]

A second type of net is the trammel net, composed of three separate walls of netting of varying-sized mesh so that fish are trapped inside. Today

14. IBID, 42.

as many as five units, each six feet high and a hundred feet long, are joined together. This kind of net can be laid out in a line or a circle and left for long periods of time. With wood floats holding up the top part of the net stone weights secured the bottom. Among these weights discovered at Bethsaida are examples of irregular-shaped basalt and limestone ranging in size from one to seven pounds and averaging about three inches in height.

The third type of net is the seine or dragnet. This commonly used type of net creates a long wall of net—in modern times as much as a thousand feet long and from five to twenty-five feet high—which is spread about a hundred yards from shore and then pulled to the shore by two teams of men. The process takes about an hour and is repeated eight to ten times a night.

Again weights are used so that fish cannot escape through gaps along the bottom. Irregular-shaped stone weights were often used including some with holes and others with grooves. However, Bethsaida has produced another type of net weight not previously catalogued by Nun. This is a dressed basalt ring weight. Five small (one to two inches in diameter) and over twenty large (four to five inches in diameter) examples have been collected.[15] A

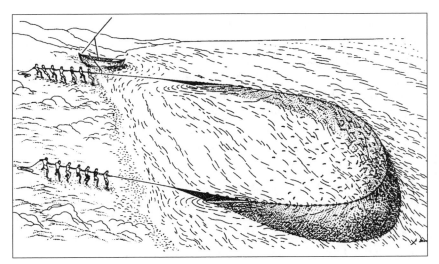

Seine net. Courtesy of Jo Moore.

15. Fortner notes that similar round stone weights appear at other sites for other functions, such as loom weights, yet she agrees that those from Bethsaida, because of size of hole and the weight of the stone, were used as net weights. Sandra Fortner, *Der Keramik und Kleinfunde von Bethsaida-Iulias am See Genezareth*, 49.

Basalt ring weights

rope slightly less than one inch in diameter would fit perfectly through the uniform-size hole in each of the large ring weights. It might seem unclear why fishermen would have gone to such an effort to work these weights when irregular shaped stones were common on the rest of the lake. This can be explained by the changing north shoreline. We would suggest that these rings working like wheels facilitated easy pulling of the nets to shore. While most of the lake floor is irregular and rocky, the silt deposits from the upper Jordan had created a more uniform surface with a gradual slope where these rings would have been effective.

The gospel accounts imply familiarity with this type of net. Jesus refers to the σαγήνη, seine or dragnet, in the parable of the net where the fishermen must separate out good and bad fish (Matt 13:47).[16] In the account of the miraculous catch of fish, a number of details suggest that the disciples were using a seine. John 21:8 states that the disciples were positioned about one hundred yards off shore and that they were dragging the nets to shore. The team of seven fishermen (John 21:1-2) would be appropriate, as would the use of two boats mentioned in the parallel account (Luke 5:7). The reference to "large fish" (John 21:11) suggests that the species was *Tilapia Galilea*, the

---

16. Lev 11:9-12 forbids certain kinds of fish including the *Clarias Lazera* or catfish.

long dorsal-finned *musht*, the largest edible fish in Galilee made popular to modern tourists as "St. Peter's Fish." Nun notes that *musht* travel in shoals during the winter months toward the warmer water fed by springs in the northern part of the lake.[17] Thus it is not surprising that the disciples found the shoal of fish on the other side of the boat (John 21:6).

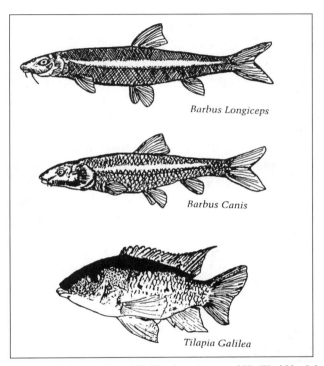

Barbus Longiceps

Barbus Canis

Tilapia Galilea

Common Fish of the Sea of Galilee from Jesus and His World by John J. Rousseau and Rami Arav copyright © 1995 Fortress Press. Reproduced by permission by Augsburg Fortress.

This episode also mentions the tearing of nets (Luke 5:6), which must have been common. Thus James and John were occupied with mending their nets (Mark 1:19) when they first met Jesus. Seven large bronze and iron needles (five to six inches long) have been found at Bethsaida. One type with a loop at one end was typical for net repair.[18] The second more

---

17. Mendel Nun, "Cast your Net upon the Water: Fish and Fishermen in Jesus' Time," *BAR* 19 (Nov/ Dec 1993), 46-56, 70.

18. Nun, *Ancient Stone Anchors,* 34.

common type with a hole in one end may have also been used in repair of both nets and sails. The location of a number of these finds on the floor of a large courtyard house complex in the center of Bethsaida may be significant. The large courtyard would provide ample space for major net and sail repair.

Fishing with hook and line

In addition to fishing with nets, hooks on lines were also employed. More than thirteen hooks ranging in size from 1 1/2 inch to 2 1/2 inch have been discovered including several in the two Hellenistic courtyard style houses. While the smaller folded lead weights may have been employed on individual fishing lines, other discovered lead sinkers of various shapes (cube, disc, "k"-shaped) were likely used. This is of special interest because of an episode contained only in Matt 17:24-27. When Peter reported to Jesus that he was approached concerning the payment of the temple tax, Jesus instructed him to cast a hook into the water and to open the mouth of the first fish that he catches to find a coin with which to pay the tax. In this case, the reference is to a second group of edible fish from the carp family known as the *barbels* because of the barbs at the corners of their mouths.[19] Since these are predators which feed on small fish, they are often caught by hook—unlike the *musht* which feed only on plankton.

0   7 cm

Fish hook

19. In the Talmud they are referred to as *biny* from the Semitic *binita* for hair. Actually there are three types of *barbels*: (a) *Barbus longiceps*—a long-headed *barbel*; (b) *Barbus Canis*—known as scaly; and (c) *Varicorhines Damascinus*. The first two are considered good Sabbath dishes, but the third which feeds on decaying matter has a poor taste. Nun, "Cast your Net," 49.

However, in one respect this story is more characteristic of the *musht*. Although the *musht* travel in shoals during the winter, they pair up during the spring months and deposit eggs in the soft bottom near the shore or in lagoons, such as around the mouth of the Jordan River near Bethsaida. After fertilization, the eggs are carried in their mouths for two or three weeks until hatched. Because of this, it is not unusual to a find foreign object in their mouth, such as a coin. It would appear then that Matthew's version of the story betrays signs of confusion about fishing practices on the Sea of Galilee.

The fishing seal

One of the most significant finds from the same courtyard house is a clay seal measuring 3/4 inch by 3/4 inch. The seal depicts two men fishing in a small *hippos* boat, like that used by Phoenicians in shallow water.[20] It may be that John 6:22-24 has this type of boat in mind when it mentions that there had been no πλοιάριον at the docks for transporting Jesus by himself to the other side after the feeding episode. This stands in contrast to the regular term for a boat, πλοῖον, which was used to describe the transport for the disciples on the previous afternoon. Likewise Josephus also mentions two occasions when he was forced to escape in a boat from Tiberias to Migdal with only two body guards (Josephus, *War* 3.618 = *Life* 96; *Life* 304). Thus the depiction on the seal is consistent with such literary descriptions.

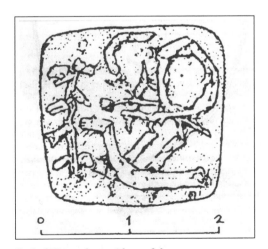

Seal of Hippos boat with two fishermen

20. Arav, "Bethsaida Excavations: Preliminary Report, 1987-1993," in *Bethsaida* (1995), 19.

Next to the boat on the left side is a reed which suggests a marshy area which is quite typical of the mouth of the Jordan River today and which was also mentioned in descriptions by Josephus (Josephus, *Life* 398-406). It may be that the reed became a symbol for the city of Bethsaida, perhaps related to the growing of flax in the alluvial plain.[21] The round objects above the men in the boat most likely are depicting the smaller cast nets (ἀμφιβληστρον), similar to that described in the call narratives of the disciples (Mark 1:16-20).

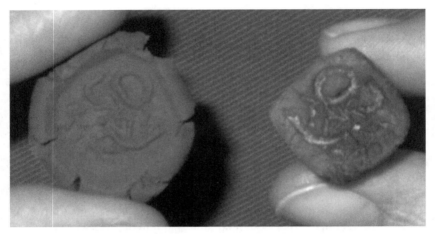

Seal of Hippos boat with two fishermen

The seal itself was made of clay and has a pyramid-shaped handle. There are several possibilities for its use. Perhaps it was used to stamp jar handles denoting the contents as fish sauce or salted fish. This was a very important industry on the Sea of Galilee, especially at Migdal (known also as Magdala, the home of Mary Magdalene). Thus this town was later given the Greek name Tarichaeae, which literally means "the place where fish are salted." John 6:9 refers to the fish in the feeding of the 5,000 as ὀψαριον, the term for dried fish. It is quite possible that Bethsaida had this kind of industry as well. Another artifact from Bethsaida is a jar handle with the mark of an anchor, perhaps also used for this purpose.

The fish used for salting are the *acanthobrama terrae sanctae*, popularly known as the Kinneret Sardine, which today make up fifty percent of the annual catch on the lake or about one thousand tons per year. Presumably this

21. Fred Strickert, "The Coins of Philip," in *Bethsaida* (1995), 185. The depiction of a reed occurs only on later coins of Philip.

species made up the three hundred fish fed to Rabbi Simeon ben Gamaliel upon his visit to Tzaidan because they are served in a single dish.[22] These fish could be easily caught and handled by a single person using the cast net as depicted on the Bethsaida seal.

Catfish

A fourth type of fish found in the Sea of Galilee is catfish, known by its Latin name *Clarias lazera.* The catfish is included among non-kosher sea life in Leviticus 11:9-12 because it does not have scales as other fish. In her analysis of bones found at Bethsaida, Toni Fisher reports that catfish bones occur in all periods of Bethsaida's history and in all areas of the tell—ranging from eight percent of all bones in the Iron Age period to four percent in both the Hellenistic and early Roman periods. Bones of other fish were not discovered, which likely means that they have not survived the ages as well as the more sturdy catfish bones—"particularly their pectoral spines and the large, sturdy supraethmoid of their skulls."[23]

Government control of fishing

Most people have a rather idyllic image of disciple fishermen on the Sea of Galilee. The impression is that they are individual workers who are in control of their own destinies, determined primarily by their own skill, effort, time investment. The fact is, just as the Roman-appointed tetrarchs controlled farming through systems of wealthy land owners, tenant-farmers, and day laborers, so the fishing industry was similarly controlled. This is one of the reasons that Antipas had built the city of Tiberias on the west shore of the Sea of Galilee. A whole pyramid of administrative structure provided control over the individual fishermen as well as those marketing the fish and those producing fish products. [24] This pyramid of control is symbolized in the name Sea of Tiberias that appears in John 6:1 and 21:1. Antipas controlled over half of the shore line, while Philip and Bethsaida had to share the rest with independent cities like Hippos and Gadara. At centers like Capernaum, tax farmers like Levi represented Antipas waiting at table to take Antipas' share of the daily catch. The partnership of Simon and Andrew with the Zebedee family, as well as hired workers, is emblematic of the bonding together of

22. PT Sheqalim 6.2,50c
23. Fisher, *A Zooarchaeological Analysis*, 177 and 217.
24. K. C. Hanson and Douglas E. Oakman, *Palestine in the Time of Jesus: Social Structures and Social Conflicts* (Minneapolis: Fortress Press, 1998), 106-10.

independent fishermen to meet quotas and high taxation. The movement of Simon and Andrew from their birth village Bethsaida to Capernaum may be related to the demands of Antipas' politico-economic expansion. The exclamation of the disciples, "We have toiled all night," is one that represents the life of the first-century Galilean fishermen.

Excursus: The Ginnosar Boat

A discussion of fishing practices in connection with Bethsaida is not complete without considering the significance of one other recent archaeological discovery: the Ginnosar boat.[25] In 1986, after a long drought when the Sea of Galilee was at its lowest elevation, members of Kibbutz Ginnosar discovered a boat in the mud in an area usually submerged. This discovery caused quite a stir, both because it is the only ancient sailing vessel ever recovered from the lake and because the process was rather exciting with the excavators battling the rising lake water caused by the renewal of rains. The boat proved to be two-thousand years old and very helpful for our understanding of first-century life on the Sea of Galilee.

The boat clearly dates to the first century. This was determined by the style of construction with mortise and tenon joints. Among the various objects in the boat were pottery shards including a complete Hellenistic cooking pot of the style which dates from the mid-first century BCE to mid-first century CE. There was also a complete Herodian lamp which dates to the first century CE.[26] Carbon-14 dating placed the construction of the boat at 40 BCE +/- 80 years or in a range from 120 BCE to 40 CE. However, the original construction, using oak for the frame and cedar for the strakes, had been repaired with other woods.[27] In other words, the boat was roughly contemporaneous with the time of the Gospels.

The boat is 25.5 feet in length, 7.5 feet wide, and 4.5 feet in depth. From the markings it appears that there had been a mast. It had a rounded stern with the fore and aft sections probably decked in, and it could easily seat seven persons. The decking was essential for fishing boats for positioning the seine nets. In the account of the storm at sea (Mark 4:36-41), Jesus is

---

25. Shelley Wachsman, "The Galilee Boat: 2,000-Year-Old Hull Recovered Intact," *BAR 14* (Sept./ Oct. 1988), 18-33. Shelley Wachsman, ed., *The Excavations of an Ancient Boat in the Sea of Galilee (Lake Kinneret), 'Atiqot 19*, 1990.

26. David Adan-Bayewitz, "The Pottery," *The Excavations of an Ancient Boat*, ed. Shelley Wachsman, 89-96 and Varda Sussman, "The Lamp," 97-8.

27. Ella Werker, "Identification of the Wood," *The Excavations of an Ancient Boat*, ed. Shelley Wachsman, 65-73.

described as sleeping in the stern probably under the decking which provided shelter while the helmsman stationed above was most exposed to the elements. The reference to "the pillow" using the Greek article suggests part of the boat's equipment which, according to Wachsman, was probably a sandbag used for ballast.

An ancient mosaic from Migdal includes a boat of the type discovered near Ginnosar. This foot-long depiction shows a boat with a mast and two oarsmen on its left side along with a helmsman holding the rudder in the water.[28] The simplicity of style suggests that the artist was working on the basis of observation rather than from a pattern book. Therefore a crew of five was usual for the typical Galilean fishing boat. This is supported also by the depiction of a boat on a coin minted in Caesarea Philippi.[29] This also fits the report of Josephus concerning his own strategy during the Jewish Revolt when he positioned 230 boats off the shore of enemy-held Tiberias. He reports that each boat was equipped with a skeleton crew of five, which nevertheless induced surrender because of the intimidating appearance of the boats some distance from shore near evening (Josephus, *War* 2.632-46 and *Life* 155-178). The typical crew therefore was five.

A larger crew was employed for fishing with others free to handle the seine nets in addition to the five-man crew. In the call of disciples, Mark 1:20 notes that James and John left behind their father Zebedee with the hired men in the boat. In that situation, there were at least five persons and probably more. John 21:2 lists seven disciples who go for a night of fishing. However, Wachsman suggests that the Ginnosar boat may have been capable of holding as many as fifteen persons.[30] When Josephus sent ten hostages from Tiberias to Migdal, he explicitly states that they went in a fishing vessel—μιᾷ τῶν ἁλιάδων—(Josephus, *War* 2.639. cf. *Life* 167). In the episode, when he tricked the Tiberians with 230 boats off-shore, he himself landed in a boat with seven soldiers and several friends in addition to the five-man crew. After the surrender, he notes that he transported 2,600 prisoners from Tiberias to Migdal which calculates to eleven prisoners per boat (Josephus, *War* 2.632-46; *Life* 155-178). So the picture in Josephus is consistent with a capacity of fifteen persons per boat. Although the Gospels never state explicitly the

---

28. J. Richard Steffy and Shelley Wachsman, "The Migdal Boat Mosaic," *The Excavations of an Ancient Boat,* ed. Shelley Wachsman, 114-8.

29. Coin minted in 220 CE under Julia Soaemias. Y. Meshorer, "The Coins of Caesarea Banias," *INJ* (1984-5), 46-7, plate 15:56.

30. Shelley Wachsman, "Literary Sources," *The Excavations of an Ancient Boat,* ed. Shelley Wachsman, 111-4.

number of disciples which accompanied Jesus on his various boat trips, such journeys with twelve disciples aboard are certainly not out of the question.

It may never be known how this boat reached its fate at the bottom of the lake. It is possible that the boat sank during one of the many storms that come up at night. One account of the disciples' nighttime struggle against the winds, which probably began at Bethsaida, describes them eventually reaching shore at Gennesaret (Mark 6:45-53), not far from the recent boat discovery. However, it is significant that partial remains of other boats were also uncovered with the Ginnosar boat. One suggestion is that the boat sank in the nautical battle which took place near Migdal during the Jewish revolt of 67 CE Josephus reports that:

> The Jews were sent to the bottom, boats and all . . . . During the days that followed, a horrible stench hung over the region, and it presented an equally horrifying spectacle. The beaches were strewn with wrecks and swollen bodies. . . . The dead, including those who earlier fell in the defense of the town numbered 6,700 (Josephus, *War* 3.392-408, 530).

It is not difficult to imagine that the Ginnosar boat was one of these boats washing ashore slightly to the north of Migdal. However, since the boat was found incomplete, it may be that a boat repair shop was located nearby and that unsalvageable wrecks were simply sunk off shore.[31]

This boat does have a Bethsaida connection. One of the coins discovered in connection with the excavation of the boat is a coin of Philip.[32] The coin depicts both Augustus and Livia and can possibly be dated to the year 30 CE when Philip officially founded the town of Bethsaida-Julias, or 33 CE at the latest.[33] This is significant since Philip's coins were meant primarily for local circulation within the Golan region. Among Philip coins discovered in archaeological excavation, this is the only example thus far found outside the territory where Philip ruled. It is quite possible that passengers on this boat had embarked from Bethsaida before it sank near Ginnosar.

Anchors

There were two anchors in the Ginnosar boat weighing about 30-40 pounds, one with a hole drilled to secure a rope and the other with a groove

---

31. Wachsman, *The Galilee Boat.*

32. Haim Gitler, "The Coins," *The Excavations of an Ancient Boat,* ed. Shelley Wachsman, 101.

33. Strickert, "The Coins of Philip," 179-81.

around the center.[34] Both types have been found at Bethsaida. Twelve basalt stone anchors ranging from thirty to sixty pounds have been discovered at various locations on the top of the Tell including the courtyard style houses.[35] Most are irregular in shape with heights ranging from ten inches to twenty inches and include a single hole in one corner for securing a rope. The uniform size of these holes from one to 1 1/4 inches in diameter suggests the size of ropes used. Such holes were generally drilled with hard flint, many of which have been found at Bethsaida. The discovery also of several large stones with partially drilled holes points to Bethsaida as a place for working anchors. One example has also been uncovered of an anchor with a groove around the middle where the rope was tied.

Missing from Bethsaida is the classical-shaped iron anchor that was common to the Mediterranean. In fact, only one example has ever been found on the Sea of Galilee, pulled up in a fishing net near Capernaum in 1970 and currently displayed at Kibbutz Ginnosar. This iron anchor has a shank five feet long with its arms extending three feet, and it weighs nearly seventy pounds—perhaps too large to be practical for these common fishing boats. Nevertheless, this shape is represented on a jar handle from Bethsaida mentioned previously. Yet this can be explained from the common depiction of anchors on Jewish coinage, influenced by interest in the Mediterranean world.

Excursus: Tabgha

The site of Tabgha on the western shore has long been associated with both the feeding of the 5,000 and the great catch of fish.[36] There the visitor is pointed to a stone, where Jesus supposedly laid the loaves and fishes, and heart shaped pillar bases on the shore, where the resurrected Jesus met with his disciples. Although this site is located a short distance south of Capernaum, it is never mentioned in the Gospels. However, the traditions are mentioned as early as the fourth century CE by the pilgrim Egeria and several churches have been built to commemorate these events.

These associations may well be the result of visits by early pilgrims who were driven less by historical accuracy than by the convenience of a site so near to Capernaum. The choice of Tabgha is not without reason. It

34. Shelley Wachsman, "The Anchors," *The Excavations of an Ancient Boat,* ed. Shelley Wachsman, 107-110.

35. By way of comparison, anchors from the Mediterranean are as large as 450 pounds and several from the Dead Sea weigh two hundred pounds. Nun, *Ancient Stone Anchors,* 17.

36. Bargil Pixner, "The Miracle Church of Tabgha on the Sea of Galilee," *BA* 48 (Dec. 1985), 196-206.

does provide a proper setting with a gradual shoreline and grassy area in the vicinity. Of greater significance is the fact that seven springs are located at this site—thus the ancient name Tabgha, short for Heptagon—which still attract shoals of fish to the waters off shore. The difficulty is that the rocky bottom of the lake at this point is not conducive to use of the common seine net even though numerous details in both Luke 5 and John 21 point to that style of net. While Mendel Nun accepts without question this location for the miracle, he concludes that a trammel net must have been used. With the artifact discoveries at Bethsaida and with the new understanding of geological and geographic changes since the first century, further exploration of the Beteiha plain near Bethsaida may be helpful in learning more about first-century fishing practices.

The mention of 153 fish in John 21:11 recalls the three hundred fish served at Tzaidan according to Rabbinic tradition. The particular number 153, however, is so unusual in such a text that it defies explanation.[37] Interestingly, the second-century Jewish-Christian Gospel of the Nazareans includes the detail that Jesus performed 53 miracles at Bethsaida. One wonders if there were something special about either the number 53 or 153 in connection with the city Bethsaida. It is easy to imagine how "100" could have been added or omitted in the passing of the traditions. Thus it is appropriate to explore further possible connections of a Bethsaida location with this account.

---

37. Raymond E. Brown, *The Gospel according to John,* The Anchor Bible (Garden City, N.Y.: Doubleday, 1970), 2:1074-6.

Chapter 7

Farming and Flax Production

The parables of Jesus frequently refer to farming. Among the best known parables are "The Sower," "The Weeds among Wheat," and "The Mustard Seed." His audience knew well farming practices and experienced them everyday of their lives. While the fishing industry played an important role around the Sea of Galilee, fields ripe for harvest could be seen all around the lake. Some of the best farm land of Galilee was located in the plain of Gennesaret on the west side of the lake, and the fertile Beteiha plain covered a narrow strip—somewhat smaller than today—along the northeast portion of the lake just below Bethsaida. The hillsides around were also farmed to such a degree that Josephus in his hyperbolic way said that every part of Galilee was being farmed—a statement he would likely make about Golan as well.

Artifacts from farming

The courtyard house in Area C was given the name "The Winemaker's House" because three pruning hooks were discovered along a kitchen wall.[1] From pollen analysis, it appears that grapes were harvested at Bethsaida already in the Iron Age. A 4.5 meter by 2.85 meter covered "cellar" to the back of the house provided a storage facility for large wine jars—with four complete jars found *in situ*. Similarly, another courtyard house in the northwest section of Area C also included a wine-cellar with jars remaining in place. While earlier residents had imported wine from places like Rhodes, these second-century BCE residents made their own.

In area A, four sickles were found. The large amount of grain discovered in the city gate chambers shows clear evidence of grain production in the

1. Sandra Fortner, *Der Keramik und Kleinfunde von Bethsaida-Iulias am See Genezareth, Israel,* (München: Ludwig-Maximilians-Universität, 2008), Tables 85, Catalog # 1449-54.

Area C
L901 B9090
09/06/93
DR# 96/369

0   5 cm

Pruning hook

Iron Age. Pollen evidence from the early Roman era points to wheat and barley cultivation.

Cattle Used in Agriculture

In her analysis of animal bone remains, Bethsaida zooarchaeologist Toni Fisher found a significant number of cattle bones through all periods

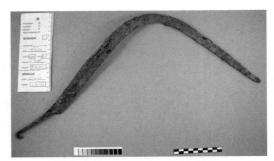

Sickle. Courtesy of Hanan Shafir, photographer, BEP.

of occupation. As a percentage of all bones, there were 38% cattle bones during the Iron Age, 44% during the Hellenistic era, and 33% during the Roman era.[2] Fisher citing the work of Rosen, notes that a percentage of twenty or higher indicates a subsistence culture employing cattle as plow-animals.[3] Since animals that are raised primarily for meat are slaughtered at a young age, the adult age detected from the cattle bones at Bethsaida supports the idea that the cattle had been raised primarily for the work as draft animals, and only secondarily for meat. In the Iron Age, cattle played an important role in grain production in the area around Bethsaida since it would take ten to fifteen acres to feed a typical family of seven.[4] This would have also been

2. Toni Gayle Fisher, *A Zooarchaeological Analysis of Change in Animal Utilization at Bethsaida from Iron Age II through the Early Roman Period.* Ph.D. Dissertation (Knoxville: University of Tennessee, 2005), 28.

3. B. Rosen, "Subsistence Economy in Stratum II," in *Izbet Sartah: An Early Iron Age Site near Rosh Ha'ayin,* ed. I. Finkelstein (British Archaeological Reports, International Series 299: 1986), 156-185.

4. Zeev Safrai, *The Economy of Roman Palestine* (New York: Routledge, 1994), 358-64.

the case during Hellenistic and Roman periods—especially with greater taxation. However, there is evidence of a new industry at Bethsaida.

Flax production

Patrick Geyer's analysis of pollens at Bethsaida in the first century CE shows a high level of flax.[5] Soundings were taken from the floor of the structure identified as the Temple of Julia. Presumably various offerings of first fruits were brought to the temple, possibly falling under the authority of Philip and his economic hierarchy. Flax, in its botanical name *Linum*, makes up 15% of the pollen. Just to the west of the temple was an oval structure, 6.8 meters by 5.5 meters, built of massive boulders in the Hellenistic era.[6] Later a ninety-centimeter wide dividing wall was added. In soundings from the north of the wall, which he calls "The Granary," the level of flax pollen was only 2%. To the south of the wall, which he called "The Bin," the level of flax pollen was 66%. It is no surprise that Geyer concludes that Bethsaida was a center of flax production.

Flax seeds are an important source of food, while the seeds—linseed oil—have both medicinal uses and can serve as a sealant on lumber, especially on boats. Linen, the cloth produced from the fibers of flax, is a most durable and flexible fabric, used for the garments of the Jerusalem high priest and burial shrouds, as well as daily garments. It is used as wicks for lamps. Yet perhaps the most significant use is for hunting and fishing nets, for ropes, and for sails for boats. Twice as strong as cotton and five times as strong as wool, linen increases in strength when wet, and then dries out quickly. The production of flax and the processing of linen make it an ideal industry for Bethsaida.

Flax production is well known from Egyptian records, yet little is known about this industry in Palestine prior to this time. Denny Clark notes that, since flax production requires large amounts of water and only certain types of soil, very few places could produce flax. The alluvial soil in the Beteiha plain along the northeast shore of the lake, however, was ideal.[7] The process involves pulling up the plants and tying them into bundles for drying and removal of the seed pods. Then the bundles are submerged in water while

---

5. Patrick Scott Geyer, "Evidence of Flax Cultivation from the Temple-Granary Complex et-Tell (Bethsaida/ Julias)," *Israel Exploration Journal* 51 (2001), 231-4; James Schoenwetter and Patrick Geyer, "Implications of Archaeology Palynology at Bethsaida, Israel," *Journal of Field Archaeology* 27 (2000), 63-73; Patrick Scott Geyer, *Bethsaida/ Julias and the Politics, Religion, and Economics of Roman Syro-Palestine (4 B.C.E.- 33/34 C.E.),* (Tempe, Arizona: Arizona State University Masters Thesis, 1998).

6. Rami Arav, "Bethsaida Preliminary Report, 1987-1993," in *Bethsaida* (1995), 16.

7. Denny Clark, "Flax Production at Bethsaida" unpublished paper.

the stalks rot and the fibers are loosened. With both the Jordan and the Meshoshim Rivers fanning out into a number of estuaries, these bundles could easily be submerged while minimizing the stink and filth. After drying, the bundles are beaten to remove the woody parts and then the stems are combed to separate the fibers—a process that is repeated through a number of cycles.

Clark notes that growing flax was especially hard on the soil[8] so that it was necessary to allow the fields to go fallow while rotating fields in the alluvial plain. Cattle then would play an important role in plowing the new fields and transporting the bundles at the time of harvest. They would then graze on the wild grasses in the fallow fields and replenish the fields with their manure. Again Geyer's pollen study is significant, since fennel made up 28% of the pollen, while general fallow field weeds made up 20% and grasses another 31% of the pollens in the granary. They also appeared in smaller amounts in the temple samples. This supports the evidence that flax production was an important industry at Bethsaida.

Weaving

While the process of flax production would have been based in the plain below Bethsaida, further steps in the preparation of linen—spinning the fibers into thread and weaving into fabric or preparing nets and ropes—likely took place in the courtyards of the residential sections. Ten pyramid-shaped clay loom weights have been discovered—five of them in Locus 570—and four shuttles made from bone are evidence of the weaving process. In addition numerous spindle weights and needles have been catalogued.[9]

Area A
B1322
29/06/88
weaving shuttle

Bone weaving shuttle

---

8. Pliny, *Natural History* 19.1.

9. Fortner, *Die Keramik* (2008), tables 88-91, catalogue # 1474-1502, pages 73-78.

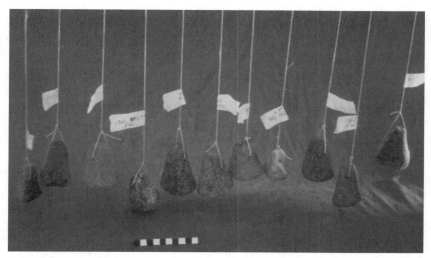

Hellenistic loom weights

Dating the Introduction of Flax to Bethsaida

The presence of flax pollens in the temple is a strong argument that flax production should be considered a government run industry at Bethsaida. With Antipas controlling the fishing market from Tiberias to Capernaum and with fish processing in Tarichaeae, it would seem that Philip found a special niche for Bethsaida along the alluvial Beteiha plain. The foundation of the city of Julias was likely related to the establishment of this industry and the Temple of Julias playing a cultic role in the political economy of the tetrarchy. Whether Bethsaida was able to export linen beyond the lake area is not known. It may be that the needs of the immediate area were sufficient for the market supply at Bethsaida.

Did Philip introduce flax to the lake region or can it be traced to an earlier date? There is good reason to think that flax production was introduced several centuries earlier. As we have seen, coastal cities like Tyre began establishing settlements inland beginning across upper Galilee and into the Huleh Valley. Why would they reach further inland to Bethsaida? What might be available at Bethsaida that could not be produced at these other settlements? What would make it worthwhile for the added time and expense of cross-country transportation of goods to the city? Flax production would provide the natural explanation. Tyre was known for its purple dye, so there would be a great need for linen to export cloth.

This industry may also link Bethsaida with the settlements in the Huleh Valley, especially Tel Anafa. The presence of spattered-wash-ware vessels at Bethsaida and no where else outside the Huleh Valley would point to that connection. In describing Tel Anafa, Andrea Berlin says,

> They apparently produced their own cloth, as excavators uncovered a considerable number of weaving-related artifacts, including spindle-whorls, bone weaving tools, over twenty-five loomweights, and a circular, sludge-filled, stone structure perhaps used for dying.[10]

Josephus describes Lake Semechonitis of the Huleh Valley as covering about thirty-two square miles and providing extensive marshlands (Josephus, *War* 4.3). The deposits of alluvial soil and large water supply would seem ideal for flax production. The silence in reports about Tel Anafa and the Huleh Valley likely is due to an absence of similar pollen tests. Only wheat, barley, and vegetables are among the presumed agricultural products, as is papyrus.[11] The need for constant rotation of fields and excessive flooding of the upper Jordan, however, would make the Beteiha plain a natural site for expansion.

The evidence from Bethsaida is not totally clear. Geyer notes that the granary samples included Roman pottery and should be considered contemporaneous with the temple. However, the granary was originally built in the Hellenistic period so that pollen samples may belong to that period. Since it had been excavated four years prior to the temple and to the taking of samples, it is quite possible that pottery shards on the floor were later contamination. Further samples of Hellenistic loci would be helpful in clarifying this question. However, most promising would be further evidence of the entire flax production process possibly to be found at the base of the Tell.

There is no question, however, that flax had become an important industry under the Tetrarch Philip—at a time when Tel Anafa had been abandoned. The production of nets, ropes, and sails would have given Philip a strategic position in the fishing economy of the Sea of Galilee.

10. Andrea Berlin, "Between Large Forces in the Hellenistic Period," *BA* 60:1 (1997), 14.

11. Wolfgang Zwickel, "The Huleh Valley from the Iron Age to the Muslim Period," in ed. Jürgen Zangenberg, Harold W. Attridge, and Dale B. Martin, *Religion, Etnicity, and Identity in Ancient Galilee: A Region in Transition* (Tübingen: Mohr Siebeck, 2007), 163-85, especially 165.

Chapter 8

Houses of Fishermen and Others

Josephus tells us that during his travels through the Galilee during the Jewish revolt of 67 CE, the Roman Cestius Gallus remarked about his high impression of the architecture of Galilean houses (Josephus, *War* 2.503-4). The common limestone and, in the Golan area, basalt made attractive and durable houses. The Gospels frequently speak of the daily life that takes place in the setting of such houses. For example a Q saying of Jesus speaks of people gathered for eating and drinking in the courtyard, others at work on the roof, women busy grinding meal, and others in bed sleeping (Luke 17:22-36). A glimpse of this setting can be seen from the Hellenistic and Roman houses uncovered at Bethsaida. It is important to remember that houses are often occupied generation after generation with rooms added on and new houses built from ruins.

The Simple House

Most people lived in a relatively simple house consisting of only one or two rooms with a small courtyard in front.[1] According to the Mishnah, the smallest size for a building designated a house was four cubits by six cubits or about two meters by two meters.[2] However, most houses were certainly larger. According to Hirschfeld's survey of simple houses, the size

---

1. A most helpful resource for understanding the architecture of first-century housing is Yizhar Hirschfeld, *The Palestinian Dwelling in the Roman-Byzantine Periods* (Jerusalem: Israel Exploration Society, 1995).
2. Baba Bathra 6:4.

could range from 25 square meters to 300 square meters.[3] Certainly this is the case at Bethsaida. An example of a simple house from Bethsaida can be seen from the plan presented below:

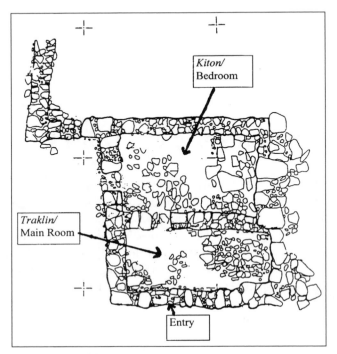

Plan of two-room house

This two-room house opened to a small courtyard which was probably shared with a number of other dwellings. It probably would have been joined to a street by narrow alleyways.[4] This house was constructed in the first century CE just on the inside of the ruins of the Iron Age wall using stones from the wall and the *Bit Hilani*. Unfortunately, as is often the case in excavations, later disturbances have made the complete picture of this house unclear.

This particular house is basically a square structure measuring about 7 meters by 7 meters. Because the walls are nearly 0.6 meters thick, this leaves a living space of only about 40 square meters. The house, with the entry to

3. Hirschfeld, *The Palestinian Dwelling in the Roman-Byzantine Periods,* 100.

4. S. Safrai, "Home and Family Life," *The Jewish People in the First Century* (Philadelphia: Fortress Press, 1976), 2:728-792.

The Roman two-room house

Roman era pottery

the south, has two main rooms. The main room was called the *traklin* which derived from the Latin *triclinium* for the dining room with three couches for reclining. Here is the area where family members sat together and where meals were taken. They usually sat on the floor around a small raised platform. Often the floors were of beaten earth though in this particular house the flooring was of stone. Matting on the floors provided a smooth surface. Dim lighting was provided by oil lamps or streams of natural light from the outside. It is thus easy to picture the unusual effort by the woman who swept her house in search of the lost coin (Luke 15:8-10).

A doorway in the north wall of the *traklin* led to the slightly smaller *kiton* or bedroom deriving from the Greek κοîτον. The residents often slept side by side on straw mattresses unrolled on the floor. Beds were also used although this was often a sign of luxury. This is demonstrated from the midrash: "The poor man sits and complains, saying, 'How am I different from so-and-so, yet he sleeps in his bed and I sleep on the ground.'"[5]

The thick basalt stone walls of the Golan were strong enough to support a second story, although there is no evidence that this was the case in this particular house. The flat roof was probably made of large timbers, possibly cedar (Isaiah 9:9) or oak, covered with reeds and clay. In Area A several large chunks of packed clay were found with the impression of reeds still embedded. It was possible to break through this kind of material as in the

5. Midrash Rabbah Leviticus 34:16.

story of the paralytic let down to Jesus from the roof (Mark 2:4). This type of roof required regular maintenance. A midrash calls attention to prepare for the winter rains: "The first rain that falls instructs the people to collect their fruit and to plaster their roofs."[6] The householder would need to patch holes and then roll the roof with a stone roller, several of which have turned up at Bethsaida. The rooftop would be used for numerous domestic activities in the warm summer months and also served for storage and drying fruits and vegetables. Peter is described as going to the rooftop for his prayers (Acts 10:9) and it was also considered a good place for study.

Courtyard Style Houses

The excavations at Bethsaida have uncovered two excellent examples of courtyard style houses built during the Hellenistic period. This type of house includes a private courtyard which is surrounded by the various rooms of the house and a stone wall which separates it from the street and creates a large private space for the family's domestic activities in a comfortable outdoor setting. This likely denotes a higher class status since in a town like Bethsaida it provided a larger living space. According to Hirschfeld's survey, courtyard style houses range in size from 65 square meters to 900 square meters with a mean of 300 square meters.

In area B, a courtyard style house has been called "the fisherman's house" because various fishing equipment was found in the courtyard.[7] The assumption is that the spacious courtyard provided ample room for business activities such as repair of nets and sails and storage of equipment. Yet the large size of this house likely does not point to the lifestyle of a common fisherman. The dimensions are 18 meters by 27 meters providing a total area of nearly 500 square meters. The courtyard itself, paved with small stones, comprises about one third of this space. Unfortunately, the house has been severely damaged so that only a single course of stones stand on the west side (the northwest corner is completely destroyed) while the best preserved part of the wall on the east side stands about a meter tall.

One of the best preserved rooms is a large kitchen on the east side where two ovens were found. There was also an abundance of shards of cooking ware including one intact Hellenistic cooking pot. Three of the four

6. Sifre on Deuteronomy 42. See also Midrash Rabbah Leviticus 35:12.

7. Rami Arav, "Bethsaida Excavations: Preliminary Report, 1987-93," in *Bethsaida* (1995), 22-3, 27.

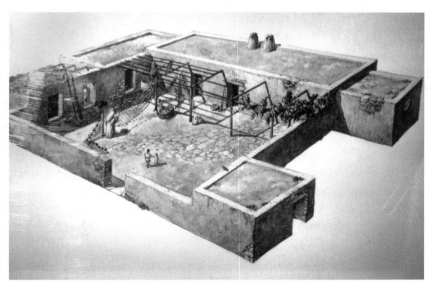

Reconstruction of the Fisherman's House (from southwest)

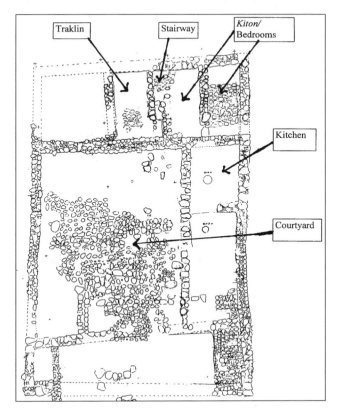

Plan of
Fisherman's House

smaller rooms on the north side of the house have been excavated and because of their size, one would guess that those on the northeast were bedrooms. The double wall in the center of these four rooms may indicate a stairway to an upper story or the roof. The high quality of life is indicated by the discovery of 156 shards of imported Roman fineware which includes fishplates and finely decorated pieces of Eastern Terra Sigillata pottery:

Hellenistic cooking pot

> The fact that half of the pieces of this fineware were found in the courtyard area demonstrates that daily life centered around this area. The highest concentration of fineware in the various rooms occurs in the third room from the east on the north side of the house. This may point to the use of this room as the *traklin*, while meals were moved outside to the western part of the courtyard in warmer weather.[8]

A second courtyard house from area C of Bethsaida has been called "the winemaker's house."[9] A narrow north-south street passes just to the west of the courtyard. The complex covers an area of about 288 square meters, measuring about 16 meters by 18 meters. Over half of this is made up by the large 12 meters by 13 meters courtyard on the southwest part of the house.

The southern wall had already been constructed in the Iron Age, so later buttresses were added for support. A well preserved spacious (4 meters by 8 meters) kitchen is on the east side of the house with walls of fine masonry standing about one and a half meters high. Among finds in the kitchen were an oven, a number of grinding stones of various sizes, and much kitchen ware. Along the southern wall were found six or seven complete broken vessels suggesting the presence of a shelf. Three rooms along the north of the house included a larger (6 meters feet by 5 meters) room in the center which may have served as the *traklin*.

8. Sandra Fortner, "Hellenistic and Roman Fineware from Bethsaida," in *Bethsaida* (1995), 99-126. Distribution patterns were presented in a paper delivered at the 1995 international meeting of the Society of Biblical Literature in Budapest, Hungary.

9. Rami Arav, "Bethsaida Excavations: Preliminary Report, 1987-93," in *Bethsaida* (1995), 29-34.

Street passing Winemaker's house

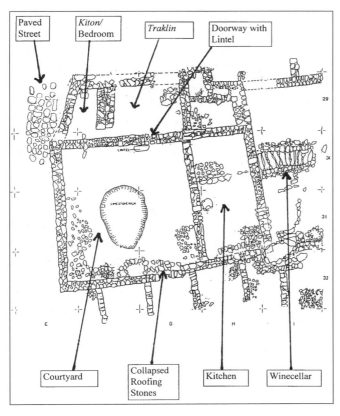

Plan of Winemaker's House

There are several unusual features about this house. Outside the house on the east was uncovered an undisturbed wine cellar with four complete Hellenistic jars and one cooking pot. The cellar was covered with ten basalt slabs, each about 3.5 meters feet long and over .4 meters in width. The use of basalt slabs for roofing is common in the Hauran although it also occurs in the Talmudic village at Qatzrin. Similar slabs of basalt were found collapsed along the southern part of the kitchen suggesting that this type of corbeling roof was employed here as well. Likewise a destruction layer of basalt slabs in the southeast part of the

Jars and cooking pot in "wine cellar"

courtyard may have covered the eastern part of the courtyard. These would have been supported by the 0.7 meter thick kitchen wall and most likely a row of pillars in the courtyard. Possibly these were made of limestone since a medieval limestone kiln in the center of the courtyard was used to make lime fertilizer for the fields from such limestone fragments.

This courtyard house also included three nicely made doorways. The main entry on the south of the courtyard is preserved only to a height of 0.6 meters. A second doorway to the rooms on the north occurs directly across the courtyard from this entry. A finely worked lintel rests where it fell just inside that doorway. The finest preserved doorway occurs in the east wall of the courtyard into the kitchen. The threshold of this 1.3 meter wide doorway is preserved and long iron nails indicate that the doorway had a wooden frame. In excavating the floor in the southeast corner of the kitchen, a Roman door key was discovered. This is the type of key described in Rabbinic literature as a *knee* or *elbow* key because there is a bend in the shaft. When the key is inserted into the keyhole, the bend makes it possible for the part with the teeth to reach around the bolt and engage the tumbler enabling the bolt to be pulled back out of the socket of the door jamb.[10] The ring on the key enabled the householder to carry it conveniently. Thus

10. Yigael Yadin, *Bar Kochba* (London: Weidenfeld & Nicholson, 1971), 194-200.

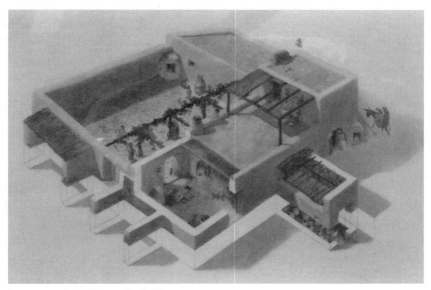

Reconstruction of Winemaker's House

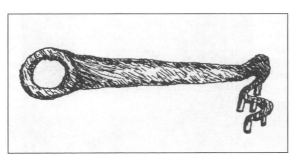

Drawing of key

Gold earring

a Rabbinic ruling states that "A woman shall not go out in public [on the Sabbath] with a key which is on her finger. If she does go out, it binds her to make a guilt offering."[11]

The inhabitants of this house displayed a rather comfortable style of life. There were also numerous examples of imported fineware as well as Rhodian amphorae. The prize find, however, was a gold earring which uses both granulation and filigree techniques and depicts an unidentified animal. The inhabitants were clearly influenced by Hellenistic culture and made use

11. Tosefta Shabbath 4:11.

of a strigilis as was common in the Greek gymnasium. There were also a few items of fishing equipment including a hook and anchors. However, there were also tools of other trades including three pruning hooks. This fits well with the presence of the wine cellar attached to the house.

The large courtyard houses demonstrate a comfortable lifestyle in the Hellenistic period. The "Fisherman's House" continued to be used in the first century CE, but this may not have been the case for the "Winemaker's House." The houses built during the Roman era on the top of the Tell are generally more modest like the two-room house. A number of Roman houses had to be removed because they had been built on rubble on the south side of the earlier Iron Age city gate. Likely more will be learned about first-century Bethsaida when the excavations are expanded to the southern slopes.[12]

12. The lack of finer Roman era architecture is a problem for some visitors to Bethsaida who expect buildings to resemble that of larger Mediterranean cities. As Markus Bockmuehl states, "the silence of the architectural record does seem deafening," "Simon Peter and Bethsaida," *Supplements to Novum Testamentum,* 115 (2005), 69.

Chapter 9

Jews and Gentiles in Bethsaida

Josephus characterizes the territory of Philip as having "a mixed population of Jews and Syrians" (Josephus, *War* 3.57; *Ant.* 17.188). The assumption has been that such a statement applies also to the town of Bethsaida. By virtue of its location on the periphery of traditional Jewish territory, one would expect Jews, but one would also expect Gentiles living side by side. Many traditional assumptions about ethnicity have been challenged in the last decades. Eric Meyers[1] and Jonathan Reed[2] have raised the question in particular about the city of Sepphoris, noting that the presence of Hellenistic culture need not be a sign of ethnic identity. A more comprehensive study by Mark Chancey has considered *The Myth of a Gentile Galilee*[3] as a whole and has found little evidence for a strong Gentile presence in the region. The inhabitants of Galilee appear to have been descendents of Judeans who migrated north under Hasmonean rule.

History of Bethsaida and surrounding area

The village of Bethsaida was founded in the Hellenistic era with a Gentile population. Early inhabitants were Phoenicians who were perhaps joined by former soldiers from a possible military occupation during the later part of Ptolemaic rule. Itureans from the north and Nabateans from the south

1. Eric Meyers, "Identifying Religious and Ethnic Groups through Archaeology," *Biblical Archaeology Today,* ed. Avraham Biram and Joseph Aviram (Jerusalem: Israel Exploration Society, 1990), 738-45.

2. Jonathan L. Reed, *Archaeology and the Galilean Jesus* (Harrisburg, PA: Trinity Press, 2000), 43-8.

3. Mark A. Chancey, *The Myth of a Gentile Galilee* (Cambridge: Cambridge University Press, 2004).

moved into the areas to the east and perhaps also some to Bethsaida. With the coming of Hasmonean rule beginning with Alexander Jannaeus in 80 BCE, Bethsaida came under the sway of Jerusalem. Yet the question of religion and ethnic changes is a matter for debate. To the east, Gamla became a community noted for its devout adherence to Judaism. To the north, Tel Anafa, remained Gentile through and through. With regard to Galilee, but also to towns like Bethsaida, Richard Horsley says, "It would be unrealistic to imagine that the extension of Hasmonean rule over Galilee resulted in a sudden or thorough conformation of social life in Galilee to 'the laws and customs of the Judeans.'"[4] His reference to following "the laws and customs of the Judeans," goes back to Josephus' comment that Aristobulus in 104-103 BCE had conquered Itureans giving them the choice of conversion or leaving. The comment reflects more the policies earlier followed with Idumeans. Yet it seems an unlikely policy for Aristobulus who ruled only a single year and even more so for Jannaeus who was concerned to develop the economic base for his expanded territory.

In the decades prior to Philip's rule over this territory, his father Herod did add Jewish settlers, bringing five hundred Babylonian Jews to settle the town of Bethyra under the leadership of Zamaris. He also settled three thousand Idumaeans in Trachonitis (Josephus, *Ant.* 16.285; 17.23-29). With a promise of liberation from taxation, Herod enticed others to immigrate to the region.

The example of Philip

As a Herodian, Philip is considered a Jewish ruler. Yet there is surprisingly little to suggest devotion to Jewish customs and practices, not even a single report of his attendance, like Antipas, at the Passover in Jerusalem. Rather the impression from Josephus is that Philip spent his entire time within his territory and won approval for his dealings with his subjects of diverse backgrounds. Unfortunately nothing is known about his mother other that her Greek name Cleopatra. Kokkinos conjectures for her a non-Jewish background, perhaps even that her roots were within this same region where Philip was chosen to rule.[5] Philip's formative years were spent in Rome and his return to Jerusalem left very little time to be shaped by the ways of Jerusalem prior to the death of Herod and his appointment as tetrarch at a very young age.

---

4. Richard Horsley, *Galilee: History, Politics, People* (Valley Forge, PA: Trinity Press, 1995), 51.

5. Nikkos Kokkinos, *The Herodian Dynasty: Origins, Role in Society and Eclipse* (Sheffield: Sheffield Academic Press, 1998), 235-236.

One incident may suggest some allegiance toward the traditions of Judaism. When Pilate attempted to install the controversial shields in the Herodian palace in Jerusalem, Philo reports that the sons of Herod appealed to Tiberius to have them removed. Whether or not Philip was included in that group of sons, is unknown. However, from practices within his own territory, Philip certainly held no scruples regarding practices that might seem offensive. Nothing speaks to Philip's attitude better than the very public action in minting coins. While the Herodians had consistently avoided human images on their coins—and until later even inscriptions that mentioned the Caesar—every coin minted by Philip includes human images: Augustus, Tiberius, Livia and even his own. Philip simply followed the custom of his territory. This is evidenced by his first coin in 1 CE which, by depicting images of Augustus and himself, imitated the coin minted by Zenodorus in 27 BCE with depictions of Octavian and Zenodorus.[6] Similarly he regularly depicted the temple to Augustus at Caesarea Philippi and then on the Julia 30 CE Sebaste coin an inscribed epithet associated with the Demeter cult. The coins themselves, to be sure reflect the attitude of Philip, and not necessarily his subjects. So what did this mean for residents in the village of Bethsaida in the southwest corner of his territory? There is only silence regarding any voices of opposition or protest, unlike the situation of Antipas who was criticized for building the city of Tiberias over a cemetery and who included forbidden images in his palace. Even in the Jewish town of Gamla, thirty-six Philip coins turned up in excavations.

More importantly, Philip's role in founding cities dedicated to Augustus and his wife Livia would have made an impact on residents. In the case of Bethsaida, the late dedication date in 30 CE would possibly point to a different character for the village during the early decades of Philip's rule than after the transformation from village to city. With the name change from Bethsaida to Julias, one would need to assume some knowledge on the part of residents about Livia and the ways of Roman rule. This would seem to be the

Philip coin 30 CE with image of Livia

6. A. Kindler, "A Coin of Herod Philip—the Earliest Portrait of a Herodian Ruler," *IEJ*, 21 (1971), 162.

case to some degree even in Judea where the procurators minted coins with Julia inscriptions and it is known that daily sacrifices were offered in the Jerusalem temple for the imperial family. The difference at Bethsaida-Julias is that Philip's coin with Demeter motifs moves from an attitude of respect for the ruler to one of toleration of non-Jewish religion, and that assumes some familiarity with those practices.

The most significant factor in determining the ethnic and religious character of Bethsaida is the identification of a pagan temple at Bethsaida. There has been reluctance by some to accept this identification,[7] but the cumulative evidence is difficult to dispute:

- The location of the temple upon the foundations of an earlier Phoenician temple.
- The reorientation of the temple in an east-west direction.
- The design of the temple to include a front porch, large hall, and back porch (*pronaos, naos,* and *opisthodomos*).
- Architectural fragments (though most are admittedly missing) including a column, dressed stones, a piece of imported marble, and a stone decorated with meander motif typical of the Augustan era.
- Vessels typical for cultic use, including two bronze incense shovels (one complete), a bronze patera, and a metal simpulum.
- A figurine showing Livia with her typical melon-like hairstyle.

Such a temple to Julia meant the transformation of Bethsaida to a center for the Imperial Cult with its rituals and associated practices impacting not only the town but the surrounding region—even attracting Gentiles from Tiberias and other parts of Galilee.

Dressed basalt stone with meander motif

7. Chancey. *Myth of a Gentile Galilee* (2004).

According to Josephus, Philip also added residents to Bethsaida at the time of its foundation as a city. So one must consider several groups in determining the make up of the city: families descending from earlier Phoenician settlers; Judeans who had migrated north under Hasmonean expansion; new residents added by Philip. With regard to the latter, who were they? Josephus offers no clues, although he does provide the earlier model of Herod who on one occasion settled Jews from Babylon into the region and on another settled Idumeans. One can begin by mentioning those that he might have excluded. Clearly, Philip would not have settled those whose religious practice would lead to criticism of the newly established temple cult and the general policies of Philip. He did not need to repeat the situation that had occurred with Antipas in Tiberias. Instead several kinds of people would certainly be included:

- administrators to implement the needs of the new polis;
- a priesthood to serve temple;
- servants to make his own life comfortable as he shifted his own residence to Bethsaida.

Presumably, many of these persons followed Philip from Caesarea Philippi and likely came from Gentile backgrounds. Philip likely also attracted Jews from Galilee who had become disgruntled with Antipas' economic policies and high taxation. However, the move to Bethsaida would mean joining Philip's tax base with the new responsibility of funding the new city. Earlier Herod had relaxed taxation to encourage immigration, but this position seems unlikely under Philip in these circumstances.

Hopefully more will be learned about these new residents in future seasons of excavation. The residential sections on the acropolis do not appear to be part of this expansion which likely occurred on the southern slope toward the lake.

The Bethsaida disciples

The designation of Bethsaida as home of several disciples and the visits of Jesus to this area demonstrate without question that Bethsaida was a Jewish town—at least partially. These Bethsaida disciples were Jews familiar with covenant history, the law and the prophets, and traditional monotheism. They kept the Sabbath and made pilgrimage to Jerusalem where they shared the Passover Seder. They appeared at home in both synagogue and temple. According to the Fourth Gospel, Andrew and possibly also Philip or John, were part of the Jewish renewal movement as followers of John the Baptist (John 1:29, 35).

At the same time, these three are the only disciples with Greek names: Philip, Andrew, and Simon—Simeon was a popular Hebrew name, but Simon is Greek. Peter could be identified in Jerusalem as a Galilean by his accent (Matt 26:73). This is often explained in terms of a careless pronunciation of gutturals, though it could be a sign of language development in an area where Aramaic was not always spoken.[8] One can assume that these disciples had a basic knowledge of the Greek language as is evidenced by the play on words with the name Jesus gave to Simon related to *Petros*, the Greek word for rock. Perhaps the most revealing information comes in John 12:20-1 when Greeks wish to see Jesus and therefore approach Philip and Andrew as intermediaries. The term here is Ἕλληνές which refers to Gentiles, not Ἑλληνίσται which would refer to Greek-speaking Jews.[9] Although John had already in chapter one identified these disciples as being from Bethsaida, he mentions this again in the Jerusalem context, which could mean that these were Greeks living in Bethsaida or at least that Bethsaida was known as a town where Jews and Gentiles lived together.

It is significant that Peter later plays a key role in the opening of the mission to the Gentiles and relaxing the requirement of circumcision. This occurs both in the Lukan account of Peter's visit to Cornelius in Caesarea Maritima (Acts 10) and the Pauline description of the Jerusalem meeting in 49 CE (Galatians 2). At the same time, Luke characterizes Peter as a follower of Kosher laws, never having previously eaten with non-Jews before he approached the home of Cornelius, and Paul points to Peter as wavering on this matter in Antioch. Still it is striking that the travels of the fisherman from Bethsaida later took him to such cosmopolitan centers as Antioch, Corinth, and Rome.

Jewish Ethnic Markers in Archaeology

Literary descriptions are often selective and sometimes shaped by the views of the authors. Knowing from literary sources only three disciples and Philip the Tetrarch,[10] how typical are they of first century Bethsaida? Clearly archaeology has helped to shape our understanding of Philip through coins

---

8. Markus Bockmuehl, "Simon Peter and Bethsaida," Supplements to Novum Testamentum 115 (2005), 53-91, especially 63-4.

9. John does not use ἔθνος to refer to the Gentiles, but to the Jewish people. Haenchen suggests that John 12:20 refers to the "Greek world in general, and thus also the pagan world." Ernst Haenchen, *John*, trans. Robert Funk, Hermeneia Series (Philadelphia: Fortress, 1984), 96.

10. The Rabbinic texts about Tzaidan likely reflect migration of Jews to the north following the destruction of the Jerusalem Temple in 70 CE.

and the excavation of the temple at Bethsaida. On the opposite end, there is yet no evidence of a synagogue like the one in nearby Gamla, nor are there any inscriptions that might identify a benefactor of the Jewish community, nor any stones decorated with Jewish symbols. What about the common inhabitants? Can the excavation of domestic space with its artifacts of daily life demonstrate the Jewishness, or lack thereof, of its inhabitants?

In his work at Sepphoris, Jonathan Reed has identified four indicators of Jewish religious identity:

- stepped plastered pools;
- secondary burial with ossuaries in loculi tombs;
- bone profiles that lack pork;
- chalk vessels.[11]

Mikvaoth or stepped, plastered ritual baths, play a central role in determining the Jewish character of Sepphoris. Present in the priestly houses excavated in Jerusalem, they are relatively rare in northern sites of this period—only found at Sepphoris, Gamla, and Qeren Naftali.[12] None have been uncovered at Bethsaida. Similarly there are no burials similar to the ossuaries of Jerusalem.

The question of diet is a bit more complicated. In her analysis of bone finds in early Roman loci at Bethsaida, Toni Fisher found that pigs make up two percent.[13] The relatively low number may be indicative of the Jewish character of the community. However, one should be careful about an argument based on the absence of something. What Fisher found is that et-Tell at no period had a high amount of pig bones. The percentage was only slightly higher in Iron Age loci and in Hellenistic loci, when the town was clearly non-Jewish. In addition, the percentage of pig bones found in loci of the Temple of Livia was basically the same as in loci from residential areas in the early Roman period, but they also show evidence of roasting in the fire. So there may be other factors. Hesse notes that other ethnic groups refrained from pork and this was also a class issue so that in Egypt priests abstained

---

11. Reed, *Archaeology and the Galilean Jesus* (2000), 44.

12. Mordechai Aviam, "Distribution Maps of Archaeological Data from the Galilee: An Attempt to Establish Zones Indicative of Ethnicity and Religious Identification," in *Religion, Ethnicity, and Identity in Ancient Galilee,* ed. Jürgen Zangenberg, Harold W. Attridge, and Dale B. Martin (Tübingen: Möhr Siebeck, 2007), 118-9.

13. Toni Gayle Fisher, *A Zooarchaeological Analysis of Change in Animal Utilization at Bethsaida from Iron Age II through the Early Roman Period* (Knoxville: University of Tennessee, 2005), 95-127.

while swineherds raised pigs for the masses.[14] Fisher notes that pigs are less common in a settlement involved in agriculture and where cattle appear in large numbers, as Bethsaida.[15] So with regard to the presence of pig bones in the Iron Age, Fisher suggests they were hunted as wild game—which may be also the case in later eras. So they are present in Roman era houses south of the gate. There is one section in Fisher's sample where there was a total absence of pig bones, loci from the northwest quarter of the Fisherman's House (the kitchen on the east side of the courtyard was not included). However, even in that house there were eight percent catfish bones—non-kosher—as is typical throughout Bethsaida. The evidence of pig bones is thus inconclusive with regard to questions of ethnicity at Bethsaida.

The one indicator of Jewish ethnicity that is clearly present at Bethsaida is chalk or limestone vessels. Carl Savage notes a particular fragment discovered in the 2000 season as a fragment of a flat-based bowl with straight sides.[16] Savage counts about ten limestone vessels discovered to this point, a number which is not that great, but which demonstrates a clear Jewish presence. In his definitive work on limestone vessels, Yitzhak Magen notes that "chalk vessels are the only components of the material culture that appear suddenly in the late first century BCE and vanish after the destruction of the Second Temple and the Bar Kochba Revolt."[17] Prior to Magen's work there was little attention to these vessels that ensured purity, so many excavations including the early years at Bethsaida, were not cognizant of the importance of such finds. Subsequently, a workshop cave at Reina near Nazareth has been excavated by David Amrit.[18] Other vessels originated in Jerusalem.

Pottery styles common to Jewish settlements

In addition to the common indicators of Jewish identity, Andrea Berlin has suggested a major cultural shift that appears with the coming of Judaism

14. B. Hesse, "Husbandry, Dietary Taboos and the Bones of the Ancient Near East: Zooarchaeology in the Post-Processural World," in *Methods in the Mediterranean*, ed. D. B. Small (Amsterdam: E. J. Brill, 1995) 197-232, especially 228.

15. Fisher, *A Zooarchaeological Analysis* (2005), 116.

16. Carl Savage, "Supporting Evidence for a First-Century Bethsaida," in *Religion, Ethnicity, and Identity in Ancient Galilee* (2007), 193-206, especially 201.

17. Yitzhak Magen, *The Stone Vessel Industry in the Second Temple Period* (Jerusalem: Israel Exploration Society, 2002), 100.

18. Aviam, "Distribution Maps," 120.

Limestone vessel fragments

and that shows itself in common household pottery.[19] This is evident primarily in two ways. First, there is the appearance of new pottery workshops
in Jewish communities, among these are Kefar Hananya in eastern Galilee,
Binyanei Ha'uma east of Jerusalem, and el-Jumeizah near Gamla. While
there is an increase in population and a need for more cooking ware, there
also appears a market for pottery that is distinctively Jewish. The second way
is that the previously common decorated ware disappears from sites that are
typically Jewish. Such a shift in pottery use appears around the middle of
the first century BCE. Among those sites that most clearly demonstrate that
shift are Gamla, where earlier pottery included Eastern Terra Sigilatta table
vessels and imported wine amphorae. By mid-century Berlin notes a shift,
"The household pottery of the subsequent phase, however, was almost exclusively undecorated, utilitarian types—storage vessels, cooking vessels, small
eating and drinking bowls."[20] The same pattern appears at Bethsaida, where
fine imported ware is replaced by Kefar Hananya ware. Berlin attributes the
change to "an increased interest in purity outside of Temple environs," and

19. Andrea M. Berlin, "Jewish Life before the Revolt: The Archaeological Evidence,"
Journal for the Study of Judaism in the Persian, Hellenistic, and Roman Period 36 (2005),
417-70.

20. Andrea Berlin, "Between Large Forces: in the Hellenistic Period," *Biblical Archaeologist* 60 (1997), 40.

refers to the practice as household Judaism. This phenomenon is significant and must be studied further. However, there is some reason to be hesitant since this pattern seems to affect a large population group where some may have initially adopted the new pottery for religious reasons and others joined in for convenience sake. It is difficult in such cases to attribute motive, especially to a whole population. It may be that the change was a reaction in opposition to Roman occupation. So the shift in pottery is significant, but the reasons are still elusive.

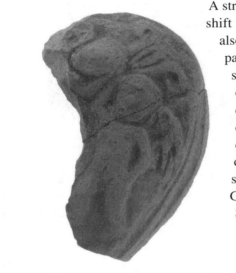

A stronger case can be made for the shift to Herodian oil lamps, known also as the wheel-made and knife-pared lamps, which, like the limestone vessels, appear at the end of the first century BCE and then disappear after the destruction of the temple in 70 CE. The chemical analysis of 176 Herodian oil lamps from Jewish sites as Jotapata, Sepphoris, and Gamla, as well as from Dor and Scythopolis, found that a high percentage were made in the pottery kilns of Binyanei Ha'uma near Jerusalem.[21] This was especially the case with Jewish sites, while some from Dor and Scythopolis were made in kilns from the north. So

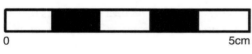

0   5cm

Hellenistic oil lamp with Erotes motif

at Sepphoris, 23 of the 30 lamps studied came from this Jerusalem area kiln, and at Jotapata 35 of 39 originated there. Most striking is that all but three of the 57 lamps studied for Gamla originated in Jerusalem. This is significant because residents of Gamla purchased lamps from Jerusalem—a long one hundred miles away—rather than make them in local kilns. It would seem that Jewish pilgrims to the Jerusalem temple would have brought

21. David Adan-Bayewitz, Frank Asaro, Moshe Wieder, and Robert D. Giauque, "Preferential Distribution of Lamps from the Jerusalem Area in the Late Second Temple Period (Late First Century B.C.E. to 70 C.E.)," *Bulletin of the American Schools of Oriental Research* 350 (2008), 37-85.

back lamps to convey a presence of the temple in their homes, perhaps especially for the Sabbath. Carl Savage notes that 34 Herodian lamps have been uncovered at Bethsaida through the 2009 excavation season, while only 3 Syro-Palestinian forms represent this same period.[22] During earlier periods decorated Hellenistic lamps, including those with Erotes motifs, had been quite common. The 92% figure of Herodian lamps in the first century corresponds to a figure of 93% at Gamla while at the non-Jewish site of Tel Anafa only 6% are Herodian. It must be noted, however, that Herodian lamps were also very common at non-Jewish Dor and Scythopolis and that one third of the Dor lamps tested had originated in Jerusalem and nearly half of those Scythopolis came from there. So again, there is evidence that Gentiles were also using lamps from Jerusalem that for Jews carried a special religious meaning. The lamps from Bethsaida have yet to be tested to see how many were brought back from Jerusalem and how many might be "imitations" from Galilean kilns.

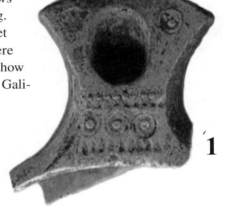

1

Herodian oil lamp

The population of Bethsaida

How large was ancient Bethsaida? The answer is comparatively small especially when one considers Josephus' comment that Bethsaida was elevated to the status of a *polis*, a city. However, the designation of *polis* was not determined by size. With regard to population, Bethsaida can best be understood as a large village, or a small town. Josephus is an unreliable reference when it comes to population estimates since he states that "the smallest village contains 150,000 inhabitants" (Josephus, *War* 3.43). This would put the total population of the Galilee in the millions. Even modern scholars do exaggerate at times. Twenty-five years ago, when the archaeology of Galilee was taking off and scholars were replacing the idyllic picture of a rural countryside with an urbanized Galilee,

22. Carl Savage, *Bethsaida: A Study of the First Century CE in the Galilee* (Lanham, MD: Lexington Books, 2010).

two of the most respected scholars projected the population of Capernaum between 12,000 and 15,000.[23]

Capernaum and Bethsaida are relatively similar in size: eight to ten hectares (= 20-25 acres). Roughly, et-Tell measures about four hundred meters by two hundred meters. Since excavations to this point have concentrated on the acropolis in the northeast quarter, it is impossible to know the extent of the city, whether or not it covered the entire tell, or whether it even went beyond to cover part of the plain below. For now, a figure of ten hectares will be assumed for the area of the city. With this base figure it is possible to estimate the population density and determine an approximate population. One study of nineteenth-century CE Palestinian villages estimated a density of about 100-150 persons per hectare.[24] By way of contrast, Roman Ostia, one of the most highly dense populations of the first century estimated at 360-435 persons per hectare. Jonathan Reed estimates a population density of 150-250 persons per hectare for first-century Sepphoris which covers between forty and sixty hectares. Accordingly, he estimates the population of Sepphoris between 6,000 and 12,000, and a similar figure for Tiberias.[25]

Bethsaida, then, would likely range between 1,500 and 2,500 persons. Capernaum would be about the same.

23. Eric Meyers and James F. Strange, *Archaeology, the Rabbis, and Early Christianity* (Nashville: Abingdon, 1983), 58.

24. Chester C. McCowan, "The Density of Population in Ancient Palestine," *JBL* 66 (1947), 425-36.

25. Jonathan L. Reed, *Archaeology and the Galilean Jesus,* 69-83. See also Richard Horsley, *Archaeology, History, and Society in Galilee* (Harrisburg, PA: Trinity Press, 1996), 44-6.

Chapter 10

Philip as Ruler

Luke 3:1 sets the historical context for Jesus' ministry during the rule of Philip, the Tetrarch of Iturea and Trachonitis. In fact, Philip's rule lasted some 37 years—corresponding almost exactly to Jesus' entire life—from 4 BCE to 34 CE. As the son of King Herod, he was one of the least expected successors, but perhaps the most effective and the best liked. With Pontius Pilate from Rome's foreign service governing Judea and Jerusalem to the south and with Philip's brother Herod Antipas ruling Galilee to the west, Philip provided the third cog of partnership under the authority of the Roman emperor.

Philip's Youth

Philip was the son of Herod and Cleopatra of Jerusalem. Little is known for certain about this Cleopatra. Her Greek name places her, like the famous Egyptian Princess, in the context of Hellenism, perhaps coming to Jerusalem with her family as part of Herod's court.[1] Cleopatra is placed somewhere in the middle of Herod's nine wives. After divorcing his first wife Doris, Herod sought political alliance with the Hasmo-

Philip coin 30 CE with image of Philip

---

1. Nikkos Kokkinos, *The Herodian Dynasty: Origins, Role in Society and Eclipse* (Sheffield: Sheffield Academic Press, 1998), 235-236.

neans through marriage to Mariamme 1 from 37 to 29 BCE and then Mariamme 2, the daughter of Jerusalem's high priest. By the mid to late 20s BCE, Herod married into his harem a Samaritan named Malthace, Cleopatra, and several other women.

Philip was likely born between 22 and 20 BCE.[2] He had an older brother named Herod who is never mentioned again by Josephus (*Ant.* 17. 21). Growing up Philip (along with Herod) would have been closest to the children of Malthace, Antipas of his own age,[3] Archelaus two years older, and the younger Olympias. By this time, Herod had already sent off to Rome, Alexander and Aristobulus, the sons of Mariamme 1, when Augustus granted Herod the right to name his successor. Augustus' policy was to educate select children of his client kings in Rome as a way of developing the future relationships essential for the smooth administration of the future empire. Josephus identifies their teacher as Pollio, presumably the well-known orator C. Asinius Pollio who had served as consul in 40 BCE and was mentioned in the dedication of Virgil's Fourth Ecologue (Josephus, *Ant.* 15.342-3).[4]

Philip was still a young boy when the Alexander and Aristobulus returned from Rome in 17 BCE to marry and begin raising their families. This was the point when palace intrigues turned hostile and Herod himself turned paranoid towards his older sons. Herod recalled his first wife Doris and sent their son Antipater to Rome as the newly named successor. By 12 BCE, Philip, Archelaus, and Antipas were also sent to Rome for their education while they missed out on Herod's execution of Alexander and Aristobulus in 7 BCE and of Antipater shortly before Herod's own death in 4 BCE. C. Asinius Pollio was still active in Rome at this time, but it is not certain whether he was involved in younger boys' education. Josephus' statement about their education has been debated so that it is not clear whether they stayed with "a private person," with "one of their own," or with "a certain Jew" (*Ant.* 17:20-21).[5]

This would have been an especially significant time for Philip and his brothers to be in Rome. Augustus had recently returned home from successful campaigns in Gaul and Spain with a new campaign to promote the

---

2. Peter Richardson, *Herod: King of the Jews and Friend of the Romans* (Minneapolis: Fortress Press, 1999), 47. Kokkinos gives an uncharacteristic early date from Philip's birth in 26 CE, 236. Harold W. Hoehner, *Herod Antipas* (Cambridge: University Press, 1972), 12.

3. On one occasion Josephus erroneously states that Philip was a full brother of Archelaus. (Josephus, *Ant.* 17.189).

4. Louis H. Feldman, "Asinius Pollio and Herod's Sons," *Classical Quarterly* 35 (1985), 240-3.

5. The Greek in the manuscript παρά τινι ἰδίῳ may be a confusion with ἰδιώτῃ or Ἰουδαίῳ.

concept of the *Pax Romana* throughout the empire. Poets like Ovid and Virgil were popularizing the idea that Rome was a divinely guided ship with Augustus at the helm. Architects were guiding a wave of great public building and artists were designing important public symbols like the Ara Pacis Augustae, dedicated in 9 BCE. On the domestic side, the Julian Laws promoted family values with Augustus' wife Livia taking on a public role. About the time of Philip's arrival in Rome, Augustus' close friend and son-in-law Marcus Agrippa had died. With Augustus thinking of succession, he named his two grandsons, Gaius and Lucius as next in line, the former about the same age as Philip. All was not bright, however. The forced marriage of Livia's son, Tiberius, to Augustus' daughter, Julia, created nothing short of a scandal with Tiberius fleeing Rome in self-imposed exile and Julia embarrassing her father through open adulterous affairs.

The three brothers returned home to Jerusalem sometime in 5 or 4 BCE to a house in turmoil. At seventy years of age, his father Herod was dying a miserable death, turning paranoid against all who surrounded him, and vacillating on the question of his succession through seven different wills.[6] The now discredited Antipater still had his father's ear and used the opportunity to poison his opinion concerning Philip and Archelaus (Josephus, *Ant.* 17.80-1). So in his sixth will, Herod named the youngest brother Antipas as successor. Then another supposed plot was uncovered with Mariamme 2, Antipater, and other family members accused and convicted. Mariamme 2 was divorced with her son Herod removed from the will and with Antipater executed—removing two more sons from contention for succession. Only in the final days before Herod's painful death in Jericho in March 4 BCE did Herod make one final change to his will, adding the names Archelaus and Philip.

Herod's Will

Upon Herod's death, three teenage sons stood poised to succeed him: Archelaus and Antipas, the sons of the Samaritan Malthace,

Philip coin 30 CE with image of Philip

---

6. Emil Schürer, *The History of the Jewish People in the Age of Jesus Christ*, vol. 1, rev. ed. by G. Vermes and F. Millar (Edinburgh: T & T Clark, 1973), 336-40.

and Philip. At sixteen years old Philip demonstrated amazing restraint and patience.[7] Eighteen-year-old Archelaus and sixteen-year-old Antipas, each vying for the title king, headed to Rome with large contingents to seek the endorsement of Augustus. Philip quietly remained at home looking after Herod's remaining administration, attempting to smooth over the mess Archelaus had already created while putting down dissent with an iron fist (Josephus, *Ant.* 17. 219-20). In the north, the Roman governor of Syria, Varus, had arrived to deal with the revolt at Sepphoris. At the recommendation of Varus, Philip eventually traveled to Rome to witness the reading of Herod's will (Josephus, *Ant.* 17. 250-98).

The estate of Herod was divided among his three sons and his sister Salome:

- Philip was named tetrarch and received the territory northeast of the Sea of Galilee including areas of Gaulanitis, Trachonitis, Auranitis, and Batanea, providing one hundred talents of annual income.
- Antipas was named tetrarch and received the territories of Galilee and Perea (east of the southern Jordan River), providing two hundred talents of annual income.
- Archelaus was named ethnarch to rule over Judea and Samaria, providing four hundred talents of annual income. Apparently he also received the right to use the name Herod as a title.
- Salome was granted control over the city of Phaselis in the Jordan Valley and Azotus and Jamnia on the southern Mediterranean coast, providing her with sixty talents of annual income.

Philip and Antipas grew into their positions and provided long, stable rule in the north: Philip from 4 BCE until his death in 34 CE, and Antipas from 4 BCE until he was deposed in 39 CE. When Salome died in 9 CE, her cities were willed to Livia the wife of Augustus—a clear sign of their close relationship.

Archelaus was not so successful. A decade of tumultuous rule followed with many Jerusalemites preferring direct Roman rule. When Archelaus divorced Mariamme to marry Glaphyra, the daughter of the ruler of Cappadocia and formerly the wife of Archelaus' older brother Alexander, the priestly elite considered this an affront. In 6 CE Augustus agreed, removing Archelaus and exiling him to Lyons. In his stead, Augustus sent a long line

7. At the most Philip and Antipas may have been 18 years old and Archelaus 20 years old.

of Roman governors to rule Judea and Samaria from Caesarea Maritima, among them Pontius Pilatus.

The Territory of Philip

Philip's territory is often identified with what is known today as the Golan Heights, an area of about 465 square miles extending about fifteen miles east of the northern Jordan River and about 35 miles north-south from Hippos to Caesarea Phillipi. Its average elevation is 900 meters above sea level, sloping from Mount Hermon (elevation 3,000 meters) down to the Beteiha plain below Bethsaida (over two hundred meters below sea level). The name Golan actually derives from a city (Deut 4:43; Josh 20:8) today to the east of the actual Golan territory.[8] The form of the name used by Josephus, Gaulanitis, likely derives from third-century BCE Ptolemaic administration which often added the *itis* suffix.

In addition to Gaulanitis, Philip ruled Trachonitis, Auranitis, and Batanea all rugged territories to the east that were granted to Herod by Augustus in about 20 BCE. At about the same time, however, Zenodorus of Iturea had sold Auranitis to Nabatea for fifty talents (Josephus, *Ant.* 15. 352). This led to considerable conflict between Herod and the Nabateans over the next decade (Josephus, *Ant.* 16. 275-99, 335-50). Herod settled three thousand Idumaeans in Trachonitis and established the town of Bethyra on the border of Batanea and Trachonitis where he settled five hundred Babylonian Jews under the leadership of Zamaris (Josephus, *Ant.* 16.285; 17.23-29). However, with the ascendancy of Aretas 4 as Nabatean king from 9 BCE to 40 CE, relations between the Nabateans and the Herodians turned relatively peaceful in the early first century CE, especially after Antipas had entered a political marriage with the daughter of King Aretas. Philip should also be credited for his role in keeping good relations in these eastern regions of his tetrarchy. Almost immediately after the death of Philip in 34 CE war broke out once again in a border dispute east of Gamla. Josephus links this battle with Antipas' decision to divorce Aretas' daughter and reports that Philip's subjects joined with Aretas to soundly defeat Antipas (Josephus, Ant. 18. 110 ff).

---

8. The modern name derives from the detailed survey carried out in the 1880s by Gottleib Schumacher for the German Society for the Exploration of the Holy Land exploring the possibility of a Haifa to Damascus railroad. His study of *Die Jaulan* comprised an even larger area of about 560 square miles. Gottleib Schumacher, *The Jaulan* (London: R. Bentley, 1888).

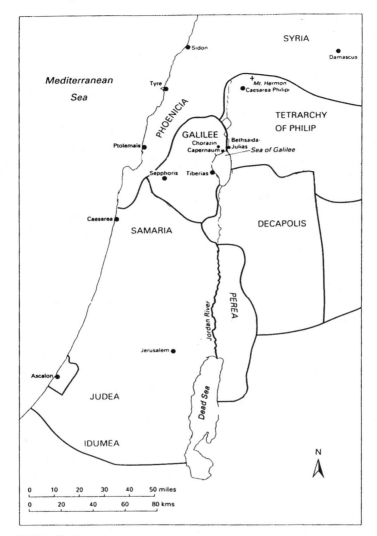

Philip's Territory

Philip's Capital: Caesarea Philippi

One of Philip's first acts as tetrarch was to establish Caesarea Philippi as his capital. It may seem surprising that Philip chose this location since this city was located in the far northwest corner of his territory, far from many of his residents. However, it was a natural choice since it was one of the first settlements by colonizers from Tyre in the fourth or fifth century BCE. Early settlers recognized the sanctity of the area with a shrine to Pan at a spring gushing from a cave and becoming one of the sources of the Jordan River—thus the ancient name Paneas (or sometimes Banias). Following the visit of Augustus to this region, Herod built a white marble Temple of Augustus. Three different sites have been suggested for this temple:

- Directly in front of the Cave of Pan.
- On a platform to the side of the Cave.
- A short distance away at Omrit.[9]

Thus the appropriateness of naming the city Caesarea Philippi, honoring both the emperor and his own role as tetrarch.

With Philip beginning his rule in 4 BCE, it is possible that he founded this city as early as 3 BCE. Many of the coins of the Roman era are dated from the founding of Caesarea Philippi where they were minted. Thus the coin of Macrinus in 217 CE is dated to year 220.[10] However, Philip himself dated his coins minted in Caesarea Philippi, not from the founding of the city, but from the beginning of his own rule. His first coin in year five may mark the dedication of the city since it includes on one side an image of Augustus surrounded by the inscription "Of Augustus Caesar" and on the other an image of Philip surrounded by the inscription "Of Philip the Tetrarch."[11] The two images correspond to the name of the new city Caesarea Philippi.

Little remains from the city of Philip's day. However, a magnificent palace from the era of Agrippa 2 has recently been excavated.[12]

Josephus' Evaluation of Philip's Rule

Josephus presents very little information about the rule of Philip itself. That can be a positive sign since it suggests there were no major controversies or military skirmishes while he was at the helm. However, Josephus no longer had as a source Nicholas of Damascus who had chronicled Herod's rule. Thus the first decades of the first century are the least documented period in Josephus' historical report.

---

9. J. Andrew Overman and Jack Olive, "A Newly Discovered Herodian Temple at Khirbet Omrit in Northern Israel," in ed. Nikos Kokkinos, *The World of the Herods* (Stuttgart: Franz Steiner Verlag, 2007).

10. Ya'akov Meshorer, *A Treasury of Jewish Coins"* (Nyack, NY: Amphora, 2001), 86.

11. *IBID,* 228, catalogue 95; plate 50: 95.

12. John F. Wilson and Vassilios Tzaferis, "Banias Dig Reveals King's Palace," *BAR* 24 (Jan./Feb. 1998), 54-61, 85.

As a kind of eulogy Josephus does provide a short summary when he reports on Philip's death, stating that Philip had the reputation of being a very popular ruler:

> In his conduct of the government, he showed a moderate and easy-going disposition. Indeed, he spent all his time in the territory subject to him (Josephus, *Ant.* 18.106).

One issue that is often a bone of contention for such rulers is that of taxation. Josephus does note that under Herod freedom from taxation had been an enticement for new settlers in Philip's eastern regions. Without having the luxury of a larger kingdom and its resources, Philip retracted this benefit:

> But when Philip, who was [tetrarch] after him, took the government, he made them pay some small taxes, and that for a little while only (Josephus, *Ant.* 17.27).

Because of Philip's moderation, this was apparently acceptable and there were no revolts during this period. Josephus does note, however, that the situation changed following Philip's death when Agrippa took a heavy handed approach. Josephus also reports that Philip often traveled throughout his territory taking with him his administrative chair which would be set up for court in various locales.

> When he went on circuits, he had only a few select companions. The throne on which he sat whenever he gave judgment accompanied him wherever he went. And so whenever anyone appealed to him for redress along the route, at once without a moment's delay, the throne was set up wherever it might be. He took his seat and gave the case a hearing. He fixed penalties for those who were convicted and released those who had been unjustly accused (Josephus, *Ant.* 18.107).

It should not be surprising that his popularity led to the use of the name Philip by his subjects, one a grandson of Zamaris who had immigrated from Babylon (Josephus, *Ant.* 17.30) and another a disciple of Jesus from Bethsaida (John 1:43).

It is ironic that the single inscription mentioning the ruler Philip comes from the eastern extremities of his territory and is written in Nabatean. It occurs on a finely decorated altar-like base for a statue and reads:

> In the year 33 of our Lord
> Philippos, there was made by Witr, son of
> Budar and Kasiu, son of Sudai

and Hann'el, son of Masak'el, and Muna, son of
Garm, this altar of the Statue of Galis
the son of Banath,
Anam, son of Ash was the Sculptor. Peace.[13]

The language of this inscription dating to 29/30 CE—"Our Lord Philip"—
denotes a positive attitude toward a relatively distant ruler.

Philip's coins

Philip reveals a considerable
amount of information about himself from the coins he minted from
his capital in Caesarea Philippi.[14]
The Romans were quite restrictive in
controlling valuable gold and silver
coins, but allowed local rulers to issue
small bronze coinage that circulated
primarily in their own territory. In a
survey of excavations in the Galilee
and Golan Danny Syon has accounted
for only ninety Philip coins.[15] Others
have appeared on the black market
and in collections. The poor quality
of Philip's coins, probably due to his
limited financial resources, results in

Pedestal from Si with inscription of Philip

coins that are often effaced and in poor quality. Philip minted coins in eight
different years of his 37-year rule, usually in two different denominations
per mint. The *As* weighed about 7.0 grams, only one fourth the size of the
large Roman bronze *Sestertius*. The *Semis* was even smaller at 3.5 grams.

13. *The Princeton Expedition of Southern Syrian (1904-1909).* Division III. Inscriptions. Section A: Southern Syria. Part 4A: Nabatean Inscriptions from the Southern Hauran.
101, p. 80.

14. Fred Strickert, "The Coins of Philip," in *Bethsaida* (1995), 165-89.

15. Danny Syon, *Tyre and Gamla: A Study in the Monetary Influences of Southern Phoenecia on Galilee and the Golan in the Hellenistic and Roman Periods,* Dissertation [Hebrew]
(Jerusalem: Hebrew University, 2004). Summary of data is available in English in Morten
Horning Jensen, *Herod Antipas in Galilee: The Literary and Archaeological Sources* (Tübingen: Mohr-Siebeck, 2006), 175-77 & 213-15.

Philip coin 30 CE with image of Tiberius and Temple of Augustus

Coin of Philip 30 CE with image of Livia

Perhaps the most striking thing about Philip's coins is that all of them portrayed human images. Generally, Jewish coins—including those of Herod, Archelaus, and Antipas—refrained from such images because of the commandment in Exodus 20:4. In his first mint in 1 CE, Philip's coins included two images: the emperor Augustus on the front and Philip on the reverse. In 8 CE, he began substituting for his own image on the reverse a simple tetrastyle temple representing the Temple of Augustus at Caesarea Philippi. This pattern continues through all of his remaining issues, with Tiberius' image replacing that of Augustus after 14 CE. One further variation occurs with the dual images of Augustus and Livia on a larger 14.0 gram *Dupondius* that does not include a date—usually the dates of Philip coins are positioned between the temple columns. In 30 CE and 33 CE, Philip added two smaller denominations for a total of four coins each year. A 2.5 gram *Quadrans* portrayed Augustus' wife Livia with the inscription "Julia Sebaste" and a 1.75 gram *Half-Quadrans* portrayed Philip himself.

It may appear that Philip chose to issue his coins randomly since they appear in only eight of his thirty-seven years. However, the following chart demonstrates that their appearance corresponds with significant events.

Several occur at the foundation of cities and others appear at times of new rulers, specifically the procurators of Jerusalem.

Year	Coins of Philip	Event
4 BCE		Philip and Antipas begin reign
1 CE	1st issue	Caesarea Philippi celebrated
6 CE		Coponius, Procurator
8 CE	2nd issue	Sepphoris Founded
9 CE		Ambibulus, Procurator
12 CE	3rd issue	Annius Rufus, Procurator
15 CE	4th issue	Valerius Gratus, Procurator
20 CE		City of Tiberias Founded
26 CE	5th issue	Pontius Pilate, Procurator
29 CE	6th issue	Death of Livia
30 CE	7th issue	Foundation of Julias
33 CE	8th issue	70th anniversary of Augustus & Livia
34 CE		Death of Philip

Coin issues at such important times serve as public relations tools, reminding his subjects of his position as the emperor's chosen ruler.[16]

Philip and the Roman procurators

When Philip's minting pattern is compared with the arrival dates of new Roman procurators, it appears that he was determined to reassert his authority lest the procurators encroach upon his territory and lest he lose his appointment as had happened to his brother Archelaus in Jerusalem. While Josephus described Archelaus' downfall in 6 CE as the result of conflict with leading Jews and Samaritans (*Ant.* 17.342-4; *War* 2.111), Dio Cassius explains it in terms of accusations by Archelaus' own brothers.[17] A contemporary of these events, Strabo, suggests that the accusations were not all one-sided, but that Herod's sons were not so successful in the arrangement as co-rulers, and that they "became involved in accusations."[18] The result of a hearing before Augustus in Rome was that Archelaus was banished while Antipas and Philip were

16. Fred Strickert, "Coins as Historical Documents," in Rami Arav and John Rousseau, *Jesus and His World: An Archaeological and Cultural Dictionary* (Minneapolis: Fortress Press, 1995).

17. Dio Cassius, *Roman History* 55.27.6.

18. Strabo, *Geography* 16.2.46.

allowed to continue their rule, yet not without difficulty—θεραπεία πολλῇ μόλις. The first procurator Coponius arrived in 6 CE, issued his own coins,[19] and carried out a census with the help of Quirinius to initiate taxation. Josephus reports that this marked the beginning of the zealot movement, through an uprising against such taxation led by Judas, a man whose father had been executed by Herod (Josephus, *Ant.* 18. 1-3; *War* 2.118). Interestingly, Josephus one time refers to him as a Galilean, but another as from Gamla in Gaulanitis, Philip's own territory. Philip's position on taxation, mentioned earlier as one of moderation, was considered acceptable by his subjects. So it would seem that his decision to issue coins in 8 CE was related to a desire to remind them that he was still in charge. So also with the arrival of Annius Rufus in 12 CE, Valerius Gratus in 15 CE, and Pontius Pilatus in 26 CE, Philip issued coins. During the eleven year interval—a significant period of time—between the arrivals of Gratus and Pilate, Philip issued no additional coins.

Year	Coins of Philip	Event	Coin of Antipas
4 BCE		Philip and Antipas begin reign	
1 CE	1st issue	Caesarea Philippi celebrated	
6 CE		Coponius, Procurator, issues coins	
8 CE	2nd issue	Reaction to Taxation	
9 CE		Ambibulus, Procurator	
12 CE	3rd issue	Annius Rufus, Procurator	
15 CE	4th issue	Valerius Gratus, Procurator	
20 CE		City of Tiberias Founded	1st issue
26 CE	5th issue	Pontius Pilate, Procurator	
29 CE	6th issue	1st Pilate coins	2nd issue
30 CE	7th issue	2nd Pilate coins	3rd issue
31 CE		3rd Pilate coins	
33 CE	8th issue		4th issue
34 CE		Death of Philip	
39 CE		Antipas Deposed	5th issue

The ten-year rule of Pilate (26-36 CE) brought about a flurry of minting activity. During Pilate's tenure, Philip issued a total of eleven different coins in four different years. During the previous 28 years, he had issued only two coins per year in four different years, for a total of eight. In addition, Antipas joined Philip in issuing coins in 29, 30, and 33 CE. This all came about in reaction

19. Ya'akov Meshorer, *A Treasury of Jewish Coins"* (2001), 168.

to Pilate's own minting practice in which he deliberately flooded the market with small bronze coins in the years 29, 30, and 31 CE. Israeli numismatist, Ya'akov Meshorer, notes that Philip and Antipas cooperated in this effort in order to "emphasize their legitimate rights as Jewish rulers."[20] Pilate was so successful that many of these small coins continue to be uncovered in excavations throughout the Galilee as well as in Pilate's own Judea. Interestingly, no Pilate coins have shown up at Bethsaida.

Philip's Leadership against Pontius Pilate

There is one particular occasion when Philip and Antipas were called upon to join forces against Pilate. This came about in response to a series of actions by Pilate which managed to offend the Jewish leadership of Jerusalem. Josephus describes how, on one occasion, Pilate ordered the troops to make their winter quarters in Jerusalem bearing the Roman standards with the image of the emperor (Josephus, *Ant.* 18.55-62), in violation of Jewish laws about images. Later he built an aqueduct, which he then chose to fund by taking money from the temple treasury (Josephus, *War* 2.167-77). Finally, he decided to display in the Herodian palace some golden shields with dedications to the emperor. Philo records this event as follows:

> One of his lieutenants was Pilate, who was appointed to govern Judea. He, not so much to honor Tiberius as to annoy the multitude, dedicated in Herod's palace in the holy city some shields coated with gold. They had no image work traced on them nor anything else forbidden by the law apart from the barest inscription stating two facts, the name of the person who made the dedication and of him in whose honor it was made (Philo, *Embassy to Gaius* 38.299).

When the Jerusalem leadership protested to no avail, Philo states that they called upon Philip and Antipas to intervene:

> But when the multitude understood the matter which had by now become a subject of common talk, having put at their head the king's four sons, who in dignity and good fortune were not inferior to a king, and his other descendants and the persons of authority in their own body, they appealed to Pilate to redress the infringement of their traditions caused by the shields and not to disturb the customs which throughout all the preceding ages had been safeguarded without disturbance by kings and by emperors (Philo, *Embassy* 38.300).

---

20. Ya'akov Meshorer, *Ancient Jewish Coinage,* vol. 2 (Dix Hills, N.Y.: Amphora Books, 1982), 38, 180.

This intervention by Philip and Antipas was successful in bringing a resolution to the problem. Philo completes the account by describing a letter of reprimand sent by the Emperor Tiberius to Pilate:

> For at once without even postponing it to the morrow he [Tiberius] wrote to Pilate with a host of reproaches and rebukes for his audacious violation of precedent and bade him at once take down the shields and have them transferred from the capital to Caesarea on the coast surnamed Augustus after your great-grandfather, to be set up in the temple of Augustus, and so they were (Philo, *Embassy* 38.305).

This episode likely took place shortly before the crucifixion of Jesus (April, 30 CE) so that at the trial of Jesus the crowds, apparently aware of the reprimand of Pilate, cried out, "If you release this man, you are no friend of Caesar" (John 19:12). The cooperation between Pilate and Herod Antipas at the trial of Jesus helped to smooth things over between the two. After reporting on Jesus' hearing before Antipas, Luke notes, "That same day Herod and Pilate became friends with each other; before this they had been enemies" (Luke 23:12). There is no indication that Philip and Pilate were reconciled. The fact is that both continued their own self-promotion by an increased frequency in coin minting.

Philip and Antipas

For thirty-seven years, Philip and Antipas ruled in adjacent territories in the north of Israel. Following the death of Philip in 34 CE, Antipas continued until he was deposed by the Emperor Caligula in 39 CE. The picture painted by Josephus is generally one of cooperation between the two brothers, especially in their dealings with Archelaus and then the Roman procurators, especially Pilate. With Philip ruling from Caesarea Philippi in the northern part of his territory and with Antipas ruling from Sepphoris in western Galilee, the two were separated by a substantial distance.

The situation changed in 20 CE when Antipas moved his capital to the newly built city of Tiberias on the western shore of the Sea of Galilee. For Antipas, this was a shrewd economic move since it gave him control over the fishing industry, symbolized by the later name for the lake, the Sea of Tiberias (John 6:1; 21:1). It appears that the economic influence of Antipas and his city Tiberias reached over into Philip's territory. No less than sixty-one coins of Antipas have been uncovered in Gamla, more than the coins of Philip.[21]

---

21. Danny Syon, *A Study of the Monetary Influence* (2004). Thirty six coins of Philip were discovered in Gamla. One coin of Antipas has been uncovered thus far in Bethsaida.

Likely the decision to build a second city at Bethsaida in southern Gaulanitis was to counteract this growing influence of Antipas. Thus, while the pattern of Philip's coins corresponds to events related to the procurators in Judea, there is also significant correspondence between the coins of Philip and Antipas with both issuing coins in 29, 30, and 33 CE—a dramatic sign of economic competition. In 36 CE shortly after Philip's death, Antipas heightened this conflict by invading Gaulanitis with his army to combat the Nabatean King Aretas 4 over a border dispute near Gamla. Yet his defeat came about not by Aretas alone, but by the men of Philip's territory who joined Aretas to check the growing ambitions of Antipas (Josephus, *Ant.* 18.113-114).

Philip and the Jesus movement

The cities of Bethsaida and Caesarea Philippi are best known for their role in the Gospels and the ministry of Jesus. The implication is that Philip created a climate within his territory that benefited the Jesus movement. Following the chronology of the Synoptics—which is shaped by Mark—the first part of Jesus' ministry is concentrated in the Galilee, the territory of Antipas (Mark 1:14–6:13). At a certain point in this Galilean ministry, Herod Antipas began to perceive Jesus as a threat and to fear that he was John the Baptist raised from the dead (Mark 6:14-16). To emphasize the implications of this threat, Mark at this point recounts the episode of the violent death of John the Baptist (Mark 6:17-29). When Jesus receives word of Antipas' growing hostility, Jesus departs from Galilee by boat for "a lonely place"—probably the less populace region near Bethsaida—where he reflects on this turn of events (Mark 6:30-32). The Matthean version is even more dramatic since it omits the report of the disciples' return and directly links Jesus' decision to cross the sea to the report about Antipas' growing hostility toward Jesus (Matt 14:13). The attempt of Jesus to seek solitude is thwarted by the crowds who follow on foot. Jesus reacts with compassion which leads him to feed the multitude (Mark 6:33-44) and to follow them back to Galilee after a night alone on a nearby mountain (Mark 6:45-52).

Yet from this point on, Jesus moves in (Mark 6:53-7:23 and 7:31-8:12) and out of Galilee (Mark 7:24-30) and soon ends up at Bethsaida once again where he heals a blind man (Mark 8:13-26). Jesus sojourns for some time in the Golan, providing the setting for two critical episodes: the confession of Peter near Caesarea Philippi (Mark 8:27-9:1) and the transfiguration near Mount Hermon (Mark 9:2-13). There is no subsequent restoration of a Galilean ministry, only a short stop passing through in secret (Mark 9:30-31). This sojourn in the Golan—the territory of Philip—allowed Jesus opportunity to reflect on his ministry and to set his face toward Jerusalem (Mark 10:1) and his inevitable arrest and death (Mark 11-15).

At no time does Jesus encounter Philip, and nowhere do we have a report about Philip's attitude toward Jesus as we do about Antipas. However, a close analysis of Jesus' itinerary does suggest at least that Jesus felt more comfortable in Philip's territory during the latter stages of his ministry. This also fits the general tolerant spirit portrayed by Philip. The arrest and execution of Jesus apparently did nothing to mend the antagonistic relationship between Philip and Pilate, as it did in the case of Antipas. As we saw above, coin evidence points to a continued suspicion of Pilate by Philip. It is not surprising that the Gospel of John reports a post-Easter return of the disciples to the shores of the lake and Matthew an encounter on a nearby mountain.

The Death of Philip

Philip's career as tetrarch began with the establishment of the city of Caesarea Philippi in the northern part of his territory. That city would serve as his capital. Later Philip's attention was redirected to the southern regions where he undertook a building campaign and founded a second city, Bethsaida-Julias. That city apparently became a favorite residence for Philip where he died in the year 34 CE. Josephus reports on his death:

> Now it was at this time that Philip, Herod's brother, died in the twentieth year of Tiberius' reign and after thirty-seven years of his own rule over Trachonitis and Gaulanitis, as well as over the tribe called the Bataneans . . . . He died in Julias. His body was carried to the tomb that he himself had erected before he died and there was a costly funeral (Josephus, *Ant.* 18:106 and 108).

To be sure, Josephus does not explicitly give the location of Philip's tomb. Some argue that it must have been located at Caesarea Philippi where he had spent most of his life. However, that city was last mentioned in *Antiquities* 18.28 and completely omitted in Josephus' summary of Philip's easy-going and populist manner as a ruler (Josephus, *Antiquities* 18.106-7). The context of *Antiquities* 18.108 suggests that Philip's tomb was close by his place of death. No sign of the tomb has yet been discovered. Nevertheless, the older Bedouins who once frequented the lower Golan recall the traditional stories which led to their choice of et-Tell as a burial ground—it had been established because it had been the burial place of a very important man from many centuries ago.[22]

---

22. These Bedouins now inhabit the village of Tuba in northern Galilee. Interviews have been recorded on videotape.

Philip's Successors

Josephus reports that Tiberius annexed the territory of Philip to the Province of Syria apparently as a temporary measure since the territory's tribute was to be kept on deposit (Josephus, *Ant.* 18.108). Still there were those who tried to fill the vacuum. Aretas of Nabatea was expanding north toward Damascus (2 Cor 11:32) and saw an opportunity to regain old territories (Josephus, *Ant.* 18.114). Antipas apparently saw his opportunity to fill his brother's shoes and appealed to the emperor to annex Philip's territory to the Galilee.

However, there was another ruler in waiting. Agrippa 1, the son of Aristobulus and Bernice had been born around 10 BCE and, like other Herodians, had been educated in Rome (Josephus, *Ant.* 18.143). His mother had been a close friend of Antonia, widow of Tiberius' brother Drusus. He therefore was raised along with (ὁμοτροφίας) the future emperor Claudius and Tiberius' own son Drusus (Josephus, *Ant.* 18.143, 146, 165). After leaving Rome in 23 CE, Agrippa 1 spent some time trying to pay off his debts before beginning his political career as supervisor of markets in the city of Tiberias (Josephus, *Ant.* 18.143-9). Agrippa then returned to Rome befriending Gaius until Tiberius' death in 37 CE when Agrippa returned to make his rule secure. Subsequently Antipas was deposed (39 CE), and Agrippa's territory began to expand so that the Golan was combined once again with the Galilee and Judea in the kingdom of Agrippa (41-44 CE). It was Agrippa who undertook one of the first persecutions of early Christians in Jerusalem in the year 42 CE, putting to death the apostle James and imprisoning for a time Simon Peter (Acts 12:1-19). Shortly thereafter Agrippa died while making a public appearance in Caesarea Maritima (Josephus, *Ant.* 19.343-52). According to the Acts of the Apostles, he was struck down by an angel and eaten by worms (Acts 12:20-23).

Since Agrippa's son was still a minor, the territory was again placed under the control of Syria until 53 CE when Agrippa 2 began to rule. For the remainder of the first century, Bethsaida was under his control (Josephus, *Ant.* 20.138; *War* 2.573). Several coins of Agrippa 2, minted across the lake at Tiberias, have been discovered at Bethsaida. During the Jewish revolt in 67 CE after Agrippa lost control of the Galilee, he retreated to the Golan where he set up a government in exile. The Bethsaida area became important for him in his strategy to regain control of the Galilee. It was at this time that Agrippa's forces under the command of Sulla camped near Bethsaida to cut off the supply routes of his opponents. Had the Galilean forces under Josephus been successful against Sulla, Agrippa's hold on the

Golan would have been weakened. However, with the defeat of Galilean forces, Agrippa secured his hold on the Golan and began to retake Galilee. Eventually, this led to the fall of Jerusalem. Agrippa 2 returned to Rome, befriending emperors and securing his rule over Bethsaida and the Golan until his death at the end of the first century.

Chapter 11

Philip's Marriage

The issue of Philip's marriage is one of the more complex interpretive problems in the New Testament. In the episode of the beheading of John the Baptist, we are told that John had criticized Herod Antipas, because he had taken Herodias "his brother Philip's wife" (Mark 6.17). In Josephus, however, we are told that Philip was married to Salome, Herodias' daughter, (*Ant.* 18. 137) and that Herodias had been married to another brother of Philip and Antipas, named Herod. (*Ant.* 18. 136). Josephus and the Gospel accounts cannot both be correct.

Various solutions have been offered which fit in the following general categories:

1. Some, who bring a presupposition that the gospels are inerrant, accept uncritically the gospel reports that Philip was the husband of Herodias.
2. Some accept uncritically the report of Josephus that Herod was the husband of Herodias, some perhaps because of their own bias against the gospel accounts and some because of preferences for Josephus' role as historian.
3. Some argue that both are correct. First, Herodias married Herod, then Philip, then Antipas.[1] This, of course, leaves the problem that Philip would have later married his own step-daughter.
4. Some have argued that both are correct by suggesting that there were two Philips: one the husband of Herodias mentioned by Josephus, thus "Herod Philip 1" and the other Philip the Tetrarch, or "Herod Philip 2."

The fact is that both Josephus and the gospel reports of Philip's marriage are filled with problems. Only by wrestling with the texts does one come to grips with the full dynamics of marriage in the world of the Herodian family.

---

1. Nikos Kokkinos, "Which Salome Did Aristobulus Marry?" *PEQ* 118 (1986), 33-50.

The gospel version of the Herodias affair

Three of the gospels include this account. Mark's version is the earliest and longest. Matthew has taken over Mark, editing it for better reading and making a few significant changes. Luke provides only a short summary.

Matthew 14:3-12	*Mark 6:17-29*	*Luke 3:19-20*
3 For Herod had arrested John, bound him, and put him in prison on account of Herodias, his brother Philip's wife,	17 For Herod himself had sent men who arrested John, bound him, and put him in prison on account of Herodias, his brother Philip's wife, because Herod had married her. 18 For John had been telling Herod, "It is not lawful for you to have your brother's wife."	19 But Herod the ruler who had been rebuked by him because of Herodias his brother's wife, and because of all the evil things that Herod had done, 20 added to them all by shutting up John in prison.
4 because John had been telling him, "It is not lawful for you to have her." 5 Though Herod wanted to put him to death, he feared the crowd, because they regarded him as a prophet.		
	19 And Herodias had a grudge against him, and wanted to kill him. But she could not, 20 for Herod feared John, knowing that he was a righteous and holy man, and he protected him. When he heard him, he was greatly perplexed; and yet he liked to listen to him.	
6 But when Herod's birthday came,	21 But an opportunity came when Herod on his birthday gave a banquet for his courtiers and officers and for the leaders of Galilee. 22 When	
the daughter of Herodias danced before the company, and she pleased Herod 7 so much that he promised on oath to grant her whatever she might ask.	his daughter Herodias came in and danced, she pleased Herod and his guests, and the king said to the girl, "Ask me for whatever you wish, and I will give it." 23 And he solemnly swore to her, "Whatever you ask me, I will give you, even half of my kingdom."	
8 Prompted by her mother,	24 She went out and said to her mother, "What should I ask for?" She replied,	

	"The head of John the Baptizer."
	25 Immediately she rushed back to the
she said	king and requested, "I want you to
"Give me the head of John the	give me at once the head of John the
Baptist here on a platter." 9 The	Baptist on a platter." 26 The
king was grieved, yet out of	king was deeply grieved; yet out of
regard for his oaths and for the	regard for his oaths and for the
guests,	guests, he did not want to refuse her.
	27 Immediately the king sent a soldier
he commanded it to be given;	of the guard with orders to bring
10 he sent and had John beheaded	John's head. He went and beheaded
in the prison. 11 The head was	him in the prison, 28 brought his
brought on a platter and given to	head on a platter, and gave it to the girl.
the girl, who brought it to her	Then the girl gave it to her mother.
mother. 12 His disciples came	29 When his disciples
and took the	heard about it, they came and took his
body and buried it; then they	body, and laid it in a tomb.
went and told Jesus.	

Luke's report occurs near the beginning of the gospel, when John the Baptist had been imprisoned by Antipas. Among the reasons: John had rebuked Antipas for taking Herodias, his brother's wife. The brevity of his report is to be expected, it would be premature at this point to report on John's death. The accounts in Mark and Matthew, however, are set in the form of a flashback. When word reaches Herod Antipas about the success of Jesus' preaching, the story of John's beheading is presented as an example of what might happen to Jesus. Both writers note that one of the reasons for John's imprisonment had been his accusation that Antipas was living with his brother Philip's wife.

Internal problems in the gospel accounts

The story itself seems to suggest the features of legendary tales: the scandal of adultery, a the promise of an over-zealous stepfather, a dancing girl, a pushy wife, the dramatic presentation of a prophet's head on a platter.[2] The fact that such details are missing from Josephus' report about John's

2. Ross S. Kraemer, "Implicating Herodias and Her Daughter in the Death of John the Baptist: A (Christian) Theological Strategy," *JBL* (125:2, 2006), 321–49.

death has been frequently mentioned as a reason to accept his credibility for accurate historical reporting.[3]

Clearly Mark did not create this story about the death of John the Baptist himself. Because of the popularity of John among the masses, it only makes sense that word of his death soon circulated among his followers and also among the fledgling Jesus community. It is true that such a story conveys inside information from Antipas' palace. However, among the early followers of Jesus were persons who could provide at least the kernel of the story of a power-hungry wife who used her daughter's dance to bring down her strongest critic, even with the grotesque image of the prophet's head on a platter. Among them were Joanna, wife of Chuza, Antipas' steward, and Manean, his life-long friend.

Yet as the story grew there were questions of accuracy. Josephus places the imprisonment and execution of John the Baptist in Herod's fortress at Machareus in the southern part of Perea while the Gospel story revolves around a birthday banquet in the new royal palace at Tiberias with the leading men of Galilee present. Perhaps it is the modern dramatic production to resolve conflicts in the space of thirty minutes that leads one to find incongruity in a party in Galilee resolved by a beheading at Machereus and the finale taking place back in Galilee with the presentation to Herodias of John's head on a platter. Yet this is the nature of good story-telling.

Yet, even without a comparison to Josephus, the gospel accounts present enough problems in themselves. Mark's language is somewhat careless—as is typical of his style—with the placement of "because Herod had married her" at the end of verse 17. Mark's report also includes inaccurate information about Herod Antipas. For example, he refers four times to Antipas as "king" and his territory as "kingdom," while the proper terms would be "tetrarch" and "tetrarchy." The use of the name "Herod" for Antipas, however, is quite common and occurs also in Josephus, though it is confusing to modern readers who associate Herod with the Christmas stories. When compared with Matthew's Gospel, it is clear that the later writer has "cleaned up" the language of Mark, omitting the final phrase of Mark 6:17 and all but one reference to Herod as "king."

---

3. Louis Feldman does not see a contradiction: "The Christians chose to emphasize the moral charges that he brought against the ruler, whereas Josephus stresses the political fears that he aroused in Herod." Louis Feldman, notes, *Josephus, Jewish Antiquities*, Books XVIII–XX, Loeb Classical Library, 433, translated by Louis H. Feldman (Cambridge, MA: Harvard University Press, 1965), note e, page 83. Elsewhere in Josephus, there is plenty of criticism for Herodias.

As is often the case in story telling, names are non-essential. The dancing daughter only receives the name Salome in the post-gospel telling of the story—albeit via the appearance of her name in Josephus as the daughter of Herodias. In popular tradition, including art, literature, and the well-known opera, she is Salome. However, few people are aware that the oldest New Testament manuscripts give her the name Herodias, not Salome, and identify her as Antipas' own daughter. Both Codex Sinaiticus and Codex Vaticanus read τῆς θυγατρὸς αὐτοῦ Ἡρωδιάδος for Mark 6:22. Yet until recent times English translations have chosen otherwise:

- the daughter of the said Herodias (KJV)
- Herodias's own daughter (New American Bible)
- the daughter of this same Herodias (New Jerusalem Bible)
- the daughter of Herodias (NIV 1984)
- Herodias' daughter (RSV 1952)
- Herodias' daughter (New KJV 1982)
- Herodias's daughter (English Standard Version 2001)

Only with the 1989 *New Revised Standard Version* is the Greek correctly translated as "his daughter Herodias." Yet tradition is so strong, that few are likely aware of this reading. A decade or so after Mark's report, Matthew 14:3—perhaps correcting what he interpreted as an incorrect reading—wrote ἡ θυγάτηρ τῆς Ἡρῳδιάδος (the daughter of Herodias). However, Matthew leaves the daughter nameless.

Yet the more serious question might be the kind of dance that elicited such a wide open promise from Antipas. Was it the sensuous dance of a perverted relationship? Or was it simply a cute bit of entertainment by an innocent child? Although the former has prevailed in traditional interpretation, Mark and Matthew's use of the diminutive κοράσιον (little girl) might suggest the latter. In this account, the gospels seem to raise more questions than provide solutions when it comes to historical information. This leaves plenty of reason for doubt with regard to the statement that Herodias had first been married to Philip.

Some would argue that the omission of Philip's name in later manuscripts of the Matthew (and Mark) should be construed as admission of error. To be fair, such transcribers may well have been influenced by knowledge of Josephus, rather than by independent sources. A more serious critique focuses on Luke's report that merely uses the expression "his brother's wife" (Lk 3:19). As the evangelist reputedly with historical interest and with specific interest in the family of Antipas, Luke's omission of Philip's name has been characterized as a correction of Mark. However, there are two common counter arguments. First is the fact that Luke's account is only a very brief notation, omitting most of the Markan material. Second is the fact that Luke 3:19 follows upon Luke's listing of government leaders in Luke 3:1, placing Jesus' ministry "when Herod was ruler of Galilee, and his brother Philip ruler of the region of Iturea and Trachonitis." There is no reason to think that in Luke's mind "his brother's wife" does not refer back to Philip the Tetrarch. For all three of the synoptics, then, their intent is to identify the first husband of Herodias as Philip the Tetrarch. However, with all the other internal problems in this account doubts persist concerning the accuracy of this identification. If Josephus names her husband as Herod, son of Mariamme 2, would it not make better sense to go with his report?

Harmonizing Josephus and the Gospels

Some have tried to solve this problem—taking the easy way out—by accepting both Josephus and the gospel reports as correct. Since there is a lot of duplication of names in the family tree of King Herod, is it not possible that the Philip, whom the gospels name as Herodias' husband, and Herod, whom Josephus names as Herodias' husband, are one and the same. Accordingly, the name of Herodias' husband was Herod Philip. In 1641 Hugo Grotius, the Dutch statesman, jurist, and philosopher, commenting on Matthew 14:3 in his *Annotationes in Libros Evangelorum*, suggests that, just as Antipas was called Herod Antipas, so there must be a Herod Philip.[4] A century later, in 1737 when William Whiston, published his English translation of Josephus, he virtually gave the name "Philip" as a second name to "Herod," the one whom Josephus identifies as the husband of Herodias.[5] "But Herodias, their sister, was married to Herod [Philip], the son of Herod the Great," (*Ant.* 18. 136). Whiston, to be sure, added the name in brackets. However, it was not based on manuscript variants or other ancient sources. It was merely his solution to the dilemma of seemingly contradictory reports in Josephus and the gospels.

The next step is that this addition to Josephus became standard in Bible Dictionaries that began to speak of "Herod Philip 1" and "Herod Philip 2." In 1863, *Smith's Bible Dictionary* included the following entry:

---

4. *Hvgonis Grotii Annotationes in Libros Evangeliorum* (Amsterdam, John and Cornelius Blaeu, 1641), 266.

5. William Whiston, translator and editor, *The Works of Flavius Josephus* (London: George Virtue, 1843), 541.

HEROD PHILIP I. (Philip) Mr 6:17 was the son of Herod the Great and Mariamme. He married Herodias the sister of Agrippa I by whom he had a daughter, Salome.
HEROD PHILIP II. was the son of Herod the Great and Cleopatra. He received as his own government Batanea Trachonitis, Aurantis (Gaulanitis), and some parts about Jamnia, with the title of tetrarch. . . . He married Salome, the daughter of Herod Philip I, and Herodias.[6]

Similarly *Easton's Bible Dictionary* in 1897 reads:

Herod Philip I (Mark 6:17), the son of Herod the Great by Mariamme, the daughter of Simon, the high priest. He is distinguished from another Philip called "the tetrarch." He lived at Rome as a private person with his wife Herodias and his daughter Salome.
Herod Philip II, the son of Herod the Great and Cleopatra of Jerusalem. He was "tetrarch" of Batanea, Iturea, Trachonitis, and Auranitis. . . . He married Salome, the daughter of Herodias. [7]

Dependence upon Whiston is clear from the reference to Herodias living in Rome, a mistranslation by Whiston of *Antiquities* 18.109. These two dictionaries along with Whiston have remained standards among conservative readers of the Bible.[8] However, they have also become some of the most accessible resources on the internet because they are all public domain.

The name "Herod Philip"

It is not unusual today to see a reference to Herod Philip—sometimes Herod Philip 1 and Herod Philip 2—in scholarly works, both among critical scholars and those of a more conservative background. However, the name "Herod Philip" simply does not appear in the ancient sources. Philip the Tetrarch is always described merely as "Philip." Herod, the son of Mariamme 2, is always referred to as Herod. The combination of names is a modern invention attempting to solve this difficult interpretive problem, but it has no basis in ancient sources. The only examples of the double name occur with the rulers Herod Archelaus, Herod Antipas, and Herod Agrippa, as a dynasty name. Archelaus, who had been designated as ethnarch (rather than

---

6. William Smith, *A Dictionary of the Bible, vol. 1* (London: John Murray 1863).

7. Matthew George Easton, *Illustrated Bible Dictionary* (London: Thomas Nelson, 1897).

8. Easton's *Bible Dictionary* was reprinted by Cosimo Classics in 2006; Smith's *Bible Dictionary* was reprinted by Thomas Nelson in 2004; and Whiston's translation of Josephus was reedited by Paul Maier and republished by Kregel in 1999.

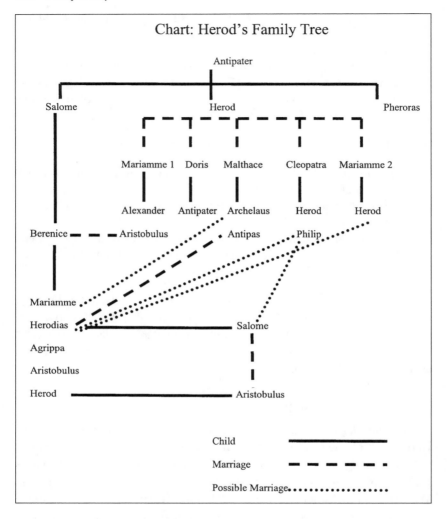

Chart: Herod's Family Tree

tetrarch), used the name Herod on his coins. Only after Archelaus was deposed in 6 CE, does Josephus begin referring to Antipas as Herod. Hoehner,
noting that Josephus signals this change, "Antipas, now called Herod" (*War*
2.167), concludes that the title was specifically given to Antipas alone and
that Philip, in a slighter lesser role, was never given permission to be called
Herod.[9] Thus it never appears on Philip's coins. Later, the title seems to
have passed from Antipas to Agrippa 1 (Acts 12:1). There is also another
way that the name Herod has appeared in recent years—and I have been

9. Harold W. Hoehner, *Herod Antipas* (Cambridge: University Press, 1972), 105-9.

guilty of this as anyone else. Because he is less well known than other sons of Herod the Great, it has become common today to use "Herod Philip" as shorthand for Philip son of Herod. However, because of the misuse of the name in trying to solve the question of Herodias' marriage, it is time that this practice be discontinued.

As for Herod, the son of Herod and Mariamme 2, there is absolutely no reason to call him Herod Philip. His name was Herod. The solution proposed by Grotius, Whiston, and many others, creates more problems than it solves. First, as noted earlier, it is clear that Luke understands the brother of Herod Antipas mentioned in Luke 3:19 to be the same as in Luke 3:1, namely Philip the Tetrarch, not another brother supposedly with the same name. Similarly, by positioning the flashback account of John's death in Mark 6 and Matthew 14, the evangelists heighten the drama of the story with the two brothers residing across the lake from each other, Antipas in Galilee and Philip in Gaulanitis. It is at this point, that Jesus' withdraws from the Galilee and begins a new phase of his ministry while seeking refuge in the territory of the more tolerant Philip. By suggesting that the gospel writers meant another Philip as the husband of Herodias, this solution ignores the context. A second problem with the "Herod Philip" solution is that it assumes Josephus was correct in identifying the wife of Philip the Tetrarch as Salome, Herodias' daughter. With Salome likely born after 10 CE this would mean an age difference of thirty years and the possibility of marriage only very late in Philip's life—a most unusual circumstance.

While Grotius and Whiston sought a simple solution to a difficult interpretive problem, they have actually done a disservice in smoothing over the difficulty when it would be better to wrestle with the Josephus texts.

Josephus on the marriage of Herodias

Critical biblical scholars have long accepted as correct Josephus' report about the marriages of Herodias and Philip. With internal problems in the gospel accounts of the death of John the Baptist, it has been natural to turn to Josephus for answers. After all, Josephus does provide a wealth of information about the family of Herod. With the "Herod Philip solution" of Whiston basically agreeing on this point, the resulting situation is that conservatives and liberals alike have treated Josephus uncritically on this particular issue. However, the difficulties with Josephus may be no less than those with the gospel accounts.

Josephus' report does include multiple references to the marriage of Herodias. The first report, similar to the gospels, is a flashback, occurring

just after Josephus' report of Philip's death in 34 CE and setting the stage
for Antipas' war with Aretas of Nabatea in 36 CE.

> The tetrarch Herod had taken the daughter of Aretas as his wife and had now
> been married to her for a long time. When starting out for Rome, he lodged
> with his half- brother Herod, who was born of a different mother, namely, the
> daughter of Simon the high priest. Falling in love with Herodias, the wife of
> this half-brother—she was a daughter of their brother Aristobulus and sister
> to Agrippa the Great—, he brazenly broached to her the subject of marriage.
> She accepted and pledged herself to make the transfer to him as soon as he
> returned from Rome (*Ant.* 18.109-110).

The second report occurs as an excursus in a genealogical section shortly
after the report about Antipas' battle with Aretas, another flashback reporting the death of John the Baptist, and a report about Antipas being removed
from office in 39 CE. After mentioning the sons of Aristobulus, whom Herod
executed, Josephus continues:

> Their sister Herodias was married to Herod, the son of Herod the Great by
> Mariamme, daughter of Simon the high priest. They had a daughter Salome,
> after whose birth Herodias, taking it into her head to flout the way of our
> fathers, married Herod, her husband's brother by the same father, who was
> tetrarch of Galilee; to do this she parted from a living husband. Her daughter
> Salome was married to Philip, Herod's son and tetrarch of Trachonitis. When
> he died childless, Aristobulus, the son of Agrippa's brother Herod, married
> her. Three sons were born to them—Herod, Agrippa, and Aristobulus (*Ant.*
> 18.136-137).

Josephus and his sources

In writing his report of Herod and his family, Josephus is much like the
gospel writers, he was not an eyewitness. Born in 37 CE, his *Jewish War*
was written in the 70s, not long after the writing of Mark and his *Jewish
Antiquities* was written in the 90s, not long after the Gospel of John. So like
the gospel writers, he was dependent on sources. The reason he was able
to provide so much detailed information about the life of Herod is that he
made use of the historical report written by Nicholas of Damascus, Herod's
own advisor. Later Josephus makes use of a source detailing the career of
Agrippa. Where Josephus is weakest is in the intervening period between
the death of Herod in 4 BCE and the rise of Agrippa 1 in the 40s CE, namely
the period covering the tetrarchies of Philip and Antipas. So it is not surprising that Josephus errs in describing Philip at one point as the full brother of

Archelaus (*Ant.* 17:189) and in referring to Philip's renaming of Bethsaida in honor of Augustus' daughter (*Ant.* 18. 28). How reliable is he on the question of Philip's marriage?

Nikos Kokkinos characterizes this section surrounding the marriage of Herodias as "poorly understood" because of "Josephus's own lack of cohesion."[10] In the genealogical section in *Antiquities* 18.130-141—of which the section above is a part—there are a number of difficulties, such as those that occur with three of Herodias' own siblings:

1. Herodias' own sister Mariamme is totally omitted.
2. Herodias' own brother Herod is listed as married to Mariamme (the daughter of Olympias, the daughter of King Herod) while elsewhere Josephus reports his marriage to the daughter of Herod's son Antipater.
3. Herodias' brother Agrippa and her nephew Agrippa are described in a confusing way (*Antiquities* 18. 132-133) which leads Niese to assume a lacuna in the text.[11]

In addition, when describing Herodias' daughter Salome (after the death of Philip) as marrying Aristobulus and bearing three sons named Herod, Agrippa, and Aristobulus, it seems too much a coincidence that Herodias' father was named Aristobulus and he had three sons of the exact same names. The rough style of this genealogy suggests that Josephus was creating the list from memory or freely editing a brief outline. Clearly his own hand is reflected in his judgment upon Herodias who acted "to confound the laws of our country" (*Ant.* 18.136).

There are also inconsistencies between the genealogy and the report of Antipas' first visit at the home of his brother. In the genealogy Herodias left her husband after the birth of Salome, which implies early in their marriage. Yet in the report of the visit, Josephus notes that Antipas had already been married a long time. The report is puzzling because it occurs in the context of a visit by Antipas to Rome, yet there is no reason given for such a trip and no other evidence that such a trip took place. Because of a mistranslation, Whiston makes it appear that Herodias was actually living in Rome at the time. Feldman correctly translates the section to read that the visit occurred en route—thus commentators suggest that Herodias may have been living in

10. Nikos Kokkinos, *The Herodian Dynasty*, 267.

11. Louis Feldman, ed. and trans., *Josephus: Jewish Antiquities, Books XVIII-XIX*, vol. IX [Loeb Classical Library; Cambridge: Harvard, 1981], 90, note a.

a coastal city as Caesarea Maritima where Antipas would embark to Rome. Yet the reason for this visit is less than clear. Assuming that Antipas did go to Rome, a more logical assumption is that he would first consult with his brother the tetrarch. When all is said and done, Josephus seems to present as many problems in this section as do the gospel writers in describing the death of the John the Baptist.

Marriage in the Herods' World

None of the answers about the marriages of Philip, Antipas, and Herodias is satisfactory resulting in a sharp divide in the scholarly world. Historical analysis leaves us with an apparent impasse. However, a broader analysis concerning marriage patterns in the world of Herod may offer new insight.

In their social science analysis of marriage in first-century Palestine, K.C. Hanson and Douglas Oakman catalogue 49 different marriages over eight generations of the Herodian family.[12] Modern ideas of marriage as an individual choice must be disregarded. Marriage is a family affair and, in the case of such a ruling family, a political affair with even the emperor Augustus or his wife Livia involved. The 22 endogamous marriages—between fellow members of the Herodian family—were designed to retain property and wealth and to consolidate power. Of the 27 exogamous marriages only six were to non-elite families with the majority arranged to improve family status or to ensure positive political relationships among allies, rivals, and even enemies. Thus in the patriarchal role, Herod arranged no less than ten marriages and prevented another.

With this background, the weak link in the arguments above—both among those who accept Josephus' account and among those who harmonize the Gospels and Josephus with the idea of two Herod Philips—is the implication that Philip remained a bachelor until late in life. This would have been unthinkable in a world where marriages were arranged by families and where marriages were meant to benefit, not so much the individual, but the families themselves, and, in the case of ruling families like the Herodians, the whole nation.

According to Suetonius, Augustus "followed a policy of linking together his royal allies by mutual ties of friendship or intermarriage, which he was never slow to propose" (Suetonius, *Augustus* 48). So it was that Augustus and Livia involved themselves in the family affairs of the Herodians by

---

12. K. C. Hanson and Douglas E. Oakman, *Palestine in the Time of Jesus: Social Structures and Social Conflicts* (Minneapolis: Fortress Press, 1998), 31-51.

encouraging the marriage of Herod's sister Salome to Alexas (*Ant.* 17. 10) even though she was in love with Syllaeus. In 4 BCE, Herod's three potential successors were all of marriageable age when they appeared before him in Rome for the reading of the will. Archelaus, was eighteen years of age, with Antipas and Philip, probably only sixteen years old. Josephus is silent on this matter, though he does mention other factors that would suggest that Augustus had a hand in arranging their marriages before they took up their appointments. Augustus did, in fact, arrange marriages for Herod's two young daughters, Roxanne and Salome, to marry sons of Pheroras and even paid for each of them 250,000 denarii as dowry (*Ant.* 17.322). With Herod's sister Salome—now the matriarch of the family—present in Rome and also benefitting from Augustus' ratification of the will, it would make sense that other marriages were also arranged at this time. Thus Emil Schürer years ago proposed that Augustus facilitated Antipas' marriage to the daughter of King Aretas of Nabatea, a country that was extremely important to keep the Parthians in check.[13] It is reasonable to think that similar arrangements were made at this time for Archelaus and Philip.

Herodias' betrothal to Herod

As granddaughter of both King Herod and his sister Salome, Herodias and her sisters were positioned for prominent roles in his kingdom. Her mother was Berenice, the daughter of Herod's sister Salome and Costobarus, whom Herod had earlier appointed as governor of Idumaea. Her father was Aristobulus, the son of Herod and Mariamme 1 from a leading Hasmonean family. Aristobulus, along with his full brother Alexander, had been sent to Rome for their education and were named in the first version of Herod's will as his successors. Returning from Rome in about 17 BCE, Aristobulus and Berenice married and had five children before Aristobulus was put to death in 7 BCE. The children were Mariamme, Herodias, Herod, Agrippa, and Aristobulus—likely in that order with Herodias born in about 14 to 12 BCE.[14]

A classic case of matchmaking took place in Jericho in 7 BCE shortly after Herod himself had ordered his two sons, Aristobulus and Alexander—heirs to the throne—to be put to death for suspicion of plotting against their father.

---

13. Emil Schürer, *The History of the Jewish People in the Time of Jesus Christ,* (Edinburgh: T. & T. Clark, 1924) 1:324, see Richardson, *Herod* (1999), 307.

14. Richardson, *Herod* (1999), 49, suggests the following order: Mariamne (16 BCE), Herod (15 BCE), Agrippa (13 BCE), Aristobulus (10 BCE), Herodias (8 BCE). However, the later reliance of Agrippa when returning from Rome seems to imply that Herodias was an older sister.

Now showing pity for their children, he set to arrange their marriages, even though most were still quite young in age.

> Herod himself brought up the children of his sons very carefully, Alexander having had two boys by Glaphyra, and Aristobulus three boys and two girls by Berenice, the daughter of Salome. And on one occasion he presented the young children to a gathering of his friends, and after bewailing the fortune of his sons, prayed that no such fate might befall their children and that by their improvement in virtue and concern for righteousness they would repay him for bringing them up. He also promised in marriage, when they should reach the proper age, the daughter of Pheroras to the elder son of Alexander, and the daughter of Antipater to Aristobulus' son, and he designated one daughter of Aristobulus to marry the son of Antipater, and the other daughter of Aristobulus to marry his own son Herod, who had been born to him by the daughter of the high priest, for it is an ancestral custom of ours to have several wives at the same time (*Ant.* 17. 12-14).[15]

What is most significant is that their spouses would come from three Herodian families—Herod's brother Pheroras, who at that time was tetrarch of Perea; Antipater, who was now named in Herod's subsequent will as successor; and Herod's son by Mariamme 2, also named Herod, who was designated in the will as second to Antipater (*Ant.* 17.53; JW 1.573).[16] The four children named by Herod were:

- Alexander's oldest son, Alexander, betrothed to Pheroras' daughter;
- Aristobulus' oldest son, Herod (of Chalcis), betrothed to Antipater's daughter;
- Aristobulus' daughter, Mariamme, betrothed to Antipater's son;
- Aristobulus' daughter, Herodias, betrothed to Herod, the son of Mariamme 2.[17]

Later, Antipater negotiated with his father Herod to change this arrangement so that Antipater himself became betrothed to Aristobulus' daughter, Mariamme. As a result, Antipater's son who had previously been promised to Mariamme, was now betrothed to Pheroras' daughter. In short, two sisters Mariamme and Herodias—granddaughters of King Herod—found

---

15. In a parallel report in *Jewish War 1. 556-59*, Josephus includes the speech Herod made on that occasion.

16. For Herod's series of seven wills, see Peter Richardson, *Herod: King of the Jews and Friend of the Romans* (Minneapolis: Fortress Press, 1999), 35.

17. The three younger sons are not mentioned at this time, one younger son of Alexander and two sons of Aristobulus, Agrippa and Aristobulus.

themselves betrothed to the two sons of Herod who were expected to succeed him. These two young girls seemed destined for power.

However, by the time Herod died just a few years later in 4 BCE, none of these families were left among those who would succeed Herod. Pheroras died a short time before Herod. Antipater was put to death as implicated in a plot against Herod. Also involved in that plot was Herod's wife Mariamme 2. So Herod responded by divorcing her, by defrocking her father from the High Priesthood, and by removing her son Herod from his father's will. This left a chaotic situation. Three sons and potential successors had been executed—Aristobulus, Alexander, and Antipater—and a fourth had been removed from his father's will—Herod. As for the two daughters of Aristobulus, Mariamme's betrothed had been executed and Herodias' betrothed was out of favor. Neither had yet reached the age of marriage. It is difficult to believe that Herodias' betrothal would have been allowed to stand, especially since this Herod was already married and Herodias would have been his second wife. This is how Josephus' statement at the end of the Jericho betrothal episode is generally taken: "for it is an ancestral custom of ours to have several wives at the same time" (*Ant.* 17. 14). His position in a priestly family would also have been seen as a liability. Herodias' grandmother Salome had never gotten along with the Jerusalem elite.

Young Herodias' sojourn in Rome

The impression given by Josephus is that Herodias' mother, Berenice, was rather ambitious for her children so that she may have spent the rest of her life in Rome until her death in about 23 CE. There she lived in close contact with the imperial family and especially "contracted a friendship with Antonia, the wife of Drusus the Great, who had his [Agrippa's] mother Berenice in great esteem, and was very desirous of advancing her son" (*Ant.* 18. 143, 165). Josephus does not specifically mention Herodias or her sister Mariamme because he is likely relying on a source highlighting Agrippa.[18] That source suggests that they had arrived in Rome prior to the death of Herod in 4 BCE. However, Josephus' earlier source suggests the possibility that Berenice and her children arrived in Rome along with the delegation deciding on Herod's successors. There he focuses on Salome, Berenice's mother and Herod's sister, who traveled to Rome "with her children" to assist in the settlement of Herod's will (*War* 2.15 and *Ant.* 17.220). Josephus paints a rather interesting

---

18. Daniel R. Schwartz, *Agrippa I: The Last King of Judea* (Tübingen: Mohr, 1990), 40.

picture with Salome and family accompanying Philip's brother Archelaus, appearing supportive on the outside, but in reality opposing him.

So there in Rome were Archelaus, Antipas, and Philip—three young men of marriageable age—and Berenice with her two daughters, Mariamme and Herodias—just moving into puberty. The girls' grandmother Salome served as the family matriarch and also the intermediary to Augustus through her good friend Livia, benefitting from the settlement by inheriting Jamnia, Azotus, Phasaelis, as well as five hundred thousand pieces of silver—in a sense becoming co-ruler along with Archelaus, Antipas, and Philip (*Ant*. 17. 321).

Josephus does not mention any details about how the three successors' marriages were arranged. However, it makes perfect sense that the political marriage of Antipas to the daughter of Aretas was arranged by Augustus, concerned as he was about a united front between Jews and Nabateans against the Parthian threat. The daughter remains nameless in literary texts, but may be named Sha'udat, one of four daughters mentioned in an inscription. As for Archelaus, Josephus records the name of his first wife as Mariamme—the same as Herodias' sister. As it turned out Archelaus later divorced Mariamme to marry out of physical attraction Glaphyra, the daughter of the King of Cappadocia and widow of his older brother Alexander. This Mariamme is never identified, whether she might have been the daughter of Aristobulus and Berenice, or an otherwise unknown daughter from the Hasmonean family, or someone otherwise unknown. However, Archelaus' marriage to his brother's wife—no different than the later charge of John the Baptist against Antipas—led to criticism against him by the Jerusalem elite and contributed to his premature recall as ethnarch in 6 CE. Josephus seems not to know of the fate of Herodias' sister Mariamme since he completely leaves her out of the genealogy in *Antiquities* 18. 130-141.

As for Herodias, we are left with two possibilities. Following Josephus, she would have left her mother in Rome sometime around the turn of the century and returned to Palestine to marry Herod, the son of Mariamme 2 and King Herod. Whiston mistranslates *Antiquities* 18.109 to locate the house of this Herod in Rome. However, as it correctly appears in Feldman, Antipas lodged with Herod before starting out for Rome. Nothing further is known about this Herod. Presumably, Herodias would have taken her place as his second wife until Antipas came to visit. The second possibility is that, according to the gospels, a marriage was arranged for her in Rome to marry Philip who was given the prestige of succeeding, along with Antipas and Archelaus, his father King Herod. From a historian's perspective, the matter remains unresolved or at best decided by which source seems most reliable. From a social science perspective, there are other criteria. From the viewpoint of Herodias and her mother Berenice, which marriage would provide honor and which marriage would carry an element of shame? From the viewpoint of Philip, what would it mean to leave Rome without an arrangement for marriage, especially when embarking on a leadership role in the Herodian family? Because of the social importance of marriage in the first century, it seems unthinkable that Philip would have remained unmarried until late in life. Yet that is the way Josephus reports on the marriage of Philip.

Archaeology also offers an important perspective. Material evidence points to growing tension between Philip and Antipas during the late 20s and early 30s CE. As will be noted in the next chapter the decision to found the city Julias on the northeast side of the lake was a response to Antipas' founding of the city of Tiberias. With both minting coins in the years 29, 30, and 33 CE, there seems to be competition which is primarily economic, but which may also be influenced by other factors. In the year 36 CE, two years after the death of Philip, Antipas engaged in a military battle against King Aretas of Nabatea (*Ant.* 18. 113-114). Josephus presents four important details about this battle:

- It took place not within areas governed by Aretas or Antipas, but near Gamla, which had been part of Philip's territory.
- The cause of the battle was attributed to revenge over Antipas' decision to divorce the daughter of Aretas.
- Defeat was interpreted as God's judgment for Antipas' execution of John the Baptist.
- Aretas was able to defeat Antipas when men from Philip's territory joined with forces of Aretas against Antipas.

What is most unusual is that Josephus describes these fighters as men from "the tetrarchy of Philip" although Philip had died two years earlier. Josephus seems to acknowledge that the roots of this conflict were not just between Antipas and Aretas, but also an earlier grudge between Antipas and Philip.

Nikos Kokkinos recognizes some of the difficulties in Josephus' report about Herodias and thus proposes that Herodias, after first being married to Herod, son of Mariamme 2, divorced him soon after the birth of Salome and married Philip, whom she later divorced for Antipas.[19] In other words, Herodias lived with three brothers in succession. Kokkinos' proposal seems a bit

---

19. Nikos Kokkinos, *The Herodian Dynasty: Origins, Role in Society, and Eclipse* (Sheffield: Sheffield Academic Press, 1998), 265-7.

complicated. However, his instincts may be correct. The more likely scenario is that Herodias' engagement to Herod ended when he was removed from his father's will and that her marriage to Philip was arranged in Rome under the watchful eye of Augustus, Livia, and Herodias' grandmother Salome. Correctly, Kokkinos concludes that Philip was never married to Salome.

Herodias' Daughter

Josephus reports that Herodias had a daughter Salome by her first husband. The date of her birth has been estimated anywhere from 1 BCE [20] to 20 CE, based on a number of factors including the age possible for Herodias' marriage—sometime between 2 BCE and 4 CE (her parents were married from 16 and 7 BCE)—and the term used in Mark for Herodias' dancing daughter—*korasion*, that could denote a young girl. Perhaps the best solution is a date around 10 CE, when her mother Herodias was about twenty-two years old and shortly after the death of her great grandmother Salome, for whom she was named.

Salome's claim to fame is she was first lady of Chalcis from 52 CE to about 70 CE. A coin from the year 62 CE portrays her image with the inscription "Queen Salome" on the reverse with the image of her husband "King Aristobulus" on the front. This confirms Josephus' report that she had married her first cousin Aristobulus—the son of Herodias' brother Herod—and together they had three children. Similar to Salome, Aristobulus' birth is generally placed around 12 and 13 CE.[21] As an ideal marriage arrangement between cousins, the likely date for them to be married was sometime in the late 20s or early 30s CE.

However, such a scenario does not correspond with Josephus' report about Philip's marriage late in life:

> [Herodias'] daughter Salome was married to Philip, the son of Herod, and tetrarch of Trachonitis; and because he died childless, Aristobulus, the son of Herod, the brother of Agrippa, married her; they had three sons, Herod, Agrippa, and Aristobulus. (*Ant.* 18.137)

From Salome's perspective, it is certainly possible from her age that she was first married to Philip prior to marrying Aristobulus. From Aristobulus' perspective, this scenario seems a bit unusual since it seems to imply that no

---

20. Kokkinos, "Which Salome Did Aristobulus Marry?" (1986), 39.

21. Contrary to Kokkinos who assumes that the gap in rule between father Herod of Chacis and son Aristobulus from 48 to 52 CE was due to Aristobulus' young age. IBID.

previous thought had been given to his marriage and that it came about only when the widow Salome was suddenly available. From Philip's perspective, the marriage to a woman thirty years younger seems highly unlikely unless a previous marriage had ended in death or divorce. There is good reason to think that Josephus must be confused here. The names of the three sons of Salome and Aristobulus are exactly the same as the three sons of Aristobulus and Berenice. Can Josephus be confused on other matters as well? It may well be that Salome did live with Philip late in his life, however, not as wife, but as daughter, seeking to escape a lecherous step-father and a manipulative mother. There her betrothal to Aristobulus would have taken place and also her subsequent marriage.

Chapter 12

The Founding of Bethsaida as Julias

On September 22 in the year 30 CE, Philip officially founded Bethsaida-Julias. This marks the most important day in the history of this seaside city and most likely it was a day of gala celebration. This is an especially significant event because it comes at the heart of the New Testament era. With the death of Jesus dated to April 7, 30 CE, there can be no doubt that the transformation of this city had an impact on Jesus and the disciples.[1] The dedication of Bethsaida as Julias, however, came late in the rule of Philip—his 34th year.

The significance of Bethsaida

Prior to it elevation to the status of a *polis*, Bethsaida must be considered a relatively insignificant village on the northern shore of the Sea of Galilee. This is a realization that has come from several decades of excavations on the top of the Tell. The northern residential area had deteriorated from its high point during the Hellenistic era and may have even been abandoned in ruins—perhaps due to a transformation to Hasmonean rule, perhaps due to a dramatic event like the 31 BCE earthquake, perhaps due to other economic factors. Whatever the cause, Bethsaida seems to have reverted in its position and size.

Philip's capital was Caesarea Philippi, a distant 45 kilometers to the north. The use of the term "distant" seems appropriate. Ramsey McMullen suggested in his study of local agrarian market economy in the Roman

---

1. Fred Strickert, "The Founding of Bethsaida-Julias: Evidence from the Coins of Philip," *Shofar: A Journal for Inter-Jewish Dialogue 13* (1995), 40-51.

Empire that a small city might influence rural peasants within a radius no more than fifteen kilometers, the distance they could travel from home to market in the early morning and then back home at the end of the day.[2] More recently David-Adan Bayewitz's analysis of the circulation of household pottery from the village of Kefar Hananya found that the pottery dominates the archaeological record of surrounding villages within a short distance, yet it is absent beyond a distance of twenty-five kilometers from the kiln.[3] When it came to establishing a sphere of influence for capital cities in these first century territories, production, trade, and taxation all played a role, and it would seem that Philip's influence would have extended out from Caesarea for about twenty-five kilometers. Josephus does note that Philip did try to extend that sphere of influence by traveling frequently through his territory and holding court wherever he went. He also minted coins, some of which carried his own image, and all of which displayed his name as tetrarch and joined him with the authority of the emperor.

Yet the village of Bethsaida, situated on the periphery of Philip's territory, was likely affected by Philip and the activities of Caesarea Philippi to only a minimal degree. Evidence for this comes from the small number of Philip coins discovered in over two decades of excavations—only five coins, all in a deteriorated condition. To be sure, earlier coins remained in circulation for generations, often centuries, and the Hasmoneans had flooded the market with their bronze coins. Yet when one thinks of Bethsaida as Philip's "second city," one would expect a better showing of coins. Then again, Bethsaida only became Philip's "second city" late in his rule.

The situation began to change in 20 CE when Antipas built the new city of Tiberias on the west shore of the Sea of Galilee. Earlier Antipas had chosen the site of his capital as Sepphoris, an old Hasmonean fortress and then government center under Herod, rebuilding it after a revolt in 4 BCE, and dedicating it in 8 CE. Josephus refers to Sepphoris as the jewel of the Galilee. Yet there was one draw back, Sepphoris was located on the western side of the Galilee. So Philip, living in Caesarea Philippi far to the north, and Antipas, in Sepphoris far to the west, were quite removed from one another. Antipas' attention also was diverted for a time to his other territory of Perea, east of the Jordan River and the northern part of the Dead Sea. As a wise builder, he waited until the completion of Sepphoris and then built

---

2. Ramsay MacMullen, "Market Days in the Roman Empire," *Phoenix*, XXIV (1970), 333-41.

3. David Adan-Bayewitz and Isadore Pearlman, "The Local Trade of Sepphoris in the Roman Period," *Israel Exploration Journal*, XL (1990), 153-72, especially 170.

a city there in honor of Livia, the wife of Augustus. The year of dedication was likely 13 CE, the year of Livia's 70th birthday.

Then after another short interval, Antipas built his third city called Tiberias. Unlike other cities which were expansions of existing villages, this city was built anew at a prominent position on the Sea of Galilee. In some ways, it may seem an unnecessary step on the part of Antipas since he already had a capital at Sepphoris. Yet as Jonathan Reed notes, "No area of Galilee lies outside a 25-km. radius of these new urban centers."[4] The result was a symbiotic relationship between the city and surrounding villages. The growing population required greater agricultural production from surrounding villages. Increased taxes from the villages helped to pay for public building projects in the city. Then a change in structure followed where villagers who once held perhaps a dozen tracts of land with diversified crops were taken over by wealthy landowners who employed the former subsistence farmers, now as tenant farmers, who now specialized in a cash crop in order to increase yields for 33% to 50% taxation. The decision to build Tiberias had important economic implications. Antipas was now tapping into the important financial resource from the lake. As noted in the chapter on the fishing industry, that whole industry was structured in a hierarchical fashion that drained the lake of the maximum amount of income to benefit Antipas and his new lakeside city, where he now lived. Symbolic of the role the city played in changing the lake culture is the name that appears in the Gospel of John, *The Sea of Tiberias* (John 6:1, 21:1).

Philip's idea of building a second city may never have arisen had Antipas not built the city of Tiberias and taken control of the fishing industry. Certainly, there would have been no need for a city at Bethsaida in the early years of his rule. However, when one thinks in terms of Reed's 25-kilometer distance of a city's sphere of influence, Tiberias, not only made its mark on western Galilee, but it also enveloped the entire lake and reached across to make an impact even on villages within Philip's territory. To be sure, Bethsaida already had a natural affinity to Capernaum, Gennesaret, and Magdala on the western shore. Peter had apparently married into a family at Capernaum, and the Bethsaida fishermen had developed partnerships with Galilean fishermen from the western side.

---

4. Jonathan L. Reed, *Archaeology and the Galilean Jesus: A Re-examination of the Evidence* (Harrisburg, PA: Trinity Press, 2000), 96. For a similar perspective of the role of Sepphoris and Tiberias, see Richard A. Horsley, *Archaeology, History, and Society in Galilee: The Social Context of Jesus and the Rabbis* (Harrisburg, PA: Trinity Press, 1996), 43-87.

Unlike Philip, who had minted coins from the beginning of his rule, Antipas minted his first coins only in 20 CE upon the dedication of the city of Tiberias.[5] Philip's coins, minted in far off Caesarea Philippi, never appear in Galilee excavations. However, the largest number of Antipas coins have turned up, not in Galilee, but in Philip's territory across the lake. Sixty-one Antipas coins were found at Gamla, just to the east of Bethsaida, nearly twice the number of Philip coins.[6] This is a clear sign that Antipas' influence had encroached on Philip's territory, and it appears that Philip took notice. In the year 29 CE, when Antipas issued his second batch of coins, Philip matched him with his own—as if they were now competing for control of the southern Golan. Again in 30 CE, they both minted coins, and then again in 33 CE. This is the context in which Philip founded the city of Julias upon the older village of Bethsaida.

A City called Julias

It is Josephus who reports that Philip named the city Julias. In *Jewish War* 2.168, written in the mid 70s CE, he describes the building efforts of both Antipas and Philip:

> On the death of Augustus, who had directed the state for fifty-seven years, six months, and two days, the empire of the Romans passed to Tiberius, son of Julia. On his accession, Herod Antipas and Philip continued to hold their tetrarchies and respectively founded cities: Philip built Caesarea, near the sources of the Jordan in the district of Paneas, and Julias in lower Gaulanitis; Herod built Tiberias in Galilee and a city which also took the name Julia in Peraea.

Omitting mention of Sepphoris, Josephus balances the report with two cities each: Philip and Antipas both named a city for the emperor, one for Augustus and the other for Tiberias, and both named a city for Julia, the wife of Augustus and mother of Tiberius. Interestingly, the cities are organized geographically in a line from north to south.

It is important to note that the context of this report is the death of Augustus and the accession of Tiberius in 14 CE. In this way the two cities Tiberias and Bethsaida-Julias are linked together. Caesarea Philippi, founded in 1 CE,

5. Ya'akov Meshorer, *A Treasury of Jewish Coins,* (Nyack, NY: Amphora, 2001), 81-2.

6. Danny Syon, *Tyre and Gamla: A Study in the Monetary Influences of Southern Phoenecia on Galilee and the Golan in the Hellenistic and Roman Periods,* Dissertation [Hebrew] (Jerusalem: Hebrew University, 2004). Summary of data is available in English in Morten Horning Jensen, *Herod Antipas in Galilee: The Literary and Archaeological Sources* (Tübingen: Mohr-Siebeck, 2006), 175-77 & 213-15.

clearly is out of place. However, there is a clear connection with the other three cities and the events of 14 CE. In mentioning first the name of Julia, the mother of Tiberius, and then the two cities named Julia and Julias, it is impossible to miss the connection.

In 14 CE, Livia Drusilla became Julia Sebaste. Her given name was Livia and she had grown to be the most powerful woman in Rome. She had married Augustus on Jan. 17, 38 BCE three days after giving birth to Drusus. Her other son by her first husband Tiberius Nero was named Tiberius—the future emperor—only three years old at the time of her second marriage. Previously Augustus had been married to Scribonia whose daughter Julia gave Augustus two grandsons, Gaius and Lucius, who were later adopted by Augustus as heirs, but who preceded him in death. Since Augustus and Livia together had no children, Tiberius was then named as Augustus' heir. Upon Augustus' death in 14 CE, the Roman Senate proclaimed the deification of Augustus and, following the wishes of Augustus, declared that Livia was officially adopted into the Julian clan. This gave her the right to use the name *Julia* as well as the title Σεβάστη (*Sebaste*), the Greek equivalent of Augusta.[7] This action indirectly made Tiberius a Julian and paved the way for his accession as emperor. At the same time, Livia/Julia was elevated to the position of empress mother and, in reality, made her co-regent with her son Tiberius.[8] This made her a person highly respected (and feared) in Rome and honored throughout the provinces.

As can be seen in this section from Josephus, Livia/Julia was highly respected also in Palestine. When referring to Livia, Josephus always uses the name Julia, even in describing events prior to her adoption. In this particular section, Josephus seems to understand the significance in identifying her as Julia, the mother of Tiberius.

The imperial family and the Herodians

King Herod had developed a special relationship with the imperial family and was dependent on them for his position of power (Josephus, *Ant.* 15.199, 361; 16.290, 338). As noted in a previous chapter, many of Herod's children and grandchildren had been sent to Rome for their education. This

---

7. Tacitus, *Annals* 1.8.14; Dio Cassius, *Roman History* 56.32.1; 46.1; 57.12.2; Suetonius, *Augustus* 101.2. Giorgio Giacosa, *Women of the Caesars: Their Lives and Portraits on Coins,* trans. R. Ross Holloway (New York: Arte e Moneta Publishers, 1983) 22-24.

8. Hans-Werner Ritter, "Livias Erhebung zur Augusta," *Chrion* 2 (1972), 313-38. See also Claudia-Martina Perkounig, *Livia Drusilla—Iulia Augusta: Das politische Porträt der ersten Kaiserin Roms* (Vienna, Cologne, and Weimar: Böhlau Verlag, 1995).

included first Aristobulus, Alexander, and Antipater; then Philip, Archelaus, and Antipas; later Agrippa and his brothers Herod and Aristobulus; and finally Agrippa 2. Augustus himself took a personal interest in their studies and directly reported back to Herod upon their completion (Josephus, *Ant.* 15.342-3; 16.6, 78-86; 17.80-2; 19.360). Thus it is not surprising that Josephus uses the term ὁμοτροφίας (raised together) to describe their relationship with the children of the imperial family including future emperors Tiberius, Caligula, and Claudius (Josephus, *Ant.* 18.165).

During this time, a number of the women in Herod's family also came to Rome developing close friendships with the women of the imperial family. This included especially Herod's sister Salome and her daughter Berenice (Josephus, *Ant.* 17.10, 134-41; 18.31, 143, 156, 165; *War* 1.566, 641-3; 2.167).[9] It was Salome who became very close with Livia. When the will of Augustus was contested, it was Salome who helped facilitate the settlement which led to the tetrarchies of Archelaus, Antipas, and Philip (Josephus, *Ant.* 17.220, 321; *War* 2.15, 98). This is rather significant since Herod's will had granted Archelaus the title "king" and greater power. Yet Salome's personal animosity for Archelaus was instrumental in reducing his status.[10] In this settlement, Salome herself received the territory of Jamnia, Azotus, and Phaselis as well as five hundred thousand pieces of silver and an annual revenue of sixty talents (Josephus, *Ant.* 17.321; *War* 2.98). When Salome died, she bequeathed her territories to Livia/ Julia (Josephus, *Ant.* 18.31; *War* 2.167).

The Founding of Betharamphtha-Livia

In view of Salome's influence with Livia and her animosity towards certain members of the Herodian family, it was politically wise for both Antipas and Philip to court Livia's respect. The timing of Antipas' dedication of the city Betharamphtha-Livia is instructive. The rebuilding of this city probably began soon after the completion of Sepphoris around 8 CE. The dedication took place certainly before 14 CE because it was first named *Livia* and then renamed *Julia* after the accession of Tiberius as emperor (Josephus, *War* 2.168).[11] Since it was customary to coordinate the founding of cities with important dates in the lives of the emperors,[12] it is likely that

9. Strabo, *Geography* 16.2.46.

10. Harold W. Hoehner, *Herod Antipas* (Cambridge: University Press, 1972), 18-39.

11. A. H .M. Jones, *The Cities of the Eastern Roman Provinces* (Oxford: Clarendon Press, 1937), 273-77. Eusebius' reference to this city as Livia suggests that this was its original name and that it was later changed to Julia. Eusebius, *Onom. Sac.* 12, 16, 44, 48 (three times), 168.

12. M. Avi-Yonah, "The Foundation of Tiberias," *IEJ* 1 (1950-51), 168-9.

Antipas chose the year 13 CE for its founding since that year marked the fiftieth wedding anniversary of Livia and Augustus and also her seventieth birthday.[13] The building of Betharamphtha-Livia thus took place between the years 8 and 13 CE.

This is significant because it followed closely after Archelaus had been deposed in 6 CE, and the Roman procurators had been established in Judea. Although Josephus explains the cause of Archelaus' downfall as a conflict with leading Jews and Samaritans (*Ant.* 17.342-4; *War* 2.111), Dio Cassius explains it in terms of accusations by Archelaus' own brothers.[14] A contemporary of these events, Strabo, suggests that the accusations were not all one-sided, but he notes that Herod's sons were not so successful in the arrangement as co-rulers, and that they "became involved in accusations."[15] The result of the hearing before Augustus in Rome resulted in the banishment of Archelaus while Antipas and Philip were allowed to continue their rule, yet not without difficulty—θεραπείᾳ πολλῇ μόλις. It is also from this point on that the title "Herod" is associated with Antipas.[16] So he came out of this situation, not merely surviving, but also benefiting.

To what did he owe this turn of events? One would expect that Salome again had played a role through the influence of Livia. This may be deduced by the fact that it was Salome who now came to control the estate of Archelais with its abundant palm groves,[17] which she then passed on to Livia several years later in her will. In other words, Antipas was greatly indebted to Augustus via Livia via Salome who not only helped him through this crisis, but even helped him to improve his lot. When Salome died several years later, and then Augustus, it was critical that Antipas cultivate his favor directly with Livia. Thus he honored her with a city named *Livia* in 13 CE, which he subsequently renamed *Julia* to celebrate her new status upon adoption into the Julian clan.

The Julia coins of the procurators

Antipas was not alone in courting the favor of Livia. The procurators of Judea began dedicating their coins to Julia after Augustus' death. From 15-26 CE, Valerius Gratus issued six different coins with ΙΟΥΛΙΑ

13. Hoehner, *Herod Antipas*, 87-91.
14. Dio Cassius, *Roman History* 55.27.6.
15. Strabo, *Geography* 16.2.46.
16. Hoehner, *Herod Antipas,* 105-9.
17. Compare Josephus, *Ant.* 17.321 with 18.31 and *War* 2.67 with 2.167.

Coin of Gratus – 17 CE

Coin of Pontius Pilate – 29 CE

inscriptions.[18] Then in the year of Livia's death, 29 CE, Pontius Pilate issued a Julia coin.[19] There was no question about his allegiance. The inscriptions were ΤΙΒΕΡΙΟΥ ΚΑΙΣΑΡΟΣ and ΙΟΥΛΙΑ ΚΑΙΣΑΡΟΣ on each side respectively. In previous years, the procurators had employed neutral symbols on their coins showing respect for Jewish custom. Pilate, however, depicted on the obverse a *simpulum,* which was a ladle used by Roman priests to pour wine over sacrificial animals. On the reverse, he depicted three ears of grain bound by stalks.

The use of grain symbolism here is extremely significant. Gertrude Grether notes that Livia was frequently associated with Abundantia (= ΕΥΘΕΝΙΑ), the goddess of agricultural plenty or identified with Demeter in the Mystery cults.[20] Statues of her have been found in the context of the Eleusian mysteries and at cult centers in Asia Minor. On coins of Augustus from 2 BCE to 14 CE, she is often depicted seated and holding ears of grain and a scepter. Following her adoption into the Julian clan, her role is that of a goddess who plays a central role in the imperial cult, especially in the provinces. Tiberius continued the practice of depicting the image of the seated Livia on the reverse of denarii bearing his own image. Since this was used for the tribute tax, it was familiar to Roman subjects even in Palestine, as the gospel accounts confirm. Thus the coin of Pilate appropriately depicts her as priestess of Augustus and the goddess of plenty.

This coin issued by Pilate is unique among the various Julia coins in that the depicted ears

18. Ya'akov Meshorer, *Ancient Jewish Coinage,* (Dix Hills, N.Y.: Amphora Books, 1982) 2:173.

19. Meshorer, *Ancient Jewish Coinage,* (1982), 180, 283.

20. Gertrude Grether, "Livia and the Roman Imperial Cult," *AJP* 67 (1946), 222-52.

Tribute Penny—Tiberius coin, © *The Trustees of the British Museum*

of grain are drooping. This occurs, of course, to commemorate the death of Livia/Julia earlier that same year. The events surrounding her death reveal a controversy concerning her relationship with her son Tiberius the Emperor. Her adoption into the Julian clan, which made possible his accession to the throne and, at the same time, elevated her status to stand in competition with him. The friction had increased to the point where he retreated from Rome and spent little time there during the last years of her life.

When she died, only a simple funeral was held for Livia/Julia and Tiberius chose not to return for it. This offered a rebuff to her own wishes for deification that would have corresponded to the situation of her husband Augustus some fifteen years earlier.[21] By staying away, Tiberius was able to deter any efforts toward an elaborate funeral and to avoid taking an unpopular public stand. At Tiberius' wish, the senate denied her request for deification and instructed only that Tiberius erect an arch in her honor—an order that was never carried out. The senate also declared an official period of mourning for one year. On the surface this order seems to demonstrate a high degree of respect for Livia/Julia. However, it was a carefully planned move which contrasted with the funeral of Augustus when mourning was forbidden because he had now ascended as a god.[22] In contrast, Livia/Julia was to be treated as a mere mortal. The Julia coin of Pilate in 29 CE, with the drooping ears of grain, shows that this mourning was taken seriously throughout the empire. It also served as a political statement. The two drooping ears of grain could easily represent Livia and Augustus; the single erect ear, Tiberius. It was essential that Pilate cultivate his favor at a time when his position was being challenged.

---

21. Dio Cassius, *Roman History* 58.2; Suetonius, *Tiberius* 51; Tacitus, *Annals* 5.1-2.
22. Dio Cassius, *Roman History* 56.41.

Coin of Philip – 30 CE – Image of Livia

Drawing of same coin

The evidence of Philip coins

Philip issued Julia coins only in the years 30 and 33 CE, both after her death. These coins carry on the obverse side the inscription ΙΟΥΛΙΑ ΣΕΒΑΣΤΗ, the name she received in 14 CE and the title as the revered one: *Augusta*. This latter title had been used on other coins of the provinces, but not on the coins of the procurators. Totally unique among Palestine coinage is the depiction of Livia/ Julia herself, the first woman to appear on a Jewish coin.[23] On the reverse are depicted three ears of grain. It would seem that Philip is here responding to Pilate's coin of 29 CE. As noted in a previous chapter, his coins follow a pattern which responds to the events surrounding the procurators in Judea. It is also significant that this is a smaller denomination of coin than Philip had previously produced, yet it corresponds to the small coins used by Pilate to flood the markets.[24]

23. Fred Strickert, "The First Woman to be Portrayed on a Jewish Coin: Julia Sebaste," *Journal for the Study of Judaism in the Persian, Hellenistic, and Roman Periods* 33 (2002), 65-91.

24. Strickert, "The Coins of Philip," in *Bethsaida* (1995), 171-8.

The imagery of three ears of grain also seems to be a response to Pilate's coin. Yet there are three differences.

- The grain is not drooping, but erect.
- They are depicted as held in a hand.
- An inscription explains the imagery: ΚΑΡΠΟΦΟΡΟΣ (Fruit-bearing).

The message is that Livia-Julia, even though she was physically dead, continues to serve as benefactress for her subjects, bestowing on them an abundance of grain through her own outstretched hand.

The difference between this coin and that of Pilate is a difference between the attitudes of the public about Livia/ Julia in Rome itself and those in the provinces. For a long time, subjects in the provinces, where ideas of divine rulers were long accepted, had granted various divine titles to Livia/ Julia. Yet in Rome deification could occur only after a ruler had died, and only in a limited number of cases. Tiberius and the senate had spoken. Livia/ Julia was a mere mortal. Yet a grassroots movement continued to persist in the provinces that supported her deification and Philip would seem to have been part of that movement. These efforts continued for several years until 41 CE when Livia's grandson, the Emperor Claudius, declared her deification.[25] It is not surprising that Philip's successor, Agrippa 1, also issued a coin in 42 CE which depicted the three ears of grain—a sign of honor for Livia-Julia.

Philip issued four different coins in the year 30 CE, unlike his pattern of issuing only two coins per mint in previous years. These four coins can be identified by the images depicted:

- Augustus and Livia
- Tiberius
- Livia-Julia
- Philip

Especially significant is the Tiberius coin, which, with the image of the emperor on the obverse and tetrastyle temple on the reverse, is identical to coins of previous mints with one exception. The inscription reads ΕΠΙ ΦΙΛΙΠΠΟΥ ΤΕΤΡΑΡΧΟΥ ΚΤΙΣ (During the rule of Philip the Tetrarch, Founder). This is the only time that those final four letters occur on a coin of Philip. The letters ΚΤΙΣ are an abbreviation for the Greek word κτίστης, meaning "founder"

---

25. Suetonius, *Claudius* 11; Dio Cassius, *Roman History,* 60.

Philip Coin—30 CE –Image of Tiberius

Coin of Philip – Undated – Image of Augustus and Livia

as "the founder of cities." In fact, in the passage from *Jewish War* quoted above, Josephus uses the same root κτίζει to describe Philip founding Caesarea Philippi and Bethsaida-Julias. The presence of this coin, along with the Julia coin, in the mint of 30 CE makes absolute the conclusion that Philip founded Bethsaida-Julias in the year 30 CE.[26]

The coin depicting both Augustus and Livia is also significant. It includes the inscription ΤΩΝ ΣΕΒΑΣΤΩΝ, which, paralleling the Julia coin, bestows upon Livia honors equal to that of Augustus. This coin makes it possible to date the founding even more precisely. Cities of client kings throughout the empire customarily celebrated the birthdays of both Augustus and Livia together in a three-day celebration in September. This began on September 22 with the recognition of Livia/ Julia and it culminated on September 24 with the celebration of Augustus' birthday and the beginning of a new year. The gala celebrations, which continued long after their deaths, often included sacrifices, games, and plays. In the year after Livia's death, it likely also included a special dedication ceremony adopting the name *Julias* for the newly expanded city of Bethsaida. September 22 in the year 30 CE, therefore, marks the likely date for the founding of Bethsaida-Julias.

As was noted above, the founding of cities often corresponded with important dates in the lives of the imperial family. Since these same coins were reissued in 33 CE, it is likely that Philip had originally intended to dedicate the city in that year which would have marked the 90th birthday of Livia-Julias and her 70th wed-

---

26. Meshorer, *Ancient Jewish Coinage*, (1982), 49, suggests that this inscription must refer to the thirtieth anniversary of the founding of Caesarea Philippi.

ding anniversary with Augustus. However, her death in 29 CE prompted Philip to celebrate its founding in the year 30 CE.

From Village to City

Josephus' first report about the founding of cities in *Jewish War* 2.168 is consistent with the 30 CE date for Julias, named for the wife of Augustus and the mother of Tiberius. Several decades later, Josephus wrote a second report in *Antiquities* 18.28:

> Philip for his part made improvements at Paneas, which is situated at the headwaters of the Jordan, and called it Caesarea; he further granted to the village Bethsaida on the Sea of Galilee both by means of a large number of settlers, and through further expansion of strength, the rank of a city and named it after Julia, the daughter of Caesar.

This report provides several critical pieces of information about Bethsaida's elevation to a city.

- The founding is interpreted in terms of extensive building projects. In particular the use of the term "strength" (δυνάμεις) may refer to the building of a Roman era wall on top of the ruins of the Iron Age wall at the southern end of the Tell. It is clear that this was not to be a new city built from scratch, but an expansion of an already existing settlement. This is consistent with the finds at et-Tell which show the Roman phase of building as a further development of the Hellenistic city. This counters the arguments of those who would like to see two separate settlements with a Hellenistic fishing village in the Beteiha plain and a later city on the acropolis about a mile away.[27]
- Josephus also mentions additional settlers, a point that cannot yet be confirmed by the current state of excavations. In fact, the northern residential section in Area C appears deserted. Future excavations on the southern slope of the Tell may be critical in determining this first-century settlement of new residents.
- Josephus describes a change in status from a village (κώμη) to a city (πόλις). It is not clear, however, what rights went with the status of *polis,* certainly not the right to mint coins.

27. James Strange, "Bethsaida," *The Anchor Bible Dictionary,* ed. David Noel Freedman (Garden City, NY: Doubleday, 1992), 1:692-3.

- Josephus notes that the founding included a name change from *Bethsaida* to *Julias*. This passage is significant because it is the only one that combines both names Bethsaida and Julias. The biblical texts consistently use *Bethsaida* and Josephus, along with Pliny and Ptolemy, use *Julias*.

City names used in first-century sources						
			Gospels	Josephus		Josephus	Pliny
4 BCE	1 CE	27	30	34		66	77
		Bethsaida	**Bethsaida/ Julias**	**Julias**	**Julias**	**Julias**	**Julias**
		Jesus' Career	Founding	Philip's Death	Agrippa's rule	Jewish Revolt Battle	Cities by Sea

The one controversial piece in Josephus' description is that he connects the name of the city not to Livia/Julia, but to Julia, the daughter of Augustus. This Julia's story is one of the great tragedies of the Augustan era.[28] As Augustus' only child she had married the highly respected Marcus Agrippa and gave birth to Augustus' own chosen heirs to the empire. In 13/12 BCE a denarius of C. Marius Tro. displayed her image flanked by Augustus' grandsons Gaius and Lucius. This would have been a high point of her life. Shortly afterwards, she was faced with the tragic death of her husband Agrippa, and she was forced to undertake a short unhappy marriage to Tiberius which by 8 BCE left only a dead newborn son and the self-exile and separation of her new husband to the island of Rhodes. In the next years her reputation unraveled as she was charged with frequent public adulterous affairs. This occurred at a time when Augustus had instituted the Julian Laws promoting family values. So serious were the accusations against her that Augustus was left with no choice but to exile his only daughter to the island of Pandateria in 2 BCE and then Rhegium, an exile which continued without reconciliation until their deaths in 14 CE.[29]

The timing of these events leaves only a narrow window when Philip might have considered naming a city for this Julia, the daughter of Augustus, between the beginning of his rule in 4 BCE and her exile in 2 BCE. As a result the traditional view for the founding of Bethsaida as Julias had once been

---

28. Arther Ferrill, "Augustus and his Daughter: A Modern Myth," *Studies in Latin Literature and Roman History,* 11 (1980), 332-46.

29. Suetonius, *Augustus* 65; Dio *History* 55.10 & 12-16; Tacitus, *Annals* 3.24.

assumed a date in 3 BCE.[30] However, such an interpretation leaves numerous problems. Does it make sense that Philip would have undertaken the building of two cities at the same time? Would not Philip have invested all his resources in completing his capital city named in the emperor's honor? Does it make sense that Philip would have named a city for a woman of this reputation? Is there any way that he would have been unaware of these events, especially in light of his presence in Rome in 4 BCE? Would not both Augustus and Tiberius have looked at him unfavorably? Why does the name Bethsaida continue in the Gospels? Would not Philip have tried to correct such a measure with another later name change? Yet the name Julias continued throughout the second half of the first century CE. Susan Wood notes, however, that Julia's footprint has all but disappeared because of her downfall. A few coins remain, as do several inscriptions in Asia where she had lived with Agrippa, but all sculptures have disappeared.[31] Likewise Wood might add: and no cities were named in her honor.

The discovery of Philip's coins from 30 CE and a fresh reading of Josephus' *War* 2.168 demonstrate that the traditional view of the founding of Bethsaida-Julias was simply wrong. Yet why did Josephus refer to Julia, the daughter of Caesar, in his description in *Antiquities* 18.28? It has been suggested that that Josephus was mistaken, as he is from time to time, or that it was a later scribal error.[32] However, the simple answer is that modern readers have misinterpreted Josephus' expression "Julia, daughter of Caesar." It is true that Augustus had only one biological daughter, Julia. However, through senatorial action Livia had also been adopted as his daughter and given the honorary name Julia. It seems odd that the same woman could be

30. Emil Schürer, *The History of the Jewish People in the Age of Jesus Christ* (Edinburgh: Clark, 1973), 2:70; Louis Feldman, ed. *Josephus, Jewish Antiquities* (Loeb Classical Library), vol. 9 (Cambridge: Harvard University Press, 1965), 25; and most recently Nikos Kokkinos, "The Foundation of Bethsaida-Julias by Philip the Tetrarch," *Journal of Jewish Studies,* 59 (2008), 236-51.

31. Susan E. Wood, *Imperial Women: A Study in Public Images, 40 BC—AD 68* (Leiden: E. J. Brill, 2000), 27.

32. An intentional scribal alteration might substitute θυγατρί for γυναίκᾳ. However, no such variants occur in the manuscripts. H.W. Kuhn and Rami Arav argue that this is a case of *homoioteleuton*, Kuhn and Arav, "The Bethsaida Excavations: Historical and Archaeological Approaches," *The Future of Early Christianity,* ed. Birger Pearson (Minneapolis: Fortress, 1991), 77-106. Mark D. Smith suggests that the expression ὁμώνυμον ἐκάλεσεν should be translated as *"he called it the same name as* Julia, the daughter of the emperor," Smith, "A Tale of Two Julias: Julia, Julias, and Josephus," in *Bethsaida* (1999), 2:333-346, especially 336-7. See also John T. Greene, "The Honorific Naming of Bethsaida-Julias," in *Bethsaida* (1999), 2:307-28, especially 316-7.

identified as both daughter and wife. Yet Josephus' use of the name Julia parallels other sources during the period after Livia's death in recognizing her dual role as wife and daughter.

In his *History of Rome*, written in 30 CE—the same year as Bethsaida's founding—Velleius Paterculus describes Livia as follows:

> Take for example Livia. She, the daughter of the brave and noble Drusus Claudianus, most eminent of Roman women in birth, in sincerity, and in beauty, she, whom we later saw as the wife of Augustus, and as his priestess and daughter after his deification.[33]

In this short description admiring Livia's virtues, Velleius recognizes her three roles in relationship to Augustus. She is wife (*coniugem*), priestess (*sacerdotem*), and daughter (*filiam*), the latter two being conferred following his death and deification. At the very end of his book, Velleius notes Livia's own death in 29 CE stating that she "in all things resembled the gods more than mankind."[34]

Similarly, an inscription accompanying a 2.13 meter tall sculpture of Livia, found at Velleia, reads:

> To Julia Augusta,
> daughter of Divus Augustus,
> mother of Tiberius the son of Divus Augustus
> and of Nero Claudius Drusus.[35]

---

33. Livia, nobilissimi et fortissimi viri Drusi Claudiani filia, genere, probitate, forma Romanarum eminentissima, quam postea coniugem Augusti vidimus, quam transgressi ad deos sacerdotem ac filiam. Velleius Paterculus, *History of Rome* 2.75.3, Trans. Frederick W. Shipley, The Loeb Classical Library (London: Heinemann, 1924).

34. Velleius, 2.130.5. *"per omnia deis quam hominibus similior."*

35. *[Iulia]e Divi*
A[ugusti] f. Augustae
matri Ti. Caesaris
[Di]v[i Au]gusti f.
Aug[usti e]t Neronis
[C]lau[di] Dru[si].

The statue with Livia towering over three other women figures, Drusilla, Agrippina 1, and Agrippina 2, is dated to the Caligulan period (37-41 CE). C. Brian Rose, *Dynastic Commemoration and Imperial Protraiture in the Julio-Claudian* Period (Cambridge: Cambridge University Press, 1997), 121-6, cat. 50; Elizabeth Bartman, *Portraits of Livia: Imaging the Imperial Woman in Augustan Rome* (Cambridge: Cambridge University Press, 1999), 123-6, cat. 33. For a view that the group is dated to the Tiberian period, see U. Hausmann, *Quaderni*

In the statue, Livia is veiled, demonstrating her role as priestess, and she wears a diadem that points to her deification following her death.

Another inscription from a statue base at Aphrodisias has been discovered, although the statue of Livia no longer survives. It reads:

> To Julia Augusta,
> daughter of Augustus,
> the [new] Hera.[36]

These three examples of the use of "daughter of Augustus" for Livia—the Velleius Paterculus passage, the Velleia inscription, and the Aphrodisias inscription—all come from the period

Velleia statue of Livia. Courtesy of Museo Arqueológico Nacional, Madrid, Spain.

following Livia's death and in one way or another they recognize Livia as having divine characteristics—perhaps contributing in some way to the movement toward her eventual deification under Claudius in 42 CE.

An analysis of Livia inscriptions demonstrates that she was most often identified as "wife of Augustus" in the period before his death in 14 CE; as "mother of Tiberius" between 14 CE and 29 CE; and then in the few inscriptions following her death as "daughter of Augustus."[37] This is consistent with the usage of Josephus in *Antiquities* 18.28 since he refers to Julia, the wife of Caesar, in relation to the founding of the city in Perea in 13 CE, but "Julia, the daughter of Caesar," in relation to the founding of Bethsaida in 30 CE. Perhaps one might argue from a stylistic standpoint, that this change by Josephus in a matter of lines from "wife of the emperor" to "daughter of the emperor," is unnecessarily confusing. However, a closer look at this section demonstrates that Josephus has knit things together rather carefully. The following chart illustrates the balanced structure of *Antiquities* 18.27-28:

---

ticinesi di numismatica e antichita classiche 18 (1989), 233-45; D. Boschung, *Die Bildnisse des Caligula. Das romische Herrscherbild,* IV (Berlin: Gebr. Mann, 1989), 97.

36. [Ἰο] υλίαν Σεβαστή [ν]
Σεβαστοῦ θυγατέ [ρα]
Ἥραν

Once again this was part of a statue group along with Agrippina, Germanicus, and M. Aemilius Lepidus, the husband of Drusilla, which suggests it is to be dated to the Caligula era. Bartman, *Portraits of Livia,* 123, also footnote 17 on page 139. Rose, *Dynastic Commemoration,* 164, cat. 104.

37. Fred Strickert, "Josephus' Reference to Julia, Caesar's Daughter: *Jewish Antiquities* 18.27-28," *JJS* 53 (2002), 27-34.

Chart: Literary Structure of Antiquities 18.27-28

Builder/	Old Name/	Location/	Building Process/	New Name/	Honoree
Herod (Antipas)					
	Sepphoris				
			ornament of Galilee		
				Autocratoris	
	Betharamptha				
			threw a wall around		
				Julias	
					for wife of Autocrator
Philip					
	Paneas				
			made improvements		
		at source of Jordan			
				Caesarea	
	Bethsaida				
			add residents and strength		
		on Lake Gennesaret			
				Julias	
					for daughter of Caesar

It is interesting to note that each ruler has dedicated two cities, the first one for Augustus, the second for Julia—and each pair is presented in correct chronological order. As a skillful writer Josephus has produced a highly parallel structure, yet he has taken pains to use a variety of expressions so that he does not repeat himself. For example, he uses ἠγόρευεν, προσαγορεύει, ὀνόμαζει, and ὁμώνυμον ἐκάλεσεν respectively for the naming of the cities – again the first two are linked linguistically, as are the last two. Likewise, as can be seen from the chart he takes care to describe the building process in four distinct ways. Herod Antipas and Philip both named a city for Augustus, yet each employed a different one of his titles in naming a city—Herod used *Autocrator* and Philip used *Caesar*.[38] Josephus, realizing this, cleverly repeated that same title in reference to the second city in each pair. Herod built a city named Autocratoris, so he constructed a second city named for "Julia . . . of Autocrator." Philip built a city named Caesarea, so he constructed a second city named for "Julia . . . of Caesar." Josephus' reference to the daughter of the Caesar should no longer be considered an

---

38. This is often lost in translation. Feldman here translates both αὐτοκράτορ and Καίσαρος with "the emperor's".

error or careless reporting. It is evidence of careful, well-structured writing consistent with historical data.

Philip's coins, the statements of Josephus, the pattern of name usage by first century authors, and the historical context following Antipas' founding of Tiberias, all point to the founding of Bethsaida as Julias in 30 CE following the death of Livia.

The Livia Cult

The practice of founding a city in honor of a member of the imperial family often led to more than just an honorary name change. The most complete evidence of the Imperial Cult comes from Asia Minor. When client kings were given permission to establish the cult, they agreed to offer worship to the emperor as well as to the goddess Roma. They would construct a temple in honor of the designated imperial family member and they would form a group of priests and officers to conduct the cult. They would also erect other structures such as a theater, amphitheater, and a stadium which would be used during the festivities taking place at the time of birthday celebrations in September.

It is not certain to what degree these practices were incorporated in Palestine. In 27 BCE, the same year that Octavian became Augustus, King Herod founded the city of Sebaste in Samaria with a temple dedicated to Augustus, a theater, and a stadium. In 13 BCE, the year of Augustus' fiftieth birthday, Herod founded Caesarea Maritima with an impressive elevated temple to Augustus, a theater, a stadium, and a hippodrome. In the case of Caesarea Philippi, the temple for Augustus was built in 20 BCE although the city was not founded until the rule of Philip.

In the case of cities founded by Antipas—Sepphoris-Autocrates, Betharamphtha-Julia, Tiberias—less is known. Jonathan Reed notes that the two Galilean cities were of a different character from Sebaste and Caesarea Martima:

> It must be noted that neither Sepphoris nor Tiberias shows the same kind of appetite for materials, buildings, and particularly decorative elements that symbolized Greco-Roman culture, compared to Caesarea Maritima or Scythopolis, the major cities in Palestine.[39]

---

39. Jonathan L. Reed, *Archaeology and the Galilean Jesus,* (2000), 93-94. For a similar appraisal see also Richard A. Horsley, *Archaeology, History, and Society in Galilee* (Harrisburg, PA: Trinity, 1996), 54-55.

Reconstruction of Roman Temple

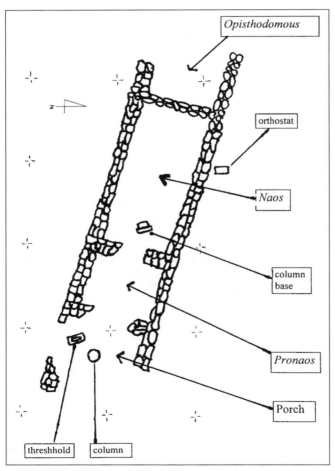

Plan of the Temple at Bethsaida

The theater at Sepphoris has been a matter of debate, but Reed places it in the late first century. Other features typical of Roman cities do not appear until after the Bar Kokhba revolt. Similarly, the only public structure discovered at Tiberias is the southern city gate with its rounded towers. Josephus does speak of a theater, but that may come later in the first century. Reed suggests that such a simple architectural style in these cities of Galilee is due to a matter of taste as well as a lack of financial resources. In both Tiberias and Sepphoris urban development is gradual.

At Bethsaida, it is important to remember that the city was founded in 30 CE, and then Philip died just four years later. There was not much time to carry out the building plans that must have been in Philip's head—especially with the limited finances of the Golan. However, there was already a temple structure from the Hellenistic era when Bethsaida came under the influence of Tyre.[40] Its size was twenty meters by five meters. While the earlier doorway had been on the north, Philip changed the orientation to face the east so that it included four major sections typical of Roman temples: a porch, an approaching hall (*pronaos*), the holy of holies (naos), and a back room (*opisthodomous*).[41]

Dressed stones from temple

40. Ilona Skupínska-Løvset, *The Temple Area of Bethsaida. Polish Excavations on et-Tell in the Years 1998-2000* (Lodz, Poland: Lodz University Press 2006).

41. Rami Arav and Richard Freund, "An Incense Shovel from Bethsaida," *BAR* (January/February, 1997), 32.

Although the structure is in a state of ruin, a segment of one column remains positioned in the exact center of the porch and several other column fragments and a column base were uncovered scattered throughout the rubble. A fragment of green marble—extremely rare in Palestine at this time—suggests the possibility of a marble floor.

Bronze incense shovel

Threshold

A few finely dressed stones point to an attractive façade that covered the rough basalt stone walls. Another stone found earlier on the surface may have been a lintel from this structure (see photo on page 116). The elongated dressed stone is covered with a meander and rosette pattern, symbolic of abundance and prosperity in the Augustan era.[42]

Area A Sq L58
L283 B4155
22/7/98
2 views

0   5 cm

Handle of 2ⁿᵈ incense shovel

As is the case when a temple goes out of use, the implements of worship are buried in nearby pits called *Favissa*. Perhaps the most significant of these implements is a complete eight-inch long, bronze incense shovel—found in May 1996—that parallels those found in the Cave of Letters and presumed by Yigael Yadin to have been among booty captured from the Roman army, who had brought them from Padua where they had been manufactured.[43] The ornate find from Bethsaida displays a Corinthian-column-shaped handle and a rectangular pan engraved with concentric circles and adorned with two protruding leaves.[44]

---

42. P. Zanker, *The Power of Images in the Age of Augustus* (Ann Arbor, MI: The University of Michigan Press, 1988).

43. Yigael Yadin, *Bar Kochba* (London: Weindenfeld and Nicolson, 1971).

44. Arav and Freund, "An Incense Shovel," 32. See also Richard Freund, "The Incense Shovel of Bethsaida and Synagogue Iconography in Late Antiquity," in *Bethsaida* (1999), 2:413-59.

Bronze patera

Clay female "Julia" figurine

Other finds include the handle of a second bronze incense shovel, a bronze ladle, two *paterae* (used for libations and sacrifices of grain), a highly decorated oil lamp filler, and high quality jugs and juglets. Paterae are often portrayed on Roman coinage as symbols of the imperial cult and it may be that a *patera* appears on one of Philip's coins that I have previously dated to 30 CE or 33 CE.[45] This coin, while depicting Augustus and Livia on the obverse, portrays a tetrastyle temple on the reverse. The temple of Augustus from Caesarea Philippi was a common feature on Philip's coins. Yet the temple on this particular coin is different in that the dates, which generally appear between the columns, are missing. Instead the columns are moved to the side to portray what has been called "an enigmatic round shape."[46] The simple appearance of a patera in the midst of a temple may well suggest the implementation of the imperial cult in Bethsaida-Julias. [47]

Several figurines were also found in the vicinity of the temple. One in particular is a rather small figurine, measuring 3/4 inch by 1 1/2 inch, showing the head of a female draped with a veil that is characteristic of depictions of Livia as priestess of Augustus.[48] Likewise her curled hair, in this case with traces of red, is of a style typical of statues of Livia/ Julia during the rule of Tiberius. Beginning with Tiberius' *Salus* coin minted in 22 CE, there was a clear development in Livia's hairstyle which has been characterized by Bartman as the tendency "to exaggerate those waves into melonlike segments that cover the head uniformly with distinguishing between side

45. The dating of the coins is based on size, Philip's minting pattern, and the correspondence with the birthday of Livia. Fred Strickert, "The Coins of Philip," in *Bethsaida* (1995), 179-81.

46. Ya'akov Meshorer, *Ancient Jewish Coinage* (1982), 2:46.

47. Previously I had wondered whether such a shape resembled the shields from the infamous incident with Pilate, which were subsequently displayed in the Caesarea temple.

48. Rami Arav, "Bethsaida Excavations: Preliminary Report, 1987-93," in *Bethsaida* (1995), 21.

Pottery from Favissa in situ

Pottery from Favissa

waves and crown."[49] Although facial features in this miniature clay figurine are clearly generic, it seems only logical to identify the figurine as Livia. Parallels for this image are the six meter high "Velletri Livia" from Wells (Norfolk), Holkham Hall and the "Velleia Livia" (see photo on page 179).[50] Because this figurine from Bethsaida was made in a mold with clay, it likely was produced for mass production for devotees to take with them.

Implications for the gospels

It is significant that the gospels all refer to this site as Bethsaida and not as Julias since the ministry of Jesus comes to an end in April 30 CE. For simplicity sake the date of Philip's *KTIS* coin is given as 30 CE, the 34th year of Philip's rule. However, with Herod's death in the spring of 4 BCE, and the time involved in the ratification of the will, his accession as ruler began only in the second half of 4 BCE. So his 34th year is more precisely dated 30-31 CE. This coincides with the general birthday festival from September 22-24 when Augustus and Livia were commemorated together. This was six months after the death of Jesus. Thus the name Bethsaida in the gospel is quite appropriate. Likewise it is interesting that Mark uses the term κώμη (village)

---

49. Bartman, *Portraits of Livia* (1999), 117. Brigette Freyer-Schauenberg, "Die Kieler Livia," *Bonner Jahrbuch* 182 (1982), 209-24, describes this development as the "Kiel type." See also Wood, *Imperial Women* (2000), 118.

50. Other parallels noted by Bartman include a gem from St. Petersburg, Bartman, *Portraits of Livia* (1999), fig. 81, cat. 105; the Paestum Livia with veil and wavy hair, fig .88-89, cat. 24; the Velleia Livia, fig. 96-97, cat. 33; the Lusitanian Aeminium Livia, fig. 150, cat. 44; and the Grumentum Livia, fig. 136, cat. 21.

to designate this location (Mark 8:23) while Luke and John designate it as πόλις (city) suggesting a later perspective (Luke 9:10; John 1:44).

The period of Jesus' ministry, therefore, corresponded exactly to this active time of building and expansion in Bethsaida that would have consumed a number of years' labor. It is difficult to imagine that Jesus and his disciples would have been unaffected by such activity. One must ask also whether this involvement would have been more than just the casual observations of those passing through. Jesus is identified in the Gospels as a carpenter. The term τέκτων (Mark 6:3) refers to various building activities including woodwork, building with stone, masonry, and the like and, therefore, Jesus may have been involved in general construction work connected with the building of such cities.[51]

It has been suggested that Joseph the carpenter settled in Nazareth because Antipas was actively building the nearby city of Sepphoris. One can imagine with a flurry of building activity taking place at Caesarea Philippi, Sepphoris, Betharamphtha-Livia, Tiberias, and Bethsaida-Julias that construction workers found themselves migrating from town to town following the work. It is all in the realm of conjecture, but one wonders if it is possible that Jesus' interest in Bethsaida stemmed from his career as a carpenter? The Gospels offer no explanation why Jesus chose to leave Nazareth and to focus his ministry on the northern Sea of Galilee area. It may well be that Jesus originally came to this area seeking work as a carpenter. His interest in this area and particularly in its inhabitants who followed him would lead him to focus his preaching and healing ministry.

51. Chester C. McCown, "ὁ τέκτων," *Studies in Early Christianity,* ed. Shirley Jackson Case (London: The Century Co., 1928), 173-89; Richard A. Batey, "Is Not this the Carpenter?" *NTS* 30 (1984), 249-58.

Chapter 13

The Multiplication of Loaves and Fishes

The Multiplication of Loaves and Fishes is the only miracle which occurs in all four Gospels (Mark 6:31-44; Matt 14:13-21; Luke 9:10-17; John 6:1-14). While Matthew and Luke derive similarities from Mark, John presents an independent witness separate from the Markan tradition.[1] Similarities in all four versions may well denote evidence of early traditions. One is also struck by the fact that in three Gospels this miracle is followed directly by the episode of the walking on the sea (Mark 6:45-52; Matt 14:22-34; John 6:16-21).[2] These factors all point to the earliness of the traditions surrounding this material.

It is also significant that this material has connections to the city of Bethsaida. In Luke 9:10, the feeding is explicitly located at Bethsaida, and, in Mark 6:45, the disciples head towards Bethsaida following the feeding. Neither Matthew nor John name the location although both include information that supports the Lucan geographical framework. It is true that such geographic references are likely additions by the evangelists. In this particular case, the contradiction suggests confusion on the part of the evangelists. For some this means that it is impossible to locate these accounts. For others, such confusion may still point to a Bethsaida connection which can only be determined by careful examination of details.[3]

---

1. The Johannine version presents enough variation to demonstrate independence from the Synoptic tradition. Raymond E. Brown, *The Gospel of John,* Anchor Bible (Garden City, NY: Doubleday, 1966), 1:236-44. Also similarities between Matthew and Luke may be evidence of a third version. Joseph Fitzmyer, *The Gospel according to Luke,* Anchor Bible (Garden City, NY: Doubleday, 1981), 1:763.

2. Only Luke omits this miracle which is part of the great omission in which Luke avoids doublets of the feeding episode and healing of a blind man in Mark 6-8.

3. Among my Bethsaida colleagues who have written on this topic, Kuhn takes the former position while Appold and Rousseau take the latter position. I am grateful for all their helpful insights.

Texts			
Matthew 14:13-21	*Mark 6:31-44*	*Luke 9:10-17*	*John 6:1-14*
13 Now when Jesus heard this,	31 He said to them, "Come away to a deserted place all by yourselves and rest a while." For many were coming and going, and they had no leisure even to eat.		1 After this
he withdrew from there in a boat to a deserted place by himself.	32 And they went away in the boat to a deserted place by themselves.	10b He took them with him and withdrew privately to a city called Bethsaida.	Jesus went to the other side of the Sea of Galilee, also called the Sea of Tiberias. 2 A large crowd
But when the crowds heard it,	33 Now many saw them going and recognized them,	11 When the crowds found out about it,	kept following him, because they saw the signs
they followed him on foot from the towns.	and they hurried there on foot from all the towns and arrived ahead of them.	they followed him;	that he was doing for the sick. 3 Jesus went up the
14 When he went ashore,	34 As he went ashore,		mountain and sat down there with his disciples.
			4 Now the Passover, the festival of the Jews, was
he saw a great crowd;	he saw a great crowd;		near. 5 When he looked up and saw a large crowd coming toward him,
and he had compassion for them	and he had compassion for them, because they were like sheep without a shepherd; and he began to teach them many things.	and he welcomed them, and spoke to them about the kingdom of God,	
and cured their sick.		and healed those who needed to be cured.	
15 When it was evening, the disciples came	35 When it grew late, his disciples came	12 The day was drawing to a close, and the twelve came	
to him and said, "This is a deserted place, and the hour is now late;	to him and said, "This is a deserted place, and the hour is now very late;	to him and said,	Jesus said to Philip,
send the crowds away so that they may go into the	36 send them away so that they may go into the surrounding country and	"Send the crowd away, so that they may go into the surrounding villages and	"Where are we
villages and buy food for themselves."	villages and buy something for themselves to eat."	countryside, to lodge and get provisions; for we are here in a deserted place."	to buy bread for these people to eat?"
			6 He said this to test him, for he himself

16 Jesus said to them,
"They need not go away;
you give them something
to eat." 17 They replied,

"We have nothing here
but five   loaves
and two fish."

18 And he said,
"Bring them here to me."
19 Then he ordered
        the crowds to sit
down
                on the
grass.

Taking the five loaves
and the two fish, he looked
up to heaven, and blessed
and broke the loaves, and
gave them to the disciples,
and the disciples gave them
to the crowds.

20 And all ate and
were filled;
        and they took up
what was left over of the
broken pieces,

---

37 But he answered them,

"You give them something
to eat." They said to him,
"Are we to go and buy two
hundred denarii worth of
bread, and give it to them to
eat?"   38 And he said to
them, "How many loaves
have you? Go and see."
When they had found out,
they said,

        "Five,
and two fish."

39 Then he ordered them
to get all the people to sit
down in groups
                on the green
grass.
40 So they sat down
in groups
of hundreds and of fifties.
41 Taking the five loaves
and the two fish, he looked
up to heaven, and blessed
and broke the loaves, and
gave them to his disciples
        to set before
the people; and he divided
the two fish among them
all. 42 And all ate and
were filled;

43 and they took up

---

13 But he said to them,

"You give them something
to eat." They said,

"We have no more than
    five   loaves
and two fish—unless we
are to go and buy food for
all these people." 14 For
there were about five
thousand men.

And he said to his disciples,
"Make them   sit
down in groups of about
fifty each."
        15 They did so and
made them all sit down.

                16 And
taking the five loaves
and the two fish, he looked
up to heaven, and blessed
and broke them,   and
gave them to the disciples
        to set before
the crowd.

17 And all ate and
were filled.

What was left over

---

knew what he was going to
do.

7 Philip answered him,
                "Two
hundred denarii would not
buy enough bread for each
of them to get a little."

8 One of his disciples,
Andrew, Simon Peter's
brother,
said to him,
"There is a boy here who
has five barley loaves
and two fish.   But what
    are they among so
many people?"

10 Jesus said,
"Make the people sit
down."
Now there was a great
deal of grass in the place;
so they sat down, about
five thousand in all.
                11 Then
Jesus took the   loaves,

and when he had given
thanks,   he
distributed them to
those who were seated;

so also the fish, as much as
they wanted. 12 When they
were satisfied, he told his
disciples, "Gather up the
fragments left over, so that
nothing may be lost."

twelve baskets full.	twelve baskets full of broken pieces and of the fish.	was gathered up, twelve baskets of broken pieces.	13 So they gathered them up, and from the fragments of the five barley loaves, left by those who had eaten, they filled twelve baskets.
21 And those who ate were about five thousand men, besides women and children.	44 Those who had eaten the loaves were numbered five thousand men.		14 When the people saw the sign that he had done, they began to say, "This is indeed the prophet who is to come into the world."

The Setting for the Miracles

Although only Luke explicitly locates this miracle at Bethsaida, the other three accounts are in agreement that the site for the feeding was reached by boat. Prior to the feeding, the evangelists describe Jesus and his disciples embarking by boat and going ashore. Afterwards Jesus sends his disciples away by boat, and, after a struggle, they reach their destination where they moor the boat. Only Luke neglects to include references to boats at the beginning, middle, and end of this section. Significantly, the same three speak of "the other side" (Matt 14:22; Mark 6:45; John 6:1) and of "crossing over" (Matt 14:34; Mark 6:53) and "going across" (John 6:17). The place of origin is not mentioned by name, but the Synoptics imply that they began on the western shore in the territory of Antipas whose growing hostility had led to Jesus' decision to withdraw for a while. Three of the evangelists report a return to the western shore at the end of this section, with Matthew and Mark specifying the destination as Gennesaret (Matt 14:34; Mark 6:52) and John mentioning their eventual arrival at the synagogue of Capernaum (John 6:59). John also reports that people had searched for Jesus on the following day, traveling by boat from Tiberias to the place of the feeding and then to Capernaum (John 6:23-24).

All of these accounts, therefore, are in agreement that the feeding took place on the eastern side of the Sea of Galilee, that is, the section east of the mouth of the upper Jordan.[4] Even Luke, who does not mention boat

---

4. Markus Bockmuehl, "Simon Peter and Bethsaida," *Supplements to Novum Testamentum* 115 (2005), 53-91, especially, 57-9.

travel at this point, confirms a location on the east side since the next episode—having omitted two chapters from Mark—is the confession of Peter which takes place at Caesarea Philippi. The difficulty in Mark 6:45—going "toward Bethsaida"—does not necessarily imply a site on the western shore, but rather one further east of Bethsaida.

Another similarity between the different versions of the feeding episode is that the crowds who wish to follow Jesus travel, not by boat, but on foot. There is a slight variation in the different accounts:

> Mark 6:33—Now many saw them going and recognized them, and they *hurried there on foot* from all the towns and arrived ahead of them.
>
> Matt 14:13—But when the crowds heard it, they *followed him on foot* from the towns.
>
> Luke 9:11—When the crowds found out about it, they *followed* him.
>
> John 6:2—A large crowd *kept following* him.

At the end of the feeding, Jesus dismissed the crowds while he sent his disciples by boat. The site therefore is one that is accessible both by land and by boat—and within a reasonable walking distance.

The Synoptics imply that the crowds walk to the site of the feeding, that they hear Jesus' teaching, that many are healed, that they are fed, and that they return to their homes—all in a single day. The account in John speaks of healing those who were sick and reserves the report of teaching until the following day in the Capernaum synagogue. Nevertheless, they agree that this was quite an undertaking for a single day. One cannot imagine a journey of more than six to eight miles each way. A typical day's journey for the Roman army was twenty-four miles. That assumed travel by Roman roads and not cross-country over mountainous terrain in the company of people who were sick and injured. In calculating distances, one must not be mislead by the modern northern shoreline of the Sea of Galilee at the mouth of the upper Jordan and the easy access by the modern road crossing into the Golan at the Aphik bridge.

When Theodosius visited the site in 530 CE, he reported the distance from Capernaum to Bethsaida as six miles. This distance implies travel by the later Roman road which went from Capernaum to Chorazin and then east to Bethsaida. With the rugged ancient coast line, this is a likely course for those described as traveling on foot in the feeding miracle. It involved a steady climb from the plains around Capernaum up to Chorazin, a steep descent down to the Jordan River, and then another climb up from the Jordan. Therefore, with those on foot coming from the place of Jesus' departure (Capernaum) as well as from towns along the way, one cannot imagine a destination too much further east of Bethsaida. Bargil Pixner has suggested Tell Khader on the east side of the lake for a feeding miracle, yet it is difficult to imagine the additional three to four miles travel on a single day.[5]

Hills, much grass, and a deserted place

The accounts also give a number of other details concerning the location. Although the site was near the sea, it was also hilly. In Mark and Matthew, Jesus ascends a nearby hill following the feeding (Mark 6:46; Matt 14:23). In John, however, Jesus climbs a hill at the beginning, and the crowds ascend to him (John 6:3). Later after coming down with the crowds, he repeats his ascent (John 6:15). Another detail is that the place was grassy where the people sat (Matt 14:19). John notes that there was "a great deal of grass" (John 6:10) and Mark notes that it was green grass (Mark 6:39). Since the entire lake is surrounded by hills, the detail about grass helps to limit the possible sites, yet it is still somewhat ambiguous.

The other significant detail is that the site is described in the Synoptics as "a deserted place" or "a lonely place," depending upon the translation. There is no question that this expression is to be emphasized since it occurs as often as three times in one account (Mark 6:31, 32, 35; Matt 14:13, 15; Luke 9:12). The term ἡ ἔρημος can be translated as desert, but because of the reference to grass, it probably denotes only a place with sparse population. Still there are farms and villages nearby. Clearly there are thematic connections with the desert feeding in Exodus, yet it is surprisingly absent in the Fourth Gospel account of the feeding. Rather, it comes in the discussion which takes place on the following day (John 6:49).

The question is raised how far Jesus originally intended to withdraw—yet compassion for the crowds drew him back to Galilee for a time. Although the later Gospel accounts refer to the crowds following Jesus to the site of the feeding, the earlier Markan account suggests that they knew of Jesus' intended destination from the beginning (Mark 6:33). Jesus' words, "Come away to a deserted place" (Mark 6:31) imply that the term ἡ ἔρημος denotes a well-known place. The crowds are aware of Jesus' destination and set out to

---

5. Bargil Pixner, "The Miracle Church of Tabgha on the Sea of Galilee," *BA* 48 (December, 1985), 199.

meet him there. Whether or not Jesus actually reached his intended destination, he and the crowds do come together in a place described as "deserted" and he spends the day in teaching and healing (Mark 6:35).

The location of the Roman road

Our earlier discussion concerning the roads near Bethsaida is helpful for understanding the feeding miracle. Especially significant is the east-west route that connected Bethsaida with Chorazin to the west and Gamla to the east. As noted, there is significant evidence that this road did not pass through Bethsaida itself, but rather followed a course about a mile to the north.

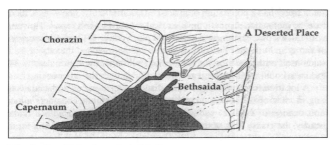

The feeding Episode: a Possible Route

If one assumes a Bethsaida locale for the feeding miracle, a likely place of encounter between Jesus, who arrived by boat, and the crowds who arrived by land, was not at the town of Bethsaida itself nor a site near the shore, but a location north of the town, perhaps near the crossroads a mile in distance. The travel of Jesus and the disciples thus included the crossing by boat, docking at the harbor of Bethsaida, making their way through the city, and hiking by foot from Bethsaida northward. This would realistically point to the possibility of the two groups beginning to come together at this junction. It would also explain Mark's notation that Jesus already saw the large crowd as he was getting out of the boat. The high ridge on the western side of the Jordan—the location of the Roman road—offers a prevailing view from et-Tell. The topography thus makes possible continued visual contact between the two groups.

This also helps to explain Jesus' reluctance to send the crowds into Bethsaida for food. For those on foot, Bethsaida was not on their itinerary and would lead to a detour and a delay of several additional hours. By feeding the crowds and directly sending them on their way, they could reasonably reach their homes that same night.

Luke's Reference to Bethsaida

This picture is complicated because Luke directs Jesus and his disciples to a city named Bethsaida. Technically it was not yet a πόλις (city), since this episode predates Bethsaida's founding on September 22, 30 CE. As some manuscripts note, it should properly be designated a κώμη (village). Clearly, modern expectations of cities should not cloud the picture. Bethsaida was a still a humble settlement with perhaps only a few thousand residents. However, with Luke's own reference to a deserted place (Luke 9:12) and his mention of farms and villages, it does not appear that he intended the city of Bethsaida itself as the location for the feeding, but rather the region nearby. The Lukan account need not be considered at odds with the other evangelists.

A location for the feeding a short distance northeast of Bethsaida is fitting in view of the details mentioned above. When one considers a location outside of Galilee, yet within walking distance and with a harbor nearby, the grassy hills of the Golan provide an appropriate setting for the feeding miracle. Because the hillsides are covered with basalt stone, there is nonetheless an abundance of grass. Yet the population was quite sparse and could easily be designated as ἔρημος.

The meal of bread and fish, although common all around the lake, is especially fitting for a location near Bethsaida. As a fishing town, one would naturally expect the presence of fish. Although the Synoptic accounts use the general term ἴχθυς (*ichthus*) for fish, John uses ὀψάριον which denotes the dried fish, possibly an export product of Bethsaida. Throughout all stages of Bethsaida's history there is evidence of grain farming and Bethsaida itself played an important role in the storage of grains. According to pollen analysis in the Hellenistic/ Roman era oval granary barley production actually exceeded that of wheat—corresponding to John's report of the young boy with five barley loaves.[6]

Other than Jesus and his disciples, the characters in this miracle story are not identified in the Synoptic accounts. John, however, includes a discussion between Jesus and Philip concerning the difficulty of feeding such a large crowd. Another disciple, Andrew, locates the boy with the loaves and fish. This is quite significant because these are Bethsaida disciples. By identifying Andrew as Simon's brother and repeating the name of Philip three times, John reminds the reader of his introduction which linked the three disciples together and established their origins at Bethsaida (John 1:40).

---

6. Patrick Scott Geyer, "Evidence of Flax Cultivation from the Temple-Granary Complex et-Tell (Bethsaida/ Julias)," *Israel Exploration Journal* 51 (2001), 231-4.

The Significance of the Feeding Miracle

The feeding of 5,000 is described as an act of compassion that Jesus has for people who have found themselves in physical need, because their spiritual hunger has led them to leave their homes in search of spiritual food. Following an afternoon of spiritual nourishment—teaching and healing—Jesus then provides the physical nourishment necessary for their long walk home. As is the case with numerous miracles, there is also a deeper symbolic or theological meaning. John alludes to this by calling the miracle a sign and by following it with a long interpretative sermon.

First, one sees in this event the plight of the masses under Antipas as the Roman client ruler of Galilee. A transition has taken place that has changed people from subsistence farmers who grew enough for their own needs to tenant farmers meeting the production expectations of the wealthy landowners. Those days of innocence are represented by the young boy willing to share what he has—meager as it is—with his neighbor. In contrast to the five loaves and two fish, the alternative is to purchase bread for all to eat. Two hundred denarii is the estimated cost, a figure that none of them has likely held in their possession or even imagined. The denarius was the silver Roman coin. Ironically, not even the tetrarchs had the right to mint such silver coins, but instead they provided the small bronze coinage that individuals might hoard to buy a loaf of bread or the daily needs no longer available because of high taxation.

Second, one sees this as the gathering of a spiritual army.[7] On Jesus' previous trip to the eastern shore, he healed a demonic possessed by spirits named "Legion"—a clear reference to the occupying forces of the Roman army (Mark 5:1-20). The political significance of the feeding miracle is suggested by the context since the preceding episode describes Antipas' execution of John the Baptist and his growing hostility toward Jesus. A retreat to the desert, in the first century, was typical for rebel movements. In the feeding miracle, the number 5,000 is thus typical of the size of a Roman legion. It also corresponds to the number of Galilean troops assembled by Josephus and Jeremiah at Bethsaida-Julias during the 67 CE revolt (Josephus, *Life* 398-406). As they eat, the crowds are divided into groups of fifty, similar to the Roman cohort. Just as the Roman army often played a role in selecting new emperors, so those who are fed seek to make Jesus their king

---

7. John J. Rousseau, "The Impact of the Bethsaida Finds on our Knowledge of the Historical Jesus," Paper presented to the Historical Jesus Section, SBL, 1995. H. Montefiore, "Revolt in the Desert," in *New Testament Studies,* (1957-8), 135-49.

(John 6:15). Supported by this spiritual army, Jesus thus returns to Galilee where he continues his ministry unafraid of Antipas' threats.

A third image is that the feeding points to a reenactment of Israel's desert experience under the leadership of Moses. They have crossed the sea just as the Israelites crossed the Red Sea. They are now located in the desert, where they are fed as Moses provided manna from heaven (John 6:26-35). Subsequently, they will cross over into the promised land. Related to this is the connection with the Christian communal meal. John notes that it is Passover time, a detail that is supported by Mark's reference to the green grass in the spring of the year. Jesus' actions in preparing the food have a liturgical ring: Jesus took the loaves. . . "he looked up to heaven, and blessed and broke the loaves, and gave them. . . ." (Mark 6:41). Superior to this food, is the nourishment that comes in his flesh and blood (John 6:47-51).

A fourth image comes from our new knowledge about Bethsaida-Julias. The Julia coins in fact depict ears of barley and designate her gift to the community in terms of an abundance of produce. The inscription reads καρπόφορος (fruit-bearing). In Livia's role as the goddess Demeter in the imperial cult, she guarantees that abundance for her community. The spring context points to the beginning of the dry season when the land becomes a desert and people wonder if the earth will ever produce again. In that desert atmosphere, Jesus also feeds the crowds. Not only do they eat, but they are full and have baskets left over. This feeding portrays Jesus as a provider superior to Livia/Julia.

Walking on the Water

The feeding episode is followed in three Gospels with the account of walking on the water. Central to the impact of this miracle is the fact that the western shore of Galilee is not readily accessible from the site of the feeding miracle. This certainly could be the case from any location on the eastern shore, but it is also the case with Bethsaida, as recent geological research has noted. The disciples have departed by boat—the only available boat according to John 6:22. The crowds have departed on foot, possibly by way of the Chorazin road. Jesus has stayed behind for a quiet evening alone in prayer on the hillside.

The disciples' arrival is hindered by the typical strong winds coming from the west. Jesus then began to make his way back to the western shore on foot. Yet Jesus does not travel by the longer Chorazin route, but makes his way by the sea—ἐπὶ τῆς θαλάσσης (Mark 6:48; John 6:19).[8] The preposi-

---

8. Stephen H. Smith, "Bethsaida via Gennesaret: The Enigma of the Sea Crossing in Mark 6,45-53," *Bib.* 77 (1996), 349-74.

tion ἔπι with the genitive can denote walking "beside the sea" or "on the sea." One can try to figure this out logistically in a number of ways as Jesus struggles along a rugged coast line or perhaps following a sandbar or dry land next to an estuary. Mark's comment that he "was going to pass them by" (Mark 6:48) suggests that Jesus' intention was merely to reach the same destination on the western shore. Yet as he sees the disciples in trouble, he comes to them on the water bringing calm in the midst of storm and courage in the midst of doubt. They arrive at Gennesaret and Jesus begins anew his ministry in the Galilee.

Chapter 14

The Healing of the Blind Man

Mark 8:23-26 presents the story of the healing of a blind man at Bethsaida. In this account, Jesus crosses the sea by boat with his disciples and arrives at the town of Bethsaida. As Jesus is passing through, a blind man is brought to him for healing. Jesus leads him outside of the town where he heals the man by spitting on his eyes. The man receives only partial sight and says that what he sees is like trees walking. After Jesus laid his hands upon his eyes, the man then was able to see. Jesus then sent him home instructing him not to return to Bethsaida.

The Text: Mark 8:22-26

> 22 They came to Bethsaida. Some people brought a blind man to him and begged him to touch him. 23 He took the blind man by the hand and led him out of the village; and when he had put saliva on his eyes and laid his hands on him, he asked him, "Can you see anything?" 24 And the man looked up and said, "I can see people, but they look like trees, walking." 25 Then Jesus laid his hands on his eyes again; and he looked intently and his sight was restored, and he saw everything clearly. 26 Then he sent him away to his home, saying, "Do not even go into the village."

The uniqueness of the Markan account

Interestingly, this is one of the few episodes from Mark which is not repeated elsewhere. Because it is attested in only one source, some might question its authenticity. However, there are several issues which explain its uniqueness. First, one must consider that this episode includes material which can be considered offensive and embarrassing. Jesus heals by spitting in the man's eyes. In two other episodes, the evangelists mention Jesus spitting in the healing process. In John 9:6, Jesus spat on the ground making a mud plaster which was applied to the eyes. In Mark 7:33, Jesus spat and touched the man's tongue. Yet here Jesus spat directly on the eyes. The New Revised Standard Version tames the language a bit stating that Jesus "put saliva on his eyes." This demonstrates that people are concerned with "offensive" language.

This episode also presents the only healing of Jesus which does not bring about complete success on the first attempt. This can be an embarrassment which seems at odds with the common image of Jesus who brings healing simply through speaking a word. In a similar way the statement in Mark 6:5 that "he could do no deed of power there" was changed in Matthew 13:58 to read "he did not do many deeds of power there, because of their unbelief." One should therefore not be surprised that later evangelists omitted this story. In fact, this is a strong argument for authenticity since the early Church would likely not have created an episode with such problematic details.

A second issue has to do with duplication. There are several miracle stories that describe the healing of blind men. All three Synoptics include the account of blind Bartimaeus at Jericho (Mark 10:46-52; Matt 20:29-34; Luke 18:35-43). Matthew alone includes the episode of two blind men in Galilee (Matt 9:27-31) and John alone includes the episode of the man born blind in Jerusalem (John 9:1-7).[1] In the Q episode of the healing of a dumb demonic, Matthew also includes the element of blindness (Matt 12:22) while Luke does not (Luke 11:14). Matthew, therefore, has three other episodes about healing the blind, which may account for this omission related to Bethsaida. In the case of Luke, the healing at Bethsaida is part of a longer section known as the "Great Omission" including the material from Mark 6:45 to 8:26. Several explanations have been offered including the possibility that there was an earlier shorter manuscript of Mark; that Luke skipped from one mention of Bethsaida to the next; or that Luke wanted to avoid a section with several doublets.[2] Even though this healing episode occurs only in Mark, there is good reason to consider it an authentic historical event.[3]

---

1. For similarities between the Markan miracle and the Johannine healing of a blind man, see Thomas L. Brodie, *The Quest for the Origin of John's Gospel: A Source-Oriented Approach* (New York: Oxford University Press, 1993), 48-66.

2. Joseph A. Fitzmyer, *The Gospel According to Luke,* Anchor Bible (Garden City, N.Y.: Doubleday, 1981), 1:770.

3. E. S. Johnson, "Mark viii 22-26: The Blind Man from Bethsaida," *NTS* 25 (1979), 370-83.

The Context in Mark

The episode of the Bethsaida blind man fits well with other geographical information in Mark 8. In verse 10, Jesus and his disciples are in the district of Dalmanutha, which is the area around Magdala on the western shore of the lake. In verse 13, they get into a boat to cross to *the other side* of the lake. In verse 22, they arrive at Bethsaida where the healing takes place. Following the healing they move further north to Caesarea Philippi where Peter offers his confession. The natural stopping-off place between the western shore of the lake and Caesarea Philippi is Bethsaida.

This episode is also appropriately located because of several theological themes in Mark. During the boat trip across the lake, the disciples realize that they had forgotten to bring bread for the journey (Mark 8:14-21). The following discussion then centers around the two feeding miracles, one which took place on the shore behind them (Mark 8:1-10) and the other near Bethsaida before them (Mark 6:30-44). The reminder about the baskets of bread left over carries a special symbolic meaning since the number of baskets is designated as twelve and seven. Usually these numbers are said to designate the Jewish world and the Gentile world respectively. The connection then with the western and northeastern shores is significant. The former is representative of Judaism and the latter is representative of the Gentile world—corresponding to Josephus' notation about the mixed population of Philip's territory.

This is especially significant in view of the previous episode that had taken place on the western side. While Jesus is still at Dalmanutha, Pharisees—as representatives of traditional Judaism—come asking Jesus to perform a miracle as a confirmation of God's approval (Mark 8:11-13). Jesus soundly rejects their request:

> Why does this generation ask for a sign?
> Truly, I tell you, no sign will be given to this generation (Mark 8:11).

Rather, Jesus immediately got into the boat and crossed over to Bethsaida. In view of this rejection of the Pharisee's request for a sign, it is especially significant that Jesus heals a blind man as soon as he sets foot on the northeastern shore. The difference to be sure is one of motive. These acts of power are not accomplished for curiosity sake, but to meet genuine human need. As in the case of his previous Bethsaida miracle, the feeding of the five thousand, Jesus acts out of compassion, not to give proof of his identity. The fact that it takes place at Bethsaida points ahead to the future success of the church in Gentile areas.

The irony of this particular miracle is that the healing of the blind was considered one of the expected messianic signs. Thus Jesus began his inaugural sermon at Nazareth by quoting Isaiah concerning the recovery of sight to the blind (Luke 4:18). In response to the question of John the Baptist in prison, Jesus instructs his followers, "Go and tell John what you hear and see: the blind receive their sight. . ." (Matt 11:4-5 = Luke 7:22). The episode of the Bethsaida healing thus is a perfect lead-in to the Caesarea Philippi confession of Peter: "You are the Messiah" (Mark 8:29). Yet just as Jesus had denied such a demonstration of proof for the Pharisees, so even in the Bethsaida miracle it is critical to note that healing takes place only outside the town and away from the crowds.

The healing of blindness thus has a deeper spiritual level. In the boat on the way to Bethsaida, Jesus notes the disciples' lack of understanding:

> Why are you talking about not having any bread? Do you still not perceive or understand? Are your hearts hardened? Do you have eyes, and fail to see? (Mark 8:17-18).

The theme of the disciples' lack of understanding, which had prevailed since the beginning, comes into focus at this critical juncture of the Gospel.

It has often been noted that the Gospel according to Mark is structured around three major sections:

1. The Galilean Ministry (Mark 1:14- 8:30).
2. The Road to Jerusalem (Mark 8:31- 10:52).
3. Death and Resurrection in Jerusalem (Mark 11:1-16:8).

Within this structure Mark has carefully positioned two healing miracles: the Bethsaida blind man at the end of section one (Mark 8:22-26) and blind Bartimaeus of Jericho at the end of section two (Mark 10:46-52). In both cases, the preceding episode highlights the disciples' lack of insight and understanding (Mark 8:14-21 and 10:35-45). The final section of the Gospel, it has been said, then leads to a third healing miracle. The disciples once again show lack of understanding in deserting Jesus at the crucifixion, but they will finally overcome their blindness when they *see* the resurrected Jesus in Galilee (Mark 16:7).

The episode of the Bethsaida blind man—although omitted by later evangelists—plays a crucial role in the organization of the earliest Gospel. The reader can only move from one section to the next when eyes are opened. It is therefore appropriate in the Bethsaida episode that healing is not altogether successful at first. True insight and understanding come about only in stages.

Therefore, the idea of sight is reinforced by the repetition and variation of words about seeing. In Greek this includes not only βλέπω, but compounds such as ἀναβλέπω, διάβλεπω, and ἐμβλέπω, as well as ὅραω. The Markan account deals with more than physical sight.

Illness in the Bethsaida Context

One should not be surprised to find a blind man waiting for Jesus in a town like Bethsaida. In the ancient world the blind were often shunned from the acceptable circles of society and joined with the lepers and lame as outcasts. Blindness was apparently rather common resulting from latent *trachoma*, a chronic contagious conjunctivitis caused by *chlamydia*.[4] Congenital blindness was also often related to various disorders which occur readily among societies struggling with economic and political oppression—as was typical in first-century Palestine. Interestingly, another report of healing a blind man includes the discussion of the commonly-held belief of a connection between blindness and the sin of parents (John 9:2).

Thus the blind were often stigmatized by their disease and forced to live as beggars gathering near cities. In the story of blind Bartimaeus, he is found begging along the main road outside the city of Jericho (Mark 10:46). As the major population center in the southern Golan, Bethsaida likely also had its share of blind beggars. It is not surprising that at the end of the episode Jesus makes a distinction between the man's home and the town of Bethsaida: Then he sent him away to his home, saying, "Do not even go into the village" (Mark 8:26). He was apparently from one of the surrounding villages and had come to Bethsaida to beg.

Mark does not state exactly where Jesus encountered the blind man. Like most travelers, Jesus likely arrived at the harbor, climbed to the top of et-Tell, made his way through the main part of the town, and continued along the main road leading north in the direction of Caesarea Philippi. One would guess that a common gathering place for beggars was the harbor area, below the actual city. There they would meet the many travelers arriving by boat. Jesus, however, took his hand and led him out of the city and away from the crowds—perhaps along the road leading north towards the east-west crossroads.

Twenty-five years ago, a stone to commemorate this healing was erected near the entry way to Hayarden Park and the access road leading to the et-Tell excavations. Subsequently it has become clear that the paved road

4. This section is highly dependent upon the work of my colleague John Rousseau, "The Healing of a Blind Man of Bethsaida," in *Bethsaida* (1995), 257-66.

leading from the Iron-Age gate on the east side of the town continued in use in the New Testament era. This road followed the eastern edge of the Tell and then turned in a northeasterly direction, several hundred meters from the current access road.

Technique of healing

In most miracle accounts in the gospels, there is not a whole lot of detail given concerning the actual technique used to bring about healing. Most often the focus is on the spoken word. Jesus simply issues a command and healing immediately follows. In several cases the actual words of Jesus, *Ephrata* or *Talitha Kumi* ("be opened" or "little girl arise"), were preserved in Aramaic by the early Church. In others, healing is related to the touch of Jesus. He takes a person's hand or lays hands upon their head. Healing even occurs when a woman touches Jesus' garment.

Several decades later in the early Church, the prayers of Christians were supplemented by the anointing of the sick with oil (James 4:14). Such use of physical intermediaries in healing also occurs in the ministry of Jesus. In the healing of the blind man recorded in John 9, Jesus applied clay to the man's eyes after forming the clay when he spit on the ground. Then Jesus follows

Paved road leading north from gate

with a command for washing. In the case of the Bethsaida blind man, Jesus spat on the eyes and placed his hands over the man's eyes.

The actions of Jesus in this miracle resemble those of many healers in the Hellenistic world. They are thus appropriate for the multicultural setting of Bethsaida. Significant parallels come from the various temples related to Asclepius, the Greek god of healing. When the blind Alcetas of Halice visited the shrine at Epidaurus, the god of healing appeared to him and ran his fingers over his eyes. When his eyes opened, he first began to see the trees of the temple precincts.[5] Aristophanes describes a healing which took place in the temple of Asclepius at Piraeus. During the night a priest, who appears with mortar, pestle, and a box, mixes a plaster of vinegar and hot spices and applies them to the eyes of the patient. A number of healed patients also describe how snakes appeared at night and licked their eyes.[6]

The use of saliva was also common, because it offered a ready fluid, but perhaps also because of the saline and enzyme content which might help draw out infection. The emperor Vespasian is reported to have restored sight to a blind follower of Sarapis in Alexandria by moistening his eyes and cheeks.[7] Pliny the Elder reports on the effect of saliva: "The best of all safeguards against serpents is the saliva of a fasting human being."[8] Saliva was frequently used to treat boils, leprous sores, and eye diseases.[9] The use of saliva by Jesus at Bethsaida to bring healing to a blind man is therefore consistent with the practice of healing in the Greco-Roman world and is especially appropriate for a town like Bethsaida.

Healing in the context of Bethsaida

A traditional Arabic name for et-Tell was *Tel e-Shafi*—translated as mound of healing. Does this reflect a belief that this location had played a

---

5. Mark Appold, "The Mighty Works of Bethsaida: Witness of the New Testament and Related Traditions," in *Bethsaida* (1995), 235.

6. Aristophanes, *Plutus*. Howard Clark Kee, *Miracles in the Early Christian World* (New Haven: Yale University Press, 1983), 81. Rousseau, "The Healing," (1995), 263.

7. Tacitus, *Histories* 4.81; Suetonius, *Lives of the Caesars, Vespasian* 7. 2; Dio Cassius, *Roman History* 65.271. Eric Eve notes that Mark was composing his gospel at the very time tales of Vespasian's healing abilities were reaching Rome in 69 CE in "Spit in Your Eye: The Blind Man of Bethsaida and the Blind Man of Alexandria," *New Testament Studies* 54 (2008), 1-17.

8. Pliny, *Natural History* 30. See also Galen, *Natural Faculties* III. 7.

9. Howard Clark Kee, *Medicine, Miracle and Magic in the New Testament Times* (Cambridge: Cambridge University Press, 1986), 104.

prominent role in healings over the centuries? The Gospel of the Nazarenes reported that Jesus performed 53 miracles at Bethsaida and a Q saying recognizes the reputation that Jesus had performed most of his miracles at Bethsaida. Yet Mark 8 records the only healing miracle specifically located at Bethsaida. Does this mean an independent healing tradition preceded Jesus? Is there something of a parallel with the episode in John 5 where Jesus healed a lame man who had waited for years by the Jerusalem pool near St. Anne's Church for the waters to be stirred by a visiting angel. Excavations have shown a rich history of that site as a health spa related to Asclepius and other deities. So Jesus' healing of the lame man provides a powerful witness against such powerful claims and unfulfilled expectations.

Oppression and poverty lead to high rates of illness and such is the case in first-century Galilee. Though no temples and healing compounds were known other than the hot springs south of Tiberias, there are certainly cases of afflicted persons who have spent years of effort and life-savings on doctors who provided no cure. Was Bethsaida such a place for anticipated healing? Hector Avalos raises this question in particular with the Bethsaida temple. Temples in general were associated with healing, he says, in three respects:

1. as a place to petition divine intervention;
2. as a place to offer thanksgiving for healing accomplished;
3. as a place where therapy is provided.[10]

0   5 cm

Small bottle

In regard to the latter, he quotes Strabo that the Temple of Asclepius at Epidaurus was "always full of the sick."[11] The role of the Hellenistic temple that stood near the gate at Bethsaida may be interpreted through the numerous figurines of pregnant women. Was there a continuation with the first-century temple? From the pollen analysis from the temple floor, 28 per cent of the pollens were identi-

10. Hector Avalos, "Bethsaida and the Study of Ancient Health Care," in *Bethsaida* (2004), 3:213-229, especially 219.

11. Strabo, *Geography* 8. 6. 15.

fied as fennel,[12] a crop that (in addition to culinary uses) was commonly employed in medicine for intestinal problems, as a diuretic, as a syrup to treat chronic coughs, and to reduce soreness and inflammation of the eyes.

Avalos also documents a number of excavated items that were commonly used for medicinal purposes:

- miniature ointment vessels that often contained pharmaceuticals;
- small bronze spatulas that could be used to apply medicines;
- a metal tweezers.[13]

Sandra Fortner has now catalogued these items and noted parallels identifying their medicinal functions.[14] Unfortunately these artifacts from the residential section in Area C also could be identified as having uses in applying cosmetics and holding expensive perfumes. Such evidence must therefore be considered inconclusive.

However, the most significant element of the Mark 8 healing story is that the blind man's associates singled out Jesus and begged him to touch him; that Jesus took him away from the city for healing; and that Jesus instructed the man not to return to the city.

---

12. Patrick Scott Geyer, "Evidence of Flax Cultivation from the Temple-Granary Complex et-Tell (Bethsaida/ Julias)," *Israel Exploration Journal* 51 (2001), 231-4

13. Avalos, "Bethsaida and the Study of Ancient Health Care," (2004), 226.

14. Sandra Fortner, *Der Keramik und Kleinfunde von Bethsaida-Iulias am See Gene-zareth, Israel,* (München: Ludwig-Maximilians-Universität, 2008), page 68, catalogue # 1435-1439, Table 82.

Chapter 15

Woe Saying against Bethsaida

It has often been suggested that Jesus focused his ministry on an area known as the "evangelical triangle." This designation is associated with an area linked between the three towns of Bethsaida, Chorazin, and Capernaum near the northern part of the Sea of Galilee. It is in this area that Jesus taught the crowds and performed most of his miracles. Nevertheless, Matthew and Luke preserve a saying of Jesus in which he berates these communities for their lack of faith. The towns of Jesus' day are compared with ancient cities with a reputation for evil deeds. Just as those ancient cities were destroyed, so also the three cities of Jesus' day are condemned.[1]

The Q Saying

The woe saying of Jesus has been preserved by two evangelists: Matthew and Luke. It therefore fits the criteria for the sayings collection known as Q. A comparison of the two versions of the saying is as follows:

---

1. This chapter is dependent in part on conversations, papers, and three published articles by my Bethsaida colleagues: Mark Appold, "The Mighty Works of Bethsaida: Witness of the New Testament and Related Traditions," in *Bethsaida* (1995), 229-42; Heinz-Wolfgang Kuhn, "Bethsaida in the Gospels: The Feeding Story in Luke 9 and the Q Saying in Luke 10," in *Bethsaida* (1995), 243-56; Kuhn and Rami Arav, "Bethsaida Excavations: Historical and Archaeological Approaches," in *The Future of Early Christianity,* ed. Birger A. Pearson (Minneapolis: Fortress Press, 1991), 77-107.

Matthew 11:20-24	*Luke 10:13-15*

20 Then he began to reproach the cities in which most of his deeds of power had been done, because they did not repent. 21 "Woe to you, Chorazin! Woe to you, Bethsaida! For if the deeds of power done in you had been done in Tyre and Sidon, they would have repented long ago   in sackcloth and ashes. 22 But I tell you, on the day of judgment it will be more tolerable for Tyre and Sidon than for you. 23 And you, Capernaum,
    will you be exalted to heaven?
    No, you will be brought down
    to Hades.
For if the deeds of power done in you had been done in Sodom, it would have remained until this day. 24 But I tell you that on the day of judgment it will be more tolerable for the land of Sodom than for you."
	13 "Woe to you, Chorazin! Woe to you, Bethsaida! For if the deeds of power done in you had been done in Tyre and Sidon, they would have repented long ago sitting in sackcloth and ashes. 14 But at the judgment it will be more tolerable for Tyre and Sidon than for you. 15 And you, Capernaum,
	    will you be exalted to heaven?
	    No, you will be brought down
	    to Hades."

In the central part of this saying, the two versions of this saying show a high degree of verbal agreement with only slight variations in the Greek text: Matthew uses ἐγένετο while Luke has ἐγενηθῆσαν. Luke has the single additional word "sitting" in verse 13. Otherwise these portions are identical. Since there is no parallel in Mark, it is most certain that Matthew and Luke have drawn upon a common source known as the sayings collection Q. Yet there are some significant differences. Matthew is the longer version including an introduction which notes that most of Jesus' miracles were, in fact, carried out in these towns. Matthew also includes a final comparison of Capernaum with the Old Testament city of Sodom.

There is good reason to believe that the shorter Lukan version reflects the earlier Q version of the saying. The introductory material in Matthew provides no additional material that could not have been derived from the saying itself. The material concerning Sodom which comes at the end parallels another saying of Jesus concerning the rejection by various unnamed towns of Jesus' disciples. They are to shake the dust off their feet because:

Truly I tell you, it will be more tolerable for the land of Sodom and Gomorrah on the day of judgment than for that town (Matt 10:15).

The same saying occurs in Luke 10:12 just prior to the Bethsaida woe saying. One could perhaps argue that Luke has omitted the final section from Q to avoid repetition. However, for Luke who has an appreciation for parallel structure, such an omission seems unlikely.[2] The introductory πλήν λέγω ὑμῖν in Matthew 11:24a betrays his hand since it is identical to verse 22a. The plural pronoun, however, is inconsistent with the use of the singular in the rest of verses 23-34 and with the context. Likewise, the final section includes the typically Matthean μέχρι τῆς ἥμερον (Matt 10:15; 27:8; 28:15). The expression "land of Sodom" (v. 24) using γή with a genitive plural is characteristic of Matthew (Matt 2:6, 20, 21; 4:15: 10:15).

Presently, Luke mentions three contemporary cities and two ancient cities while Matthew mentions three each. It is more likely that Matthew has added material to create an appearance of parallelism. Nevertheless the parallelism is somewhat lacking since there is no reference to repentance as in the first part. Just as Luke is closest in preserving the sayings of Q in general, so in the case of the woe saying about cities it is likely that the Q version is represented by Luke.

The matter of Q has also become quite complicated with recent research focusing on several layers of materials. In this light, the present prophetic saying is something of an intrusion into an earlier layer of wisdom material and therefore may belong to a second edition of Q known as Q-2.[3] Nevertheless, it shows the marks of an originally independent saying which was only later joined with other such sayings.

The question of authenticity

There is considerable debate whether this saying was actually spoken by Jesus or whether it represents the words of the spirit-led community of the early Church. The work of the Jesus Seminar and its recently published *The Five Gospels: The Search for the Authentic Words of Jesus* concludes that this saying was not in character with the preaching of Jesus and that it likely stemmed from early Christian prophets in frustration over a lack

---

2. John Kloppenborg, *Q Parallels: Synopsis, Critical Notes, and Concordance* (Sonoma, CA: Poleridge, 1988), 74.

3. Burton Mack, *The Lost Gospel of Q*, (San Francisco: Harper and Row, 1993), 36; Helmut Koester, *Ancient Christian Gospels*, (Philadelphia: Trinity Press, 1992), 140; John Kloppenborg, *The Formation of Q*, (Philadelphia: Fortress Press, 1987), 195-6.

of acceptance of their message.[4] Among my colleagues at Bethsaida, Mark Appold is in general agreement with this view while Heinz-Wolfgang Kuhn argues that the saying was actually spoken by Jesus.

It is significant that both Matthew and Luke place this saying in the context of mission activity of Jesus' followers. Matthew 10 reports Jesus' commissioning of the twelve who are sent out into neighboring towns and villages. This is followed in chapter 11 by the question of the imprisoned John the Baptist, a section of sayings about the followers of John, and then the Bethsaida woe saying. Luke 10 reports Jesus sending out the seventy. The saying follows directly after the advice concerning their response to towns who are not receptive. The contexts, of course, are the creation of the evangelists. Yet they are appropriate since the saying does speak about Jesus' mighty works as if they are already accomplished events. The saying thus gives the impression of presenting the point of view of the early church looking back on the ministry of Jesus.[5]

At the same time, one could argue that it would be surprising for the early church to focus entirely on one phase of Jesus' ministry, his miracles, at the expense of his teaching ministry. Yet this is the case in this particular saying. These towns are condemned because they have seen his mighty acts and have not believed. Yet not a word is said about his teaching activity in these same areas. This is ironic in one sense because the sayings collection emphasizes the teaching of Jesus and includes only a few references to miracles. However, current study on the Fourth Gospel calls attention to early interest in the signs of Jesus and an early signs collection which does focus on that aspect of his ministry. One cannot exclude a connection between this particular saying and the signs tradition.

Another critical issue concerns the actual situation of these particular towns. What do we know about them both in terms of Jesus' ministry and in the history of the early Church? Rudolf Bultmann argued that this saying could not be authentic because it assumed a later situation when preaching in Capernaum ended in failure.[6] The synoptic picture is exactly the opposite. Capernaum is described as the center of Jesus' activity and this ministry meets with amazing success so that crowds of people are always surrounding

4. Robert W. Funk, Roy W. Hoover, *et al.*, *The Five Gospels: The Search for the Authentic Words of Jesus* (New York, Polebridge Press, 1993).

5. David A. Catchpole, *The Quest for Q*, (Edinburgh: T. and T. Clark, 1993), 172.

6. Rudolf Bultmann, *The History of the Synoptic Tradition*, (Oxford: Blackwell, 1968), 112. Bultmann gives three arguments against authenticity: 1. the saying describes Jesus' activity as already completed; 2. it assumes the failure of preaching in Capernaum; and 3. it would be difficult for Jesus to imagine Capernaum as exalted because of his preaching activity.

Jesus. Unfortunately, the Acts of the Apostles and the canonical epistles are silent with regard to further developments in Capernaum, as also Bethsaida and Chorazin. Yet archaeological work since the time of Bultmann suggests a picture of a continuation of Jesus ministry by the early church in Capernaum and no evidence of any interruption in that community.

Capernaum, of course, is not the only town mentioned in this saying. In fact, a case can be made that it plays only a secondary role. The actual saying focuses primarily on a parallelism between the two ancient cities of Tyre and Sidon and cities contemporary to Jesus: Chorazin and Bethsaida. Since sayings against Tyre and Sidon were typical in the Old Testament prophets (Isa 23; Jer 47:4; Ezek 26-28; Joel 4:4-8), their inclusion here adds to the dynamic of early Christian prophets. Thus a connection with cities of Jesus' day was natural. Because of the similarity in sound between *Sidon* and *Tzaidan* (Bethsaida), the role of this city dominates the saying. Also striking is the fact that Bethsaida is compared with Chorazin, since Bethsaida is usually linked by its connections across the sea. Chorazin and Bethsaida would be linked by a Roman road, one city to the west of the Jordan in Galilee and the other to the east of the Jordan in the Golan. The saying may not derive then from the experience of fishermen apostles, but from those later itinerant preachers with sandals on feet and staff in hand walking from town to town—and speaking the word of the risen Jesus.[7]

With Bethsaida and Chorazin linked together, a contrast is marked from Capernaum on the sea. The two former sites are cities set on a hill.[8] With their lights shining at night, they cannot be hid and therefore have a grandeur about them. Capernaum, in contrast, sits below next to the sea. Thus the significance of Jesus' words, "Will you be exalted to heaven?" Capernaum is condemned, not to tumble with mountains into the sea, but to sink to Hades with the earth opening up around it. Implicit here is a comparison with the prophetic condemnation of Babylon in Isaiah 14:13-14. However, Capernaum is treated only briefly. Later Matthew

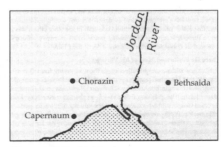

The evangelical triangle

---

7. Gerd Theissen, *Social Reality and the Early Christians,* (Minneapolis: Fortress Press, 1992), 37-59.

8. Although Bethsaida was located near the sea, it was situated on a mound rising over 100 feet above the level of the Sea of Galilee.

has drawn another connection with the destruction of Sodom by the side of the Dead Sea and thus expanded the saying.

This saying points to a flurry of activity not reported in depth by the New Testament writers. It is a reminder that the evangelists have reported only one small part of that story and that archaeology may be the only means available to capture even a glimpse of that total picture. This is underscored by the mention of Chorazin. Absolutely nothing is reported about the ministry of Jesus in this first-century town, apart from this saying. Here it is said that Jesus worked miracles, but not a single story survives. In this case even archaeological excavations have not been able to take us back further than a third-century site. So the picture is only partial. In the case of Bethsaida, we are much better off. We do have a number of episodes in the gospels to supplement and expand on the Q saying, and we now have archaeological evidence. Yet one would be mistaken to think that Jesus' ministry in Bethsaida, as also in the other cities, was limited to these few reports. This saying points to an extensive ministry by Jesus and its continuation in the early days of the Church.

Where he performed most of his miracles

Matthew includes an introduction to the woe saying from Q in which he states that Jesus had performed most of his miracles in the area of this evangelical triangle bounded by Chorazin, Bethsaida, and Capernaum (Matt 11:20). The version of this saying in the second-century Jewish-Christian Gospel of the Nazareans gave the number of miracles performed in Bethsaida as fifty-three. In previous chapters, we have already given attention to three miracles connected with Bethsaida: the feeding of the five thousand; the walking on water; and the healing of the blind man.

Is there evidence for other miracle traditions to be connected with Bethsaida? One episode that fits the context of Bethsaida is the story of the miraculous catch of fish in relation to the risen Jesus' appearance to seven disciples (John 21). Like many miracles, the story itself does not indicate specifically the location. The context of the story is that the disciples have gone back to their former lives, careers, and homes. Under the leadership of Peter they return to the Sea of Galilee and a night of fishing. It is natural to assume that Peter would choose to return to his home, Bethsaida—though the Church of the Primacy of Peter would make a case for a site on the western shore at Tabgha. The dawn breakfast encounter with Jesus on the shore parallels the episode of the feeding of the five thousand since Jesus offers the disciples a meal of bread and fish. Even the language is similar:

"He took the bread, and gave it to them" (John 21:13). Finally, there may be a connection between the number of fish 153 and the tradition of 53 Bethsaida miracles. It is common in textual transmission for a number like 100 to be added or omitted from a text. These clues suggest a Bethsaida context for this miracle.

One other miracle which has been linked to Bethsaida is the healing of the lame man lying beside a pool of water where there were five porches (John 5:1-18). Archaeological excavations at St. Anne's church near Stephen's Gate in Jerusalem point to the existence of such a pool and also the presence of a healing cult in this place. The Jerusalem location is fitting since a subsequent discussion in the temple concerns the issue of healing on the Sabbath. From Josephus we learn that the northeast quarter of the city near the temple was named *Bezetha* (Josephus, *War* 2.15). From the Dead Sea scrolls we learn about a pool named *Bet 'Esdatayin* (plural) on an eastern hill in Jerusalem.[9] However, the manuscript evidence for both of these names John 5:2 is rather weak. Another name *Bethesda* is attested only by the fifth century codices Alexandrinus and C. The name *Bethzatha* is attested by the fourth century codex Sinaiticus and *Belzetha* by Manuscript D. The strongest manuscript evidence points to the name *Bethsaida*, attested in P66 from around 200 CE and the important third-century P75 and the fourth-century Codex Vaticanus among others.

Thus the translators of the Vulgate and King James Version included *Bethsaida* for John 5:2. One could perhaps argue for a Bethsaida locale for this miracle based on the complexity of issues concerning an early Jerusalem ministry of Jesus and the presence of a Synoptic parallel for this miracle in Galilee (Mark 2:1-12). However, John's knowledge about Bethsaida (John 1:44; 12:22) would argue against the possibility of such an error. Because of the witness to the site in both ancient literature and archaeology,[10] it is generally assumed that the name of the pool associated with this miracle was *Bethzatha*.[11] With the spread of Christianity there was less familiarity with the geography of Palestinian sites. Already in the early

---

9. 3 Q15 xi 12-13. J.T. Milik, *Discoveries in the Judean Desert III* (Naperville, Il.: Allenson, 1962), 271.

10. Remains of the pool have been uncovered near the Church of St. Anne. There was located a pool divided by a bedrock causeway (thus the Qumran plural notation) so that five porches stood upon it, two on each side and one on the causeway. Yigael Yadin, *Jerusalem Revealed* (Jerusalem: Israel Exploration Society, 1976).

11. Raymond E. Brown, *The Gospel According to John,* The Anchor Bible (Garden City, NY: Doubleday, 1966), 1:206-7.

third century CE the grammarian Aelius Herodianus (born in Alexandria and living in Rome), wrote:

> Every pronunciation of written words beginning with the syllable "b" combined with "h" are such as: Bethlehem, Bethesda, Bethsaida, Bethphage, which are names of **places in Jerusalem** (my emphasis).[12]

Apparently the less familiar name would have been replaced by later scribes with the more familiar *Bethsaida*. There is even more reason to expect such a change if Bethsaida had gained such a reputation associated with the miracles of Jesus.

The Gospels do present significant evidence for the miracle tradition at Bethsaida. By nature of the gospel materials, one can only expect that a small segment of the Jesus tradition has been passed down. In the case of Chorazin, there is none. However, in the case of Bethsaida there is ample evidence of miracle tradition.

Later citation of the woes against Bethsaida

Within the early church, there was frequent citation of Jesus' saying of woe against the cities including Bethsaida. The early fifth century biblical scholar Jerome considered the question of miracles:

> "Woe to you, Chorazin, woe to you, Bethsaida. . . ." Chorazin and Bethsaida, cities in Galilee, were lamented over by the Savior because, after so many signs and virtuous works, they would not do penance. Tyre and Sidon, cities given to idolatry and other vices, were preferred. They were preferred because Tyre and Sidon had only trampled upon natural law, whereas in the case of Chorazin and Bethsaida, after they transgressed against both natural and written law, they paid little heed to the signs done among them. We may ask where it is written that the Lord did signs in Chorazin and Bethsaida. We read above: "And he traveled among all the cities and villages, curing all the sick" and the rest. Among the other cities and villages, therefore, the Lord had done signs in Chorazin and Bethsaida. . . . Whereas Chorazin and Bethsaida are condemned because they would not believe in the Lord when he was present, Tyre and Sidon are justified because they believed his apostles.[13]

---

12. Aelius Herodianus, *Partitiones* 5.14, edited by Jean Francois Boisonade (originally published in 1819; reprint Amsterdam: Hakkert, 1963).

13. Jerome, "Commentary on Matthew 2.11.22-24," (Commentaire sur s. Matthieu [translated and edited by Emilie Bonnard; vol. 1; Sources chrétiennes 242; Paris: Cerf, 1977]).

On the basis of the general summary statements about the healing of the sick, such as Matthew 9:35, Jerome accepts without question that most of his miracles were done in these cities. Yet it is because of the people's lack of faith in spite of Jesus' very presence that they are condemned.

This was a similar view as that of the third-century Origen of Alexandria, who saw Jesus' foreknowledge of their later faithfulness and judgment:

> "Woe to you Chorazin; woe to you Bethsaida, for if the signs that happened in you had taken place in Tyre and Sidon, they would long ago have clothed themselves in sackcloth and ashes and repented. But I say to you, it will be better for Tyre and Sidon than for you," etc. For the Savior, having foreknowledge of the faithlessness of those in Chorazin and those in Bethsaida, and those in Capernaum, and that it is better for the land of Sodom on the day of judgment than for those cities, what marvelous things took place in Chorazin and in Bethsaida, seeing that, because of these things, it is better on the day of judgment for the Tyrians and Sidonians than for the citizens of these cities?[14]

The famed fourth-century preacher John Chrysostom was particularly fond of Jesus' woes against the Galilean cities, quoting them in his published sermons no less than five times. Yet his focus was not so much on the destruction of Bethsaida, but on his sorrow for Bethsaida in much the same way that he wept for Jerusalem:

> So also over Bethsaida, he did not treat its future with counsels or with signs, but with sorrow alone, repeatedly pronouncing the woe over the cities just as we ourselves do over those who are on death's door.[15]

The condemnation, however, was not irreversible, but led to forgiveness:

> And Christ came to reproach the cities, saying, "Woe to you Chorazin; Woe to you Bethsaida," in order that he might set them free from reproach.[16]

It was not that the residents' nature was evil, for from Bethsaida came five apostles:

---

14. Origen, "Fragments of Commentary on Exodus," MPG 12: 280, line 28.

15. John Chrysostom, "Quod Reulares Feminae Viris Cohabitare Non Debeant 2.68" (Jean Dumortier, *Saint Jean Chrysostome* [Paris: Les Belles Lettres, 1955]). See also "Exposition of Psalms" MPG 55:260, lines 60 ff.

16. John Chrysostom, "Homily on Ephesians" (MPG 62: 74, lines 38 ff.). See also "On Isaiah 1.3" (Jean Dumortier).

> Jesus came to reproach the cities in which most of his miracles were per-
> formed, because of their lack of repentance, saying, "Woe to you, Chorazin.
> Woe to you, Bethsaida." Then, in order that you might learn that it was not
> from their nature that these cities were so cursed, he sets forth the name of
> the city, from which came five apostles. For Philip and those two pairs of
> leaders were from there.[17]

Of course, it is the Fourth Gospel that had introduced the idea that Peter, Andrew, and Philip had come from Bethsaida. So drawing on that tradition, as also on one including the place of origin of James and John, Chrysostom could virtually ask, how bad was Bethsaida?

Interestingly, Eusebius in the early fourth century does not mention the woe saying in relation to Bethsaida although he does refer to the city in four different works. In his *Onomasticon*, he does, however, make a connection with the city of Chorazin:

> Chorazin (Matt 11:21). A village in Galilee which Christ cursed, according to
> the Gospel. It is now deserted, separated from Capernaum by two mile stones.[18]

Eusebius of Caesarea has no similar statement about Bethsaida. However, in a discussion of the expression "Galilee by the sea" in his Commentary on Isaiah, Eusebius comments on the three cities of the evangelical triangle:

> Indeed Capernaum and Bethsaida and Chorazin and the rest of the villages,
> which the evangelical writing refers to as around the Lake of Tiberias, are
> still now pointed out.[19]

The final clause is somewhat ambiguous, perhaps suggesting that Bethsaida was still in existence in his day, yet possibly being a reference merely to the location of ruins.[20]

---

17. John Chrysostom, "Homily on Matthew," MPG 57: 424, lines 45 ff.

18. Eusebius, *Das Onomasticon der biblishen Ortsnamen*, edited by E. Klostermann, vol. 3.1 of *Eusebius Werke*. GCS 11.1 (Leipzig and Hildesheim: Georg Olms, 1966), 174, line 23.

19. Eusebius, *Der Jesajakommentar,* edited by J. Zeigler, vol. 9 of *Eusebius Werke*. GCS (Berlin: Akadmie-Verlag, 1975), 1.54.

20. Mark D. Smith, "Eusebius of Caesarea and the Fate of Bethsaida," in *Bethsaida* (2004), 3:253-71.

Chapter 16

The Early Church, a Communal Meal, and the Sayings of Jesus

The New Testament no where explicitly mentions the existence of a Christian community in Bethsaida. For that matter, none of the other communities connected with the ministry of Jesus—with the exception of Jerusalem—is mentioned by name. This should not be surprising since the picture of the early church preserved in the canonical writings is predominated by the mission activity of Paul. The communities that Paul visits are scattered throughout the Mediterranean area. The focus of Luke in The Acts of the Apostles—influenced by the Pauline picture—likewise moves throughout these Mediterranean cities.

The Acts of the Apostles and early Christian letters

The picture of Pauline Christianity assumes the existence also of a Palestinian Christian community. When Paul reports in Jerusalem concerning the success of his missionary endeavors in Gentile regions, James replies, "There are thousands of Jews who have become believers" (Acts 21:20). One can pick up on later references to Jewish- Christian communities that imply some kind of early activity. For example, Eusebius mentions relatives of Jesus living in Galilee at the end of the first century.[1] Likewise, Jerome

---

1. Eusebius, *Ecclesiastical History* 1.7.13. See also Justin Martyr, *Dialogue* 38; Tosefta Hullin 22; Kohelet Rabbah 1.24; 2 Baruch 41.3; 83.8. Albert I. Baumgarten, "Literary Evidence for Jewish Christianity in the Galilee," in *The Galilee in Late Antiquity,* ed. Lee I. Levine (Cambridge: Harvard University Press, 1992), 39-50; L. E. Elliott-Binns, *Galilean Christianity* (Chicago: Alec R. Allenson, Inc., 1956).

notes that the Jewish Christians referred to Hillel as unholy, a play on words made possible by the distinctive Galilean pronunciation of the first letter of his name.[2] However, the impression given by Acts is that these Christians are concentrated in the area around Jerusalem.

Here one has to understand the theological focus of Luke who wants to portray the spread of Christianity from Jerusalem to Rome. Thus the risen Jesus even instructs the disciples not to part from the city of Jerusalem. The first seven chapters of Acts are restricted entirely to the episodes about the church in that locale. Then the movement is gradually expanded into the Judean coastal regions, Samaria, Phoenicia, and Syria until the Mediterranean journeys of Paul are taken up. It is ironic that by the end of Acts, Christian communities have been planted in areas totally surrounding the Galilee and the Golan. They are in Damascus, Sidon, Antioch, and Caesarea, but the Galilee is mentioned only once in passing (Acts 9:31). In a summary statement, it is mentioned that the church in Galilee, along with Judea and Samaria, experienced a time of peace and growth following the conversion of Paul. Paul likewise, who has been entrusted the ministry to the uncircumcised (Gal 2:7), asserts his independence from the Palestinian church as well as the leadership of the apostles and thus minimizes his attention of this segment of Christianity. At the same time, the Acts of the Apostles does suggest an even more complex picture by describing Gentile Christianity emerging, not only among the Pauline communities, but even in Palestine (Acts 10). The picture of the growth of Christianity from Acts and the letters of Paul is anything but complete.

Inferences from the Gospels

The four Gospels present the ministry of Jesus and are not intended to include historical reporting about the early church. Yet since the Gospels were not put into writing until forty years later and more, they too must be treated like an archaeological tell with careful attention to various layers and strata.[3] The stories of Jesus offer helpful clues that can fill in gaps about early church history.

For example, the resurrection appearance stories are a helpful corrective to the Jerusalem-centered picture of Acts. In Mark 16:7, in contrast to the

---

2. Jerome, *Commentary on Isaiah* 8.14.

3. Howard Clark Kee, "Early Christianity in the Galilee: Reassessing the Evidence from the Gospels," in *The Galilee in Late Antiquity,* ed. Lee I. Levine (Cambridge: Harvard University Press, 1992), 3-22.

Luke-Acts position, the disciples were told to go to Galilee where they were to see Jesus. They returned to the same place where they had encountered Jesus before—the Sea of Galilee—and he appeared to them there (John 21). They met on a Galilean hillside and they were sent out from there into all the world (Matt 28:16-20). The picture assumes a continuation between the communities where Jesus found followers and the communities of the early church—which is only logical. It assumes a concentration in these same areas and then movement outward.

As we saw in the previous chapter, there are sayings in the gospels that present a perspective of the church looking back on the completed ministry of Jesus. Thus the sayings collection Q assumes knowledge of Christian communities in Bethsaida, Chorazin, and Capernaum (Matt 11:20-24 = Luke 10:13-15). In a similar way, the emphasis in Mark on a Capernaum-centered ministry implies some knowledge of a community there in the mid-first century. Archaeology supports this with the discovery of the early house church, described in an earlier chapter by its popular name as "The House of Peter."

The Fourth Gospel: Philip and Andrew, leaders in Bethsaida

Surprisingly, it may be the fourth Gospel, the last to be written, that provides a more detailed picture of an early Christian community—specifically that of Bethsaida.[4] The identification of this city as the home of several disciples likely is included because the community there continued to recognize and preserve their contribution. It is important to pay attention to the order in which the disciples are identified: "Now Philip was from Bethsaida, the city of Andrew and Peter" (John 1:44). That Peter is mentioned last reflects less his prominence in the stories of Jesus than his later absence from Bethsaida in view of his leadership position in the Jerusalem church (Gal 2:9; Acts 1–12). On the other hand, Philip, who is barely mentioned in the Synoptics, is now the prominent disciple from Bethsaida. He is mentioned no less than four times in the Fourth Gospel, three times in connection with Andrew, but his name always occurs first (John 1:44; 6:5; 12:20; 14:8). The inner circle of Peter, James, and John in the Synoptics is replaced by a special role assigned to Philip and Andrew.

---

4. Mark Appold, "The Mighty Works of Bethsaida: Witness of the New Testament and Related Traditions," in *Bethsaida* (1995) 239; Karl Kundsin, *Topologische Überlieferungsstoffe im Johannes Evangelium* (Göttingen: Vandenhoeck and Ruprecht, 1925); Klaus Wengst, *Bedrängte Gemeinde und verherrlichter Christus* (Neukirchen-Vluyn: Neukirchener, 1983).

Bethsaida and early Christian communal meals

The role of these two disciples in the episode of the multiplication of loaves and fishes (John 6:1-15) sheds light on that special status. The fact that this is the one miracle occurring in all four gospels points to its early date. In the Fourth Gospel, Jesus questions Philip about what to do in this difficult situation and Andrew brings to Jesus the young lad with loaves of bread and fish. Their roles are not essential to the story since the Synoptics do not name them. It would seem that their role is not as historical characters in the miracle event, but as liturgical leaders of the community reenactment of that same event.

In order to understand this, one must see the connection between the feeding of the five thousand and the miraculous catch of fish in John 21. Both miracles have the same theme: Jesus provides for his followers in abundance. Both have a link to the Sea of Galilee, and quite possibly a setting near Bethsaida. The situation of the latter miracle is that the disciples have returned to their homes following the death of Jesus. Peter, the Bethsaida fisherman, has invited six others for a night of fishing on the sea. Five of the seven disciples are named. The two nameless disciples may well be Philip and Andrew (John 21:2). What happens in the miracle is clear: after a night of failure, they meet success; out of nothing they find abundance. The disciples then join Jesus on the shore for a meal of bread and fish; they recognize Jesus; and they are commissioned for their tasks.

In the same way that the Jerusalem communities commemorated Jesus' Last Supper with a regular gathering of bread and wine, it is not difficult to see how the Bethsaida community might offer a varied form of commemoration sharing bread and fish. Early Christian art in fact depicts this variation in Lord's Supper representations. Thus the feeding of the five thousand is told in John as a liturgical meal.[5] The reader in fact is told that it is the time of Passover. The words of Jesus call forth a response from the people; a young boy delivers a basket of loaves and fish; Jesus offers a eucharistic blessing; "when they had given thanks" (John 6:11); the disciples distribute the food; and the people on the grass eat their fill. Later the Eucharistic Prayer of Didache 9:4 reflects a connection with the feeding episode and especially notes the element of gathering the fragments. The eucharistic understanding is underscored later when the crowds refer to "the place where they had eaten the bread after the Lord had given thanks" (John 6:23). That they remembered, not just the action, but also the place is significant. In

5. Raymond E. Brown, *The Gospel According to John,* The Anchor Bible (Garden City, N.Y.: Doubleday and Company, 1966), 1:247-9.

summary, these texts point to an early Christian community that gathered under the leadership of Philip and Andrew at Bethsaida, the place where the risen Jesus revealed himself through mighty deeds, and where he continued to reveal himself through the sharing of a liturgical meal of bread and fish.

Sayings

In recent years there has been a lot of attention given to the sayings of Jesus. This includes primarily study of the sayings collection known as Q, which was used by Matthew and Luke, and also careful analysis of the Gospel of Thomas collection of 114 sayings discovered at Nag Hammadi, Egypt in 1945. This work has been popularized by the Jesus Seminar which undertook the careful examination of each individual saying and published findings in *The Five Gospels: The Search for the Authentic Words of Jesus.*[6]

Philip and the sayings tradition

The early Christian community at Bethsaida-Julias provides a possible context for the gathering of sayings about Jesus. The Apostle Philip is an appropriate character to bring about the gathering process. Bishop Papias of Hierapolis in the early second century placed Andrew and Philip, along with Peter, at the beginning of the collectors of these sayings:

> If, then anyone came who had been a follower of the elders, I inquired into the sayings of the elders—what Andrew said, or what Peter said, or what Philip, or Thomas, or James, or John, or Matthew, or any of the other disciples of the Lord said.

The first three names are those mentioned in John 1:44—"Now Philip was from Bethsaida, the city of Andrew and Peter." While the names of Thomas and Matthew are most often mentioned in connection with the sayings tradition, Philip plays no less a prominent role.

Philip is highlighted in the Nag Hammadi document *Pistis Sophia* where he is introduced as "the writer of all the words which Jesus spoke and of all that he did."[7] The following words are then addressed particularly to Philip:

> Hear, Philip, you blessed one, that I may speak with you, for you and Thomas and Matthew are they to whom the charge is given by the first mystery, to

---

6. *The Five Gospels: The Search for the Authentic Words of Jesus,* ed. Robert W. Funk, Roy W. Hoover, et al. (New York: Polebridge Press, 1993).

7. Edgar Hennecke, *New Testament Apocrypha,* ed. Wilhelm Schneemelcher (Philadelphia: The Westminster Press, 1963), 1:272.

write down all the things which I shall say and do. . . "Through two and three witnesses shall everything be established;" the three witnesses are Philip and Thomas and Matthew.[8]

Philip is placed alongside the two best-known gatherers of sayings. Thomas is well known today because of The Gospel of Thomas and Matthew is identified in Papias as the one who wrote "the sayings of Jesus in the Hebrew language for each one to interpret as he could." It is not surprising, then, that the Nag Hammadi Library also includes a Gospel of Philip. In later tradition, Philip was in fact remembered for his role in preserving the sayings of Jesus.

This also is made clear in the fourth Gospel. In addition to the three occasions when Philip and Andrew are mentioned together (John 1:44; 6:6-8; 12:21-22), Philip's name occurs by itself in the farewell discourse in John 14. There Philip is depicted in the role of gathering the sayings of Jesus as he makes the following request:

Lord, show us the Father, and we will be satisfied (John 14:8).

Jesus responds:

The words that I say to you I do not speak on my own; but the Father who dwells in me does his works (John 14:10).

A little later as the discussion progresses, Jesus speaks directly to the sayings collection process:

I have said these things to you while I am still with you. But the Advocate, the Holy Spirit, whom the Father will send in my name, will teach you everything, and remind you of all that I have said to you (John 14:25-26).

Here are addressed two central components of the sayings gathering process. First, is remembering. Although the disciples have not always understood the significance of Jesus' teaching and actions at the time they happened, the function of the Holy Spirit is to remind them and help them to understand their significance (John 2:22; 12:16). Second, the Holy Spirit functions as a teacher so that, as the community continues to speak and to apply itself to new situations and contexts, the words of Jesus are being spoken through them.

Philip is very much involved in the Fourth Gospel in the sayings gathering process. Since remembering is key to that process, the author has called attention to Philip at critical junctures throughout the gospel—chapters 1, 6, 12, and 14—where he serves as witness to the words of Jesus.

8. IBID.

A nucleus of sayings: John 12

In John 12 Philip appears in a context, along with Andrew, where the sayings gathering process begins. The two disciples bring Greeks to see Jesus who then responds with a series of three early sayings:

> Very truly, I tell you, unless a grain of wheat falls into the earth and dies, it Remains just a single grain; but if it dies, it bears much fruit. Those who love their life lose it, and those who hate their life in this world will keep it for eternal life. Whoever serves me must follow me, and where I am, there will my servant be also. Whoever serves me, the Father will honor (John 12:24-26).

The Fourth Gospel is not often viewed as a source of authentic sayings of Jesus. In fact, the Jesus Seminar in its publication *The Five Gospels* has printed only four Johannine sayings in gray, denoting possible authentic words of Jesus, at least reflecting his teaching, though not necessarily with the exact words. Among these four are the first two of these sayings of Jesus in John 12.[9] Although the Fourth Gospel is removed from the historical Jesus by some six or seven decades, it is generally assumed that these three sayings were taken from a pre-Johannine source.[10] Schnackenburg has identified these three sayings as "a unit, firmly rooted in the tradition and catechesis of the primitive church."[11] The dying grain saying of verse 24 will be treated in detail in the next chapter.

What stands out the most about the latter two sayings is that parallels occur in Mark 8:34-5, but in reverse order. These sayings occur in the context of the confession of Simon Peter which is linked geographically to the area of Caesarea-Philippi, just north of Bethsaida. That episode is preceded in Mark 8 by the second feeding miracle and the healing of the blind man at Bethsaida.[12] Even though it is a major revision from Mark, Luke 9 places the confession of Peter and the sayings about losing one's life and being a servant directly after the Bethsaida feeding of the five thousand episode. Further study is needed to explore in depth the relation of these three sayings to a possible early Bethsaida sayings source.

9. Funk, *Jesus Seminar*, 431-32.

10. Raymond E. Brown, *The Gospel According to John,* The Anchor Bible (Garden City, N.Y.: Doubleday, 1966), 1:471-74; Ernst Haenchen, *John,* Hermeneia Series (Philadelphia: Fortress, 1984), 2:97.

11. Rudolf Schnackenburg, *The Gospel According to St. John* (N.Y.: The Seabury Press, 1980), 2:384.

12. See Thomas L. Brodie, *The Quest for the Origin of John's Gospel: A Source-Oriented Approach* (N.Y.: Oxford University Press, 1993), 48-66.

At this point, however, we can make three observations. First, it is significant that the theme of the necessity of the death and resurrection of Jesus is at the heart of these sayings. This stands in contrast to recent studies which portray Jesus as a Cynic teacher for a community where death and resurrection was not at the core of its teaching.[13] At Bethsaida, however, one expects that reflection about the death and resurrection of Jesus would have occurred in light of discussions about Livia's death in 29 CE and her subsequent deification. Second, these sayings are linked to the concept of martyrdom, not only to the result of bearing much fruit, but also with the model of discipleship. This suggests a context of possible conflict with the Livia cult and perhaps in association with the persecutions carried out under Agrippa in 44 CE. What did discipleship mean, when leading figures like James had been put to death for his beliefs and when Peter had been imprisoned and forced to flee to another place (Acts 12)? Third, it points to a possible connection with Q, the synoptic sayings source, since the second saying has parallels in Q (Matt 10:37 = Luke 14:26 and Matt 10:39 = Luke 17:33).

Matthew 10:37	*Luke 14:26*
	Whoever comes to me and does
Whoever loves father or mother more	not hate father and mother,
than me is not worthy of me; and	
whoever loves son or daughter more	wife and children, brothers and sisters,
	yes, and even life itself,
than me is not worthy of me.	cannot be my disciple.
Matthew 10:39	*Luke 17:33*
Those who find their life	Those who try to make their life
will lose it,	secure, will lose it,
and those who lose their life	but those who lose their life
for my sake, will find it.	will keep it.

Bethsaida and Q

Perhaps the most intriguing area for studying the sayings of Jesus in relation to Bethsaida is the Q document used as a source for Matthew and Luke, yet unknown to Mark. A vast amount of research, analysis, and re-

13. John Dominic Crossan, *Jesus: A Revolutionary Biography* (San Francisco: Harper Collins, 1994); Burton L. Mack, *The Lost Gospel: The Book of Q and Christian Origins* (San Francisco: Harper Collins, 1993).

flection has led to the recreation of the text of about two hundred verses that reveal clues about its own origin. The consensus today seems to be that expressed by Udo Schnelle that "The Sayings Source presumably originated in (north) *Palestine*, since its theological perspective is directed primarily to Israel."[14] The sites most commonly suggested include cities of the Decapolis, Sepphoris, Tiberias, Capernaum, cities along the north shore of the Sea of Galilee, and Bethsaida.[15] The case for Bethsaida is a natural one since the only Galilean place names mentioned in Q are Bethsaida, Chorazin, and Capernaum—occurring in the woe saying that reflects the frustration of early Christian prophets against a lack of response in these cities. However, one finds clues that point to both the itinerant nature of the early preachers and the idea of settled communities. So the quest to locate Q more specifically has been somewhat elusive.

Clearly the focus in Q is on Israel, with statements of judgment, often with barbs against the Pharisees, balanced by a belief that the Q community itself understands what it means to keep the law. Yet there is clearly interaction with Gentiles who are held up as examples for virtuous living, such as the centurion of Capernaum. The implication is that the community has engaged itself in the Gentile mission and looks forward to the day when "people will come from east and west, from north and south, and will eat in the kingdom of God" (Matt 8:11 = Luke 13:29). Although there are frustrations, the sayings provide hope of abundant growth, especially with the parable of the mustard seed. While the Markan and Thomas versions closely reflect the authentic words of Jesus, the Q version (Luke 13:18-19) turns the parable into an allegory based on Daniel 4 and Ezekiel 17. The seed grows into a large tree that provides shelter and sustenance for Gentiles. This theme is reflected also in the parable of the great supper (Matt 22:1-14 = Luke 14:15-25), where outsiders are welcome at the meal.

It should not be surprising therefore that Q was originally written in Greek.[16] There is no question that Jesus' teaching was originally in Aramaic, but attempts to project an early Aramaic form of Q have failed, and studies

---

14. Udo Schnelle, *The History and Theology of the New Testament Writings* (Minneapolis, Fortress, 1998), 186.

15. Jonathan L. Reed provides bibliography for these suggestions in *Archaeology and the Galilean Jesus: A reexamination of the Evidence* (Harrisburg, PA: Trinity, 2000), 170, note 1. For Bethsaida, see Dale Allison, *The Jesus Tradition in Q* (Harrisburg, PA: Trinity, 1997), 53, and Ivan Haevner, *Q: The Sayings of Jesus* (Wilmington, DE: Michael Glazier, 1987), 42-5.

16. John Kloppenborg, *The Formation of Q: Trajectories of Ancient Wisdom Collections* (Philadelphia: Fortress, 1987), 41-88.

have shown a dependence on the Septuagint and not the Hebrew Scriptures.[17] So the language of Q would point to a context on the boundary where the community interacts with Gentiles and Greek-speaking Jews.

As would be expected for the mainly rural character of Galilee and the Golan, Q contains numerous agricultural metaphors including threshing floors, millstones, cultivated fields, the harvest, trees bearing good fruit, and many others. Yet as Jonathan Reed has noticed, it seems that the view of agrarian life comes from the perspective of the city, where day laborers are sent out into the harvest, where storehouses and granaries are located, and where the impersonal passive is used to describe the actions of those engaged in agriculture.[18]

Q sayings speak directly about cities, where there are gates, market places, and plazas where money-changers are present, courts are held, and prisons are located. Jesus asks the people what they *went out* to hear and to see when they encountered John the Baptist, and Jesus himself is criticized because his city-oriented dining practices are contrasted with those of John (Luke 7:33-34). In contrast to these encounters with John and his simplicity of dress, those in the cities are used to seeing kings walking around in fine clothes.

Clearly, this description of the Q community fits very well the city of Bethsaida. One can easily visualize the tetrarch Philip walking around the city in his fine clothes and people gathering for market-day with a buzz of activities. Yet, the one thing missing from Bethsaida and the territory of Philip is the element of conflict. With Josephus describing Philip as a populist ruler and with Jesus and his disciples finding refuge in his territory during the later stages of his ministry, a setting for Q within the territory of Antipas seems more likely. A convincing argument has been made by Gerd Theissen[19] that the prominent image of a reed, displayed on the coin of Antipas minted in 20 CE at the dedication of his capital Tiberias, is behind Jesus' question to the crowds:

> "What did you go out to the wilderness to look at?
> A reed shaken by the wind?" (Matt 11:7 = Luke 7:24)

---

17. Christopher M. Tuckett, *Q and the Early History of Christianity: Studies on Q* (Edinburgh: T & T Clark, 1996), 567-8.

18. Jonathan L. Reed, *Archaeology and the Galilean Jesus* (2000), 189-91.

19. Gerd Theissen, *The Gospels in Context: Social and Political History in the Synoptic Tradition* (Minneapolis: Fortress, 1991), 26-42.

The royal palaces, the soft robes, and the life of luxury could fit both Philip and Antipas, but the whole picture seems to fit Antipas best.

An early Christian cross?

By the early middle ages, pilgrims reported seeing a church at Bethsaida. Of course, permanent structures are rare prior to the time of Constantine. Early Christians still gathered in local synagogues and in the houses of members. Thus one would not expect any physical remains from the early Christian movement. From his first survey of et-Tell in the early 1980s Bargil Pixner reported his observation of an oblong slab of stone on the surface with an incised cross—two intersecting lines with "V" shaped extensions at the end of each arm. Because the stone had been removed prior to the beginning of excavations, this report adds little to our knowledge about Bethsaida.

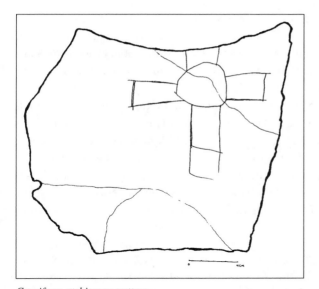

Cruciform etching on pottery

In May 1994, however, a cruciform incision appeared on a pottery shard during excavation of a room on the north-side of the courtyard of "the Winemaker's House" in Area C. Needless to say, this find attracted a lot of interest. The somewhat rough and imperfect cross inscription measures 4 1/4 inches by 5 1/2 inches although the top portion has broken off. It is composed of a circle in the center with four extended arms each made up of two connected parallel lines. The "circle" in the center is imperfect with a 1.65 inch horizontal diameter contrasting a 1.42 inch vertical diameter. Yet all three complete arms extend 2.12 inches from the center. Fainter lines continue another 1.30 inches from the lower arm which alter the appearance from a "Greek cross"—all arms equidistant—to a "Roman cross"—horizontal arms intersecting the vertical at a distance of one third from the top.

Four factors enter into the evaluation of this etching: the period of occupation for this house; the date of other finds from Locus 924; the type and age of the pottery itself; and a comparison of the form of the etching with parallels from the ancient world. One of the complications in determining the extent of occupation for a house like this is that many forms of pottery can only be dated to a general range that may cover several centuries. For example, the sealed locus of the wine cellar included pottery generally dated from the first century BCE to the first century CE. After more careful analysis, Sandra Fortner has dated the jars from the wine cellar from the third to first centuries BCE and the two casseroles, one from 50 BCE to 100 CE and the other from 25 BCE to 25 CE.[20] It now appears that the house was no longer occupied in the first century. Locus 924 itself included a second-century BCE coin of Antiochus 3; numerous pieces of Hellenistic pottery including a tall neck cooking pot, flask, shallow bowl, jugs, oil lamp, and wide-neck jar, and many others; but also one Roman decorated oil lamp. The evidence strongly points to a first-century BCE context, but the single Roman piece allows for a little ambiguity. As for the etched pottery, no rim or handle was found. Five shards can be pieced together to suggest an amphora or storage vessel. The largest shard measures fifteen by six inches, and the rim fragment points to an opening of over five inches. It does appear to be a large vessel such as an amphora or a storage vessel probably from the Roman period.[21] The figure was not part of the original design of the vessel, but was etched after firing.

20. Sandra A. Fortner, *Die Keramik und Kleinhundevon Bethsaida-Iulias am See Gennesaret, Israel* (München: Ludwig-Maximilians Universität, 2008), 85-86, catalogue # 443, 1075, 1088, 1103, 1104. In the preliminary reports, Rami Arav noted that "The jars and the casserole [in the wine cellar] date from the end of the second to the early first century BCE." Rami Arav, "Bethsaida, Preliminary Report, 1994-1996," in *Bethsaida* (1999), 2:99. In my earlier monograph I dated the jars from 100 BCE to 70 CE and the casserole to the first century CE. I chose the later part of the range. Strickert, *Bethsaida: Home of the Apostles* (1998), 150-151.

21. Petrographic analysis found no basalt fragments in the clay, so it was likely brought to Bethsaida from another location. The components suggest that it was made in western Galilee The clay was composed of marly (containing calcium carbonate) and also include terra rosa (a mixture containing iron) mudballs for thinning the clay. It was fired at a very hot temprature, 1,000 degrees C. Petrographic analysis was carried out by Dr. Yuval Goren of the Israel Antiquities Authorities in Jerusalem.

Regarding the form of the design, one must begin with the knowledge that the cross symbol was rarely used by Christians prior to the time of Constantine.[22] None of the few examples of cross designs by early Christians even closely resembles the form from Bethsaida. There are numerous cruciform figures also in other cultures. However, the form of a circle with four arms extending outward appears nowhere during this general period. While the form may appear through Christian eyes to resemble a cross, it could also be the symbol of the sun with rays reaching outward, or another such figure.

The cruciform etching must therefore be considered inconclusive.

22. Graydon F. Snyder, *Ante-Pacem: Archaeological Evidence of Church Life Before Constantine* (Mercer University Press, 1985), 27; Jack T. Sanders, *Schismatics, Sectarians, Dissidents, Deviants: The First One Hundred Years of Jewish-Christian Relations* (Valley Forge, PA: Trinity Press, 1993), 31-9; Jack Finegan, *The Archaeology of the New Testament* (Princeton: 1969), 220-60.

Chapter 17

John 12:24 and Livia *Karpophoros*

In the days shortly before his death in Jerusalem, Jesus spoke these interpretive words:

> Very truly, I tell you, unless a grain of wheat falls into the earth and dies, it remains just a single grain; but if it dies, it bears much fruit (John 12:24).

This saying was spoken when Philip and Andrew, two Bethsaida disciples, reported that there were "Greeks" wishing to see Jesus. A saying about grain sown and bearing fruit is by no means unusual—as the parables of the sower, mustard seed, and seed sown secretly. What is unique is the connection to the death and resurrection of Jesus. This can be understood against the background of Livia's death in 29 CE and the renaming of Bethsaida in her honor.

An Early Saying of Jesus

According to *The Five Gospels* of the Jesus Seminar, John 12:24 is one of only four Johannine sayings considered possibly authentic.[1] This saying is printed in gray, which means that it reflects the ideas of Jesus although not his exact words. This is surprising because there is no synoptic or Thomas parallel; however, a Pauline saying demonstrates that the imagery "has deep roots in the Christian tradition."[2]

---

1. Robert W. Funk, Roy W. Hoover, *et al.*, *The Five Gospels: The Search for the Authentic Words of Jesus* (New York: Polebridge Press, 1993), 431-32. Only John 4:44 received a pink or "probably" designation, while John 12:25 and 13:20 are both colored gray, which means that the ideas are close to those of Jesus.

2. Funk, *Jesus Seminar* (1993), 411.

> What you sow does not come to life unless it dies. And as for what you sow, you do not sow the body that is to be, but a bare seed, perhaps of wheat or of some other grain (1 Corinthians 15:36-37).

Since 1 Corinthians is usually dated to the early 50s CE, this would point to wide use of the saying in the first two decades after the death of Jesus on April 7, 30 CE.[3]

Years ago, Dodd asked whether John 12:24 also "should not be accepted as representing an element in the tradition as primitive and authentic as any-thing" contained in the Synoptics. He noted that in form it is very similar to a number of synoptic parables (salt, kingdom divided, eye, lost sheep) which he refers to as the form of an "observed invariable sequence" or "law of nature" that "if A occurs, then B occurs."[4] So there is a high degree of similarity with the Synoptic seed parallels: ὁ κόκκος τοῦ σίτου [the grain of wheat] is not unlike the κόκκος σινάπεως [a grain of mustard seed] of the mustard seed parable (Mark 4:31) and πεσὼν εἰς τὴν γῆν [falling into the earth] is almost identical to ἔπεσεν εἰς τὴν γῆν [it falls into the earth] of the parable of the sower (Mark 4:8). Only the introductory "very truly I say to you" and "it remains alone" (John 15) have a distinctively Johannine ring.[5] More important is the similarity in motif with the mustard seed parable that the one becomes many. According to Dodd, "It appears, therefore, that we have here a *pericope* which in form, in the character of its imagery, and in the whole manner in which it is presented . . . associates itself closely with the tradition of parabolic teaching as we know it from the Synoptics."[6]

The final words in the John 12:24 text καρπόν φέρει [it bears fruit] are significant. The actual epithet καρπόφορος [fruit bearing] occurs only in Acts 14:17—a sermon by Paul in the town of Lystra in Asia Minor against the backdrop of a temple of Zeus in which Paul points to the one creator

---

3. Hans Conzlemann, *1 Corinthians,* trans. James W. Leitch, Hermeneia Series (Phila-delphia: Fortress, 1975), 281, notes that the analogy of human life and the cycle of nature is common in the ancient world, yet what is new in the Christian saying is the necessity of death as a condition of life.

4. C. H. Dodd, *Historical Tradition in the Fourth Gospel* (Cambridge: Cambridge Uni-versity Press, 1963), 366-9. See also Rudolf Schnackenburg, *The Gospel according to St. John* (New York: The Seabury Press, 1980), 2:383; Raymond E. Brown, *The Gospel According to John,* The Anchor Bible (Garden City, NY: Doubleday, 1966), 1:471-3.

5. J. N. Sanders, A Commentary on the Gospel according to St. John (New York: Harper & Row: 1968), 292; Brown (1966) 1:471.

6. Dodd (1963), 369. Similar opinions are expressed in Brown (1966), 1:471-3; Schnack-enburg (1980), 383.

God worshipped in Judaism as καρπόφορος. Likewise in Romans 7:4, 5 and Colossians 1:6, 10 he uses the metaphor for Christian behavior—with the verbal form καρποφορέω.

The predominant expression used in the Synoptics is καρπόν ποιεῖν [to produce fruit], used a total of fourteen times in Q (Matt. 3:8 = Luke 3:8; Matt 3:10 = Luke 3:9; Matt 7:16-20 = Luke 6:43-44), Matthew's unique material (Matt 13:36; 21:43), and Luke's unique material (Luke 13:9). The Markan parable of the sower uses καρπόν δουναῖ [to give fruit] (Mark 4:7, 8; Matt 13:8 while Luke 8:8 has καρπόν ποιεῖν [to produce fruit]). Only in the final verse of the explanation to the parable of the sower do all three writers use καρποπορέω (Mark 4:20; Matt 13:23; Luke 8:15). This same expression is repeated by Mark in the parable of the seed sown secretly (Mark 4:28).

John uses exclusively καρπος φερεῖν [to bear fruit]. The first occasion is the Passover week dying grain saying (John 12:24). Three chapters later, Jesus gives the "I am the vine; you are the branches" discourse, which employs καρπός φερεῖν seven times (John 15:1-16). This is clearly a favorite Johannine expression. With John's often subtle sacramental theology, one can see a clear link between the two sayings, one focusing on the fruit of sown grain and the other on the fruit of the vine. The dying grain saying thus provides an introduction to the grain and vine motifs common to both Passover and Eucharist. The point is that through the single grain and the single vine comes much fruit.

Unlike the Synoptics, there is no reference to a Thursday evening Passover meal nor to the Eucharistic words in John 12-15. Rather one is directed back to the previous Passover when Jesus stayed behind at Bethsaida (John 6), where the same disciples Philip and Andrew played leadership roles, and when Jesus fed the five thousand taking the grain of the field and producing much fruit.

The Demeter myth

John 12:24 is very similar to other sayings of Jesus, but there is one critical difference. The grain does not represent the word or the kingdom as in the Synoptic parables. Rather it represents a person whose death is inevitable and necessary. The parable not only speaks of the seed "falling into the earth," but twice it is also mentioned that the seed "dies."[7] The use of the article ὁ κόκκος του σίτου [the grain of wheat] makes it clear that

---

7. Brown (1966), 1:472, states, "the peculiar feature of this parable is the insistence that only through death is the fruit borne."

the parable is not about seeds in general, but about one particular seed,[8] whose death will lead to bearing much fruit.

The closest parallels for this symbolism are found in a Hellenistic religious background and especially mystery religions where the annual cycle of death and rebirth was dramatized with an ear of grain.[9] In the mysteries of Eleusis Demeter[10] traveled to the underworld to bring back her daughter Kore so that the earth could bring forth corn. In time, hopes of individual immortality were thus linked to this agricultural festival.[11] The grain myth is known from the eighth-century BCE Homeric *Hymn of Demeter* which details the abduction of Demeter's daughter Kore to the underworld, her rescue, and finally the explanation of the life cycle of grains with the four-month period in which the fields are barren corresponding to the return of Kore to the underworld each year. The planting thus is understood as a mystery in which the seed is sown to its death below the surface of the ground, yet sprouts new life and an abundant crop for another year.[12] The sanctuary became prominent in the religious life of Athens. A late fifth-century BCE document describes how Athenians made regular grain payments to support the sanctuary:

> Resolved by the council and the people. . . , on the proposal of the drafting committee: that the Athenians give first-fruits of the grain to the Two Goddesses according to the ancestral custom and the oracle of Delphi.

After explaining the details of this transaction, the document concludes:

> May there be many good things and an abundance of grain of good quality to those who do this. . . . [13]

8. Cf. Brown (1966), 1:467, who refers to "a parabolic use of the article" as in Luke 8:5, 11. See also C. K. Barrett, *The Gospel According to St. John* (London: S.P.C.K., 1960), 352.

9. H. J. Holtzmann, *Evangelium, Briefe und Offenbarung es Johannes* (Tübingen: Mohr, 1908); Brown (1966), 1:472; Barrett (1960), 352; Sanders (1968), 293.

10. Also known as Brimo, Ceres [Roman], Deo, and Doso, and sometimes identified with her daughter, Kore, Kore Persephone, and Isis [Egypt].

11. Herbert Jennings Rose, "Demeter," *The Oxford Classical Dictionary*, 2nd ed. N. G. L. Hammond and H. H. Scullard (Oxford: Clarendon Press, 1970), 324.

12. David G. Rice and John E. Stambaugh, *Sources for the Study of Greek Religion* (Chico, CA: Scholars Press, 1979), 171-83; Marvin W. Meyer, ed., *The Ancient Mysteries: A Sourcebook* (San Francisco: Harper & Row, 1987), 20-30.

13. *[IG] Inscriptiones Graecae. 1873.* (Berlin: W. de Gruyter, 1873) I, 76.1-46. Translation in Rice and Stambaugh (1979), 185-87.

At about the same time, Herodotus documents the festive nature of the annual processions from Athens to Eleusis (*Hist.* 8.65). This same procession is alluded to a generation later (405 BCE) by the playwright Aristophanes in *The Frogs*. Here Dionysius, on a journey to the underworld, encounters initiates into the Eleusinian mysteries who celebrate in death as they did in life. The chorus sings a processional hymn to Proserpina:

> March, chanting loud your lays,
> Your hearts and voices raising,
> The Saviour goddess praising
>> Who vows she'll still
> Our city save to endless days,
> Whate'er Thorycion's will (lines 378-83).

The leader then responds to introduce another hymn, this time to Demeter:

> Break off the measure, and change the time, and now with
>> chanting and hymns adorn
> Demeter, goddess mighty and high, the harvest-queen,
>> the giver of corn (lines 384-85).

Here in the final line, the epithet καρπόφορος is used of Demeter. She is "the harvest queen, the giver of corn" [τὴν καρποφόρον βασίλεαν].

The same basic expression had been used of Demeter by Herodotus in describing fertile Mesopotamia which abundantly brings forth the grain of Demeter (Δήμητρος καρπὸν ἐκφερειν) an expression repeated several lines later (*Hist.* 1. 193). From inscriptions from Pessinus[14] and Paros[15] it would appear that the epithet καρπόφορος was well known for Demeter. In the second century CE, Pausanius mentions in Tegea a temple of Demeter and Kore which was called καρπόφορος (*Description of Greece,* 8.53.7).

A similar situation occurs in Rome with Demeter's equivalent Ceres—literary references point to the spread of this cult in Rome by at least the fifth century BCE.[16] It was understood that the name Ceres itself derived (with the similarity of "c" and "g" sounds) from the idea of bearing fruit. The Augustan scholar Varro quotes the poet Ennius as saying "She, because she

---

14. [CIG] *Corpus Inscriptionum Graecarum,* ed. Broeckh, August, *et. al.,* (Berlin: Berolini, 1828), 4082.

15. IG 12 (5).226.

16. Barbette Stanley Spaeth, *The Roman Goddess Ceres* (Austin: University of Texas Press, 1996), 1.

bears fruits, (is called) Ceres."—*Quae Quod gerit fruges, Ceres.*[17] The Latin *frugifera* [bearing fruit]—equivalent of καρπόφορος—is used as an epithet of Ceres.[18] As Barbette Stanley Spaeth notes, "The Greeks gave Demeter the epithet *Karpophoros* (Bearer of Fruit), while the Romans called Ceres *Frugifera* (Bearer of Fruit)."[19] The impact of the dying grain myth is widespread.

There are two major problems with the Demeter cult as background for the grain saying in John 12:24. First, its Hellenistic character does not seem to fit the other evidence of an early, possibly authentic saying of Jesus. Second, the emphasis in John is on an action which really risks losing one's life and requires a death that is real. As Raymond Brown has pointed out, this is weakened by "the automatic and immutable character of this [Hellenistic] cycle."[20] It does seem far-fetched to make a connection with this saying of Jesus and Hellenistic mystery religions.

The Greek connection

An adequate explanation for the connection between the grain imagery of one becoming many and death becoming life has long eluded scholars. John offers a clue by setting this saying in the context of the Jerusalem Passover when Greeks[21] wish to see Jesus. The mention of Greeks is highly significant. On the one hand, it is totally unexpected from a historical perspective because Greeks would not be permitted to eat the Passover meal,[22] and it is unusual from a literary perspective because the Greeks are not mentioned again after this introduction. Their place in the episode is more symbolic than historical. The author seems to be giving the reader a clue perhaps to the upcoming gentile mission, but perhaps also to the significance of this saying. This is underscored further by including as intermediaries Philip and Andrew—the only disciples with truly Greek names. Likewise the author

17. Varro *Ling.* 5.64. See also Cicero *Nat. D.* 2.26.67; 3.30.52; 24.62.

18. *Sen. Phoen.* 219; *Claud. Rapt. Pros.* 2. 138; *Germ. Arat* 38; Similary Ovid (*Met.* 5.490) makes use of the epithet *frugum genetrix.*

19. Spaeth, *The Roman Goddess Ceres* (1996), 130.

20. Brown (1966), 1:472.

21. The term here is Ἕλληνές which refers to gentiles, not Ἑλληνίσται which would refer to Greek-speaking Jews. John does not use ἔθνος to refer to the gentiles, but to the Jewish people. Haenchen suggests that John 12:20 refers to the "Greek world in general, and thus also the pagan world." Ernst Haenchen, *John*, trans. Robert Funk, Hermeneia Series (Philadelphia: Fortress, 1984), 96. See also Brown (1966), 1:466; Schnackenburg (1980), 381; Barrett (1960), 351; Sanders (1968), 290; E. D. Hoskyns, *The Fourth Gospel* (Lonon: Faber & Faber, Ltd., 1947), 423.

22. Exodus 12:48; Josephus *War*, 6.422-7; Schackenburg (1980), 381.

reminds the reader that these disciples are from Bethsaida—a piece of information that had already been mentioned once in John 1:44—an area noted for its "mixed population" (Josephus, *War,* 3.57). In order to understand the saying of Jesus in John 12:24, the reader should look to the Greek cultural and religious setting of Bethsaida.[23]

Livia Cult

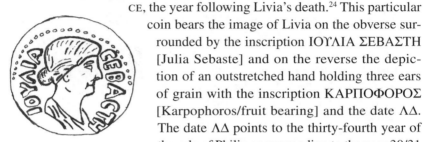

The mention of Bethsaida in John 12 is significant because the tetrarch Philip had founded Bethsaida as Julias and issued a Julia Sebaste coin in 30 CE, the year following Livia's death.[24] This particular coin bears the image of Livia on the obverse surrounded by the inscription ΙΟΥΛΙΑ ΣΕΒΑΣΤΗ [Julia Sebaste] and on the reverse the depiction of an outstretched hand holding three ears of grain with the inscription ΚΑΡΠΟΦΟΡΟΣ [Karpophoros/fruit bearing] and the date ΛΔ. The date ΛΔ points to the thirty-fourth year of the rule of Philip corresponding to the year 30/31 CE—a year in which Philip minted at least two and possibly three other coins:[25]

- A small coin with Philip's image.[26]
- A coin with Tiberius' image and the temple at Caesarea Philippi with the letters ΚΤΙΣ denoting the founding of the city.[27]

Philip coin – 30 CE – Image of Livia

23. The reference to Bethsaida of Galilee perhaps focuses on "Galilee of the Gentiles" as a territory of mixed culture and should be contrasted with Jerusalem rather than making a distinction between Galilee and Golan. Brown (1966), 466; Barrett (1960), 351.

24. Fred Strickert, "The First Woman to be Portrayed on a Jewish Coin: Julia Sebaste," *Journal for the Study of Judaism in the Persian, Hellenistic, and Roman Periods* 31 (2002), 65-91; Ya'akov Meshorer, *A Treasury of Jewish Coins* (Nyack, NY: Amphora Books, 2001), plate 51, number 107.

25. Arie Kindler, "The Coins of the Tetrarch Philip and Bethsaida," *Bethsaida: A City* (1999), 2:245-9, notes two parallels, one minted by Agrippa for his wife Kypros and another minted by Agrippa 2—both are likely dependent on the Philip coin. Ya'akov Meshorer, *Ancient Jewish Coinage* (Dix Hills, NY: Amphora Books, 1982), 2:246, 250.

26. Meshorer, *Ancient Jewish Coinage* (1982), plate 8, number 12.

27. Arie Kindler, "A Coin of Herod Philip: The Earliest Portrait of a Herodian Ruler," *IEJ* 21 (1971), 162-63. Coins with Augustus' image were minted in 1, 8, and 12 CE and with

- A large coin with the double image of Augustus and Livia under the legend ΣΕΒΑΣΤΩΝ.[28]

The *KARPOPHOROS* legend and the grain symbolism on the Julia Sebaste coin point to Livia's role as a Demeter/Ceres figure. As Gertrude Grether has noted:

> The tendency of the art of the period seems to have been to stress her office as priestess of Augustus and her association with the deities of plenty and fertility. The general idea expressed is that, since Augustus is no longer on earth but has taken his place among the divinities, his blessings must come to the Roman people through the mediation of his priestess, Julia Augusta.[29]

Coin of Philip – 30 CE – Image of Livia

The extent of the assimilation of Livia with the goddess Demeter/Ceres is confirmed by inscriptions from throughout the empire:

- From the island Gaulos near Malta:
  CERERI IULIAE AUGUSTAE DIVI AUGUSTI MATRI TI CAESARIS AUGUSTI
  Translation: [dedicated to] "Ceres Julia Augusta, wife of the deified Augustus, mother of Tiberius Caesar Augustus."[30]
- From Lampsacus:
  Ἰουλίαν Σεβαστὴν Ἑστίαν νέαν Δήμητρα
  Translation: [dedicated to] "Julia Augusta Hestia, the new Demeter."[31]

Tiberius' image in 15, 26, 29, 30, and 33 CE. Meshorer, *Ancient Jewish Coinage* (1982), plate 8, number 10a.

28. Meshorer, *Ancient Jewish Coinage* (1982), plate 7, number 6; Jacob Maltiel-Gerstenfeld, *260 Years of Ancient Jewish Coins* (Tel Aviv: Kol Printing Service Ltd., 1982), 148-9.

29. Gertrude Grether, "Livia and the Roman Imperial Cult," *American Journal of Philology* 67 (1946), 222-52, especially 245.

30. Spaeth (1996), cat. 1.1; Elizabeth Bartman, *Portraits of Livia: Imaging the Imperial Woman in Augustan Rome* (Cambridge: Cambridge University Press, 1999), Epig. Cat. 50.

31. Spaeth (1966), cat. 1.2; Bartman (1999), Epig. Cat. 55.

- From Amphrodisias:
  Θεᾶς Ἰουλίας νέας Δήμητρος
  Translation: [dedicated by the priests] "of the goddess, Julia, the new Demeter."[32]
- From Nepet:
  Cereri August
  Matri Agr
  Translation: [offerings dedicated] "to Ceres Augusta, mother of the fields."[33]
- From Cyzicus:
  Αὐτοκράτορα Καίσαρα θεόν θεοῦ υἱόν
  Σεβαστὸν καὶ Λιουίαν θεὰν Δήμητηρά . . .
  Translation: "The god Imperator Caesar Augustus, son of a god, and the goddess Livia, Demeter . . ."[34]

The impression is quite clear that the fruits of Demeter/Ceres are now bestowed through the benefactress Livia/Julia.

The cult of Ceres had arrived in Rome as early as the fifth century BCE with worship at the Aventine where Temples of Ceres, Liber, and Libera paralleled the Eleusinian triad. Nine different coin types of Ceres were used already for the years 48 through 42 BCE.[35] It was Augustus himself who initiated the link between Livia and Demeter/Ceres after he himself had been initiated into the Eleusian mysteries in 31 BCE, just after the battle of Actium (Dio Cassius, *Hist.* 54.7). On that occasion, the people of Eleusis erected statues to both Octavian and Livia. An inscription on the base for the latter read:

> Ὁ δ[ῆμ]ος
> Λιβίαν Δρουσίλλαν
> [Αὐ]τοκράτορος Καίσαρος
> γυναῖκα
> Translation: "The people [dedicated the] statue of Livia Drusilla, wife of Imperator Caesar."[36]

---

32. Spaeth (1996), cat.1.3.
33. Spaeth (1996), cat. 1.6; Bartman (1999), Epig Cat. 63.
34. Bartman (1999), Epig Cat. 7.
35. Spaeth (1996), 98.
36. Bartman (1999), Epig Cat. 1.

Her statue does not survive. Susan Wood argues that Livia herself may have been initiated into the Eleusinian rituals when she accompanied Augustus on a second trip to Eleusis in 19 CE.[37]

Following the return of Augustus from campaigns in Spain and Gaul, the Senate decreed in 13 BCE the erection of the *Ara Pacis Augustae* to celebrate the return of peace—the *Pax Romana.* This altar is the first time that identifiable mortal men and women were to appear on an official state relief in Rome. No less than ninety figures make up a stately procession on the north and south friezes with Augustus and Livia dominant, projecting the image of a ruling couple with shared powers—they alone wear both veil and laurel wreath—and emphasizing the relation between lasting peace and the continuation of this dynasty.[38]

The larger-than-human status of Livia is emphasized by the similarity in her depiction with a mother figure on the eastern panel often named *Italia*[39] who, crowned with a wreath of wheat and poppies, holds two children in her lap. Flanked by nymphs, with a grazing sheep and a reclining lamb at her feet, and surrounded by various plants and fruits such as pomegranates, grapes, and nuts, the *Italia* figure clearly portrays the ideal nurturing figure which Barbette Stanley Spaeth identifies as the goddess Ceres.[40] The Augustan visual message is paralleled in writing by Ovid:

> Peace nourishes Ceres
> and Ceres is the nursling of peace.[41]

Likewise Horace writing in 13 BCE, the year of Augustus' campaigns in Spain and Gaul, declares:

> The fatherland yearns for Caesar. (For when he is here),
> the cow in safety roams through the fields, Ceres and
> nourishing Prosperity nurture the fields, the ships fly
> over the pacified sea (*Carm.* 4. 5.16-19).

37. Susan Wood, *Imperial Women: A Study in Public Images, 40 BC-AD 68* (Leiden: E. J. Brill, 2000), 92-93; Dio Cassius, *Hist.* 54.9.10.

38. Bartman (1999), 86-93.

39. Both figures are veiled and crowned in a similar fashion. A. Bonnano, *Roman Relief Portraiture to Septimus Severus.* British Archaeological Reports Supplement 6 (Oxford: Oxford University Press, 1976), 28.

40. Barbette Stanley Spaeth, "The Goddess Ceres in the Ara Pacis Augustae and the Carthage Relief," *American Journal of Archaeology* 98 (1994), 65-100.

41. *Pax Cererem nutrit, Pacis alumna Ceres.* Ovid, *Fast.* I, 704.

Upon Augustus' return, Horace declares the promise fulfilled: "Your era, Caesar, has brought back abundant fruits to the fields" (*Carm.* 4. 15.4-5).

To underscore the connection between Livia and Ceres Augustus chose to dedicate the altar on January 30, 9 BCE, the birthday of Livia. In 7 CE, following the adoption of Tiberius by Augustus, the emperor dedicated two other altars in Rome, the *Arae Cereris Matris* and *Opis Augustae*, serving to link Livia and the goddess Ceres.[42] Likewise Augustus restored the ancient Temples of Ceres, Liber, and Libera which were then rededicated by Tiberius in 17 CE (Tacitus, *Annals* 2.49).

The identification of Livia with Ceres was very useful in that the goddess seemed to represent a variety of symbols. Not only was the connection with fertility, *karpophoros*, peace and prosperity, but the ancient myth of Ceres and Proserpina (Demeter and Kore) represented the virtues of chastity and motherhood. Ceres was the ideal symbol for the Augustan program, and Livia as the grand mother played the role perfectly.[43] With the death of Drusus, the heir apparent, on a military campaign in 9 BCE, Livia along with her son Tiberius moved into the spotlight.

Beginning in 2 BCE and continuing to his death in 14 CE, coins of Augustus depicted on the reverse a seated female who holds a scepter in her right hand and wheat stalks in the left.[44] This same imagery was adopted on official state coins of Tiberius—the tribute coin[45]—and of Claudius in 42 CE after the deification of Livia.[46] The inscription on the latter—*Diva Augusta*—makes clear the figure is Livia.[47] A coin from Alexandria in 10/11 CE depicts Livia on the obverse with Euthenia/Abundantia on the reverse.[48]

---

42. Grether (1946), 226.

43. Spaeth (1996), 113.

44. Spaeth (1996), fig. 40—[RIC] *Roman Imperial Coinage,* ed. Harold Mattingly *et al.,* (London: Spink, 1923), 1:56.219; [BMCRE] *Coins of the Roman Empire in the British Museum,* ed. Harold Mattingly (London: The British Museum, 1975), Augustus 544.

45. BMCRE 1, 124-7, nos. 30-60, plates 22.20-23.9; RIC 1:95.25-29.

46. BMCRE 1, 195, no. 224, plate 37.7.

47. BMCRE 1:91; Spaeth (1996), 171; Bartman (1999), 103; Wood (2000), 88-89; Grether (1946), 227; For a contrary view, see John Pollini, "Man or God? Divine Assimilation and Imitation in the Late Republic and Early Principate," *Between Republic and Empire: Interpretation of Augustus and His Principate* (Berkeley: University of California Press, 1990), 334-57, especially 350. In the provinces during the rule of Tiberius, a number of imitations of this figure include the name Livia in the inscription. [RPC] *Roman Republican Coinage,* ed. M. H. Crawford (New York: Cambridge University Press, 1974), 341 –Caesaraugusta; 711 –Hippo Regius; 3919 –Cyprus. Bartman (1999), 118, n. 25.

48. RPC 5053.

Tribute Penny – Tiberius Denarius, © The Trustees of the British Museum

Susan Wood notes that "during the period of her widowhood, Livia first began to be explicitly identified as 'Ceres Augusta.'"[49] According to Elizabeth Bartman, "Ceres was Livia's most politically innocuous (and consequently, most widespread) divine evocation."[50] In addition to coin images, Bartman has catalogued a large corpus of sculpted portraits of Livia which include a significant representation of Ceres/Demeter figures. Perhaps the most common mark of identification of Ceres in art is the *corona spicea*—a crown of wheat. Here Ovid's rendition of the myth of Ceres and Proserpina seems to have been influential. He describes the daughter's return as affecting the land:

> Only then did Ceres recover her expression and her spirit and she put the wheat sheaf garland on her hair; and a great harvest was produced in the fallow fields and the threshing floor scarcely received the heaped up wealth (*Fast.* 4.615-18).

This is depicted well by a sardonyx cameo from the Tiberian era which presents Livia facing left, veiled, and wearing a very distinct floral wreath.[51] This is common in numerous statues.

In Tibullus, where *Pax* is given the attributes of Ceres, the stalk of wheat is held forth in the hand—as in the case of the seated women on the imperial coins mentioned above. Tibullus describes the role of *Pax* including a descriptive reference to the wheat imagery:

49. Wood (2000), 112.
50. Bartman (1999), 93.
51. Bartman (1999), 190, fig. 185 = Spaeth (1996), fig. 10—from Museo Archeologico 14549- Florence. Height 4.5 cm.

"Livia on sardonyx." Courtesy of Museo
Archeologico di Firenze, Italy.

*Ceres Borghese "Portrait de l'Impératrice Livie figurée en Cérès, éspouse d'Octave-Auguste
en 38 av. JC," Paris, Musée du Louvre], Réunion des Musées Nationaux/Art Resource, NY*

Meanwhile let Peace tend our fields. Bright Peace first led under the curved
yoke the cows about to plow the fields; Peace nourished the vine plants and
stores the grape juice so that pure wine might flow for the son from the father's
jar. In peace shine the hoe and plowshare, but decay masters the sad arms of
the harsh soldier in the darkness. . . . Then come to us, nourishing Peace,
and hold the wheat stalk in your hand, and let fruits pour out of your shining
breast (*Corpus Tibullianum, Book Two:* 1.10.45-50, 67-68).

The *corona spicea*, hand-held wheat stalks, cornucopia, and other floral
arrangements, when employed in sculptural representations of Livia, serve
to identify her with Ceres/ Demeter.

The Ceres Borghese with a likely provenance near Rome brings together several of these characteristic symbols.[52] Wearing the floral wreath,
Livia stands erect while clutching a cornucopia of fruit to her left side and
extending her right hand with stalks of wheat. Bartman suggests that this

52. Bartman (1999), 45, fig. 45, cat. 3—Musee du Louvre (Paris) Ma 1242. Height 2.53
meters, probably from near Rome.

"Velletri Livia." Courtesy of
Holkham Hall, Wells-next-the-Sea,
Norfolk.

"Cameo of Livia." Courtesy of Vienna
Kunsthistorisches Museum.

"reflects an important portrait of Livia" in Rome since a similar figure has been discovered near Spanish Cordoba.[53]

In contrast to the highly decorated Ceres Borghese, the Velletri statue is highlighted alone by the stalks of wheat held erect in the left hand.[54] The figure of Livia is dressed in chiton and himation, veiled, and with waves of hair framing her face. Yet there is no question. It is Livia in the guise of Ceres.

Perhaps the closest parallel to the depiction on the Philip coin commemorating the city of Bethsaida/Julias is a cameo figure from Vienna.[55] The figure of Livia, enthroned and diademed, faces to the left gazing at a bust of Augustus that she holds in her right hand—thus providing a dating

53. Bartman (1999), 106.

54. Bartman (1999), 152, fig. 132, cat. 15—Wells (Norfolk), Holkham Hall. From the Villa Ginnetti in Velletri, white marble, height 2.08 meters.

55. Bartman (1999), 104, fig. 79, cat. 110 – Sardonyx from Vienna, Kunsthistorisches Museum IX A 95. Height 10 cm.

for this piece shortly after Augustus' death in 14 CE. It is the depiction of the stalks of grain, however, that is important here. Unlike other parallels where the ears of grain are bunched together, here the artist has depicted three distinct ears. Like the depiction on the coin of Philip, they are held in the left hand—in this case oversized perhaps for emphasis. One should also not overlook the similarity in context. Just as the gem depicts Livia in mourning following the death of Augustus, so also the coin of Philip, dated to the year 30 CE, is clearly a response to Livia's death.

The Ceres/Demeter imagery serves to convey ideas of fertility, prosperity, and peace as well as virtues of motherhood and chastity—all of which were important in the Augustan program. At the same time, one should not overlook the role of the Ceres/Demeter myth focusing on life and rebirth. So while the gem depicts Augustus in his deified state, that message of continuity of life is affirmed in the symbol of the wheat stalks. There is mourning, yet there is also a message of hope. The program of Augustus will continue on in the role of Livia as benefactress.

Karpophoros Epithet

As seen above, *karpophoros* [fruit bearing] was the dominant slogan associated with the goddess Demeter. The coin of Philip dedicated to Julia/Livia is the only known example of ΚΑΡΠΟΦΟΡΟΣ on a coin. It is important to note that the epithet does not merely call attention to the goddess Demeter, but it explicitly describes Livia herself as *karpophoros*, identifying the imperial mother with the goddess.

An inscription on a large stele from Ephesus dating from 19 to 23 CE offers a parallel. While dedicated to Livia, the decree describes the special favors granted to the *Demetriastai* [priests of Demeter] among whom several are named including

ἱερεῖς. . . τῆς Σεβαστῆς Δήμητρος Καρποφόρου
[Priests. . . of Augusta Demeter Karpophoros][56]

This is the beginning of a trend in which the epithet *karpophoros* is appropriated by women of the imperial family so that later inscriptions will designate in a similar way the following imperial women:

- Agrippina the Elder, wife of Germanicus and mother of Caligula:
  Αἰολὶς Καρποφόρος (from Mytilene on Lesbos);

---

56. [SEG] *Supplementum Epigraphicum Graecum* (Leiden, 1923), 4.515; Bartman (1999), Epig. cat. 45; Spaeth (1996), cat. 1.4.

- Agrippina the Younger, sister of Caligula, daughter of Agrippina the elder, wife of Claudius, mother of Nero:
  Αἰολίς Καρποφόρος (from Thermae); and
  Αἰολίς Καρποφόρος (from Mytilene);
- Sabina, wife of Hadrian:
  Δημητήρ Καρποφόρος (from Tchelidjik); and
  Καρποφόρος (from Athens).[57]

These later examples indicate that the use of the epithet for Livia herself may have been more extensive. Certainly Philip's subjects must have had some frame of reference to have understood the *karpophoros* inscription on his coin.

Livia coins in a Jewish provenance

There is a well-known episode when Jesus, confronted by Jerusalem authorities concerning taxes, calls for a coin and says, "Render unto Caesar, the things that are Caesar's and to God the things that are God's" (Mark 12:15). The saying revolves around the image of Caesar Tiberius depicted on the coin. A lesser-known detail is that the reverse depicts an image of Livia, seated and in the guise of *Pax*.[58] For over thirty years, this particular coin type had circulated throughout the empire and served as the "tribute penny" (see photo, page 246) presented to Jesus in Jerusalem. Livia was a well-recognized figure even among those living far on the eastern edges of the Roman Empire on Palestinian soil. The Roman procurators of Judaea residing in Caesarea Maritima also issued their own coins among which were a number dedicated to Livia. In deference to Jewish

*Coin of Procurator Gratus –
17 CE*

custom no images of Livia were depicted. Yet during the years 15 through 26 CE, Valerius Gratus issued no less than six different coins with a ΙΟΥΛΙΑ [Julia] inscription.[59] The symbols employed were inoffensive cornucopia,

---

57. Spaeth (1996), cat. 4.1; 6.1 and 2; 12.3 and 4.
58. BMCRE, no. 35.
59. Meshorer (1982), 2:173; Gratus coin for year 17 CE, Meshorer (1982), plate 31, no. 16.

Coin of Pontius Pilate – 29 CE

amphorae, vine leaves, and olive leaf wreathes. Still those symbols did point to the concept of fertility and abundance associated with the empress mother.

In the year 29 CE and again in 30 CE, following Livia's death, the new procurator Pontius Pilate continued the practice of issuing Livia coins now with a ΙΟΥΛΙΑ ΚΑΙΣΑΡΟΣ [Julia of Caesar] inscription.[60] Pilate, known for his willingness to test the boundaries of Jewish law (Josephus, *Ant.* 18.55-62; *War* 2.167-77; Philo, *Embassy to Gaius* 38.299-305), did not refrain from images that were associated with the imperial cult such as the *simpulum* and the *lituus*. In addition, imagery of three ears of grain, which are significant for Livia, appear on Pilate's coins. The frequency of these Livia coins in modern coin markets attests to their wide circulation. The holders of such coins were surely aware of the importance of this individual named Julia.

The Death of Livia

The Demeter myth of the dying grain was spread throughout the Roman Empire through its appropriation by Livia the wife of Augustus; and the impact of Livia on Palestinian soil was communicated through the naming of cities and the minting of coins. It is, however, at the point of her death in 29 CE that the connection of Livia and the dying grain myth is made explicit. The evidence for this is the use of grain imagery on Livia coins both by Pilate and by Philip in 29 and 30 CE.

It is well known that Livia sought apotheosis for herself, as had been the case with Julius Caesar and her husband Augustus. In the eastern provinces, she was already treated as a goddess while living. Yet in Rome, these attributes of Ceres and other goddesses were still seen as more symbolic. However, a falling out between Tiberius and Livia during her latter years resulted in Tiberius going into exile himself in 26 CE to Capreae from where he ruled. Even news of her death was not enough to bring him back to Rome. Fear that her followers might stage a grandiose funeral and pressure for her apotheosis, he stayed away only sending orders that her funeral be kept

---

60. Meshorer (1982), 2:180, 283; Pilate coin of 29 CE, Meshorer (1982), plate 31, no. 21.

simple and he asked the Senate to declare the year of mourning (Dio *Hist.* 58.2; Suetonius, *Tiberius* 51; Tacitus, *Annals* 5.1-2) – a significant move in contrast to the declaration forbidding mourning following Augustus' death since he was to be seen as a god (Dio *Hist.* 56.41). It was the continued popularity of Livia and a grassroots movement that eventually led to her deification by Claudius in 41 CE (Dio *Hist.* 60; Suetonius, *Claudius* 11).

The Pontius Pilate coin of 29 CE is appropriate for a year of mourning to commemorate Livia's death. Thus the inscription ΙΟΥΛΙΑ ΚΑΙΣΑΡΟΣ [Julia of Caesar] notes her special role as wife of Augustus and mother of the emperor and the *simpulum* on the obverse points to her role as priestess in the imperial cult. Yet it is the use of grain imagery on the reverse that identifies Livia as the new Demeter.

The motif of drooping ears of grain on this particular coin resembles the Vienna gem where Livia, holding the bust of Augustus, was clearly in mourning. In contrast, Ceres Borghese and Velletri statues portray Livia with erect stalks of wheat. What is especially interesting about the Pilate coin is that three distinct ears of grain are depicted rather than the common, less-distinct bunches found on many statues.

"Livia with Augustus and the bust of a young man on a sardonyx"—
St. Petersburg, Hermitage, The State Hermitage Museum,
St. Petersburg. Photograph © The State Hermitage Museum.

A gem from St. Petersburg also portrays a trinity of figures.[61] The positioning of Livia and Augustus –this time an actual figure rather than a bust—closely parallels the Vienna gem. Here Livia, bedecked with the Ceres *corona spicea,* is portrayed as priestess with the veil and her uplifted right hand. New to this depiction is the central character of a young boy. His identity, while debated for years, must remain uncertain. The obvious connection with Tiberius cannot be proven because of lack of facial resemblance and the incongruency of age.[62] Nevertheless, the youthful figure surely represents the promise of the Augustan dynasty. With both Augustus and Livia depicted with divine attributes, the empire's future will be in the hands of youthful mortals—including Tiberius. The coin of Pilate would seem to follow this idea. The single erect ear of grain in the center would likely represent the living Emperor Tiberius while the two drooping ears would represent the now fallen Augustus and Livia. Such a depiction is not unlike the Vienna gem where, in Livia's hand-held bundle, the lower ear of grain seems to recede giving way to two stronger, healthier looking stalks. Here this lower receding stalk would represent the deceased, though deified Augustus. The Pilate coin has taken that one step further in response to the death of Livia in 29 CE and the Roman Senate's declaration of a year of mourning. The representation of the drooping ears of grain on the coin of Pilate was thus consistent with that decree. With Augustus and Livia now dead, Pilate's future was clearly dependent upon his favor with Tiberius.

Coin of Agrippa 1—42 CE

Like the Pilate coin, Agrippa 1 also employed the imagery of three grain stalks in a coin minted in 42 CE. Only this time all the stalks of grain are

---

61. Bartman (1999), 105, fig. 81, cat 105—sardonyx gem – St. Petersburg, Hermitage Z 149. Diameter 8.3 cm.

62. Bartman (1999), 103.

presented as erect.[63] The timing of this coin is significant. In 41 CE Livia finally achieved her goal of apotheosis when her grandson Claudius became emperor and declared her deification. On that occasion, Claudius reissued the common Tiberian and Augustus state coin which depicted the seated Livia in the guise of Ceres holding an ear of grain.[64] The inscription *DIVA AUGUSTA* [goddess Augusta] makes the explicit connection with her role as the new Demeter and her deification. It was thus fitting that Agrippa 1—who had been educated in Rome alongside Claudius—would commemorate Livia's deification far away on Palestinian soil.

Diva Augusta—Dupondius of Claudius—Rome: 42 CE,
© *The Trustees of the British Museum*

On the other hand, it is somewhat surprising that Philip was to employ the symbolism of three erect ears of grain on his Julia Sebaste coin of 30 CE—eleven years prior to Livia's apotheosis. Presumably Philip was part of a grassroots movement in support of Livia's deification—a movement at odds with the official position of the emperor and the Roman Senate. Yet there is no ambiguity concerning the coin of Philip. The ears of grain are presented more in the traditional pose of Ceres/Demeter, erect and held in an outstretched hand—a sign of vitality and health. The two legends ΙΟΥΛΙΑ ΣΕΒΑΣΤΕ [Julia Sebaste] and ΚΑΡΠΟΦΟΡΟΣ [karpophoros/fruit bearing] underscore the continued benevolence of the Livia figure.

The Demeter motif also made a natural connection with the establishment of a new city. Before grain was discovered, people wandered without boundaries. The settled farming society was thus the beginning of law, the beginning of civilization. Thus in commenting on Vergil's *Aenead* 4.58, Servius writes:

---

63. Meshorer (1982), plate 10, number 11.
64. BMCRE (1975), 224.

Ceres . . . is in charge of the founding of cities,
as Calvus teaches: "She taught the sacred laws."[65]

This idea led to the well-known custom of encircling the boundaries of a city with the furrow of a plow. What better way to demonstrate stability and prosperity—and to ensure Philip's continuation as ruler—than to found a city and to dedicate it to the empress mother.[66] By incorporating the motifs of Ceres/Demeter on the Julia Sebaste coin, Philip was also recalling the great virtues of the Augustan program—the recognition of motherhood, peace, and prosperity, the natural progression of the life cycle.

Livia and the dying grain saying of John

The role of Livia as priestess in the imperial cult helped to spread the Demeter myth throughout the empire, including first-century Palestine. There is now strong evidence that the depiction of stalks of grain on sculptures and on coins and the common epithet *karpophoros* were commonplace. Because of the coincidence of the respected Livia's death in 29 CE less than a year before the death of Jesus of Nazareth (April 7, 30 CE), one must take seriously this phenomenon as background for the dying grain saying in John 12:24. The mention of "Greeks" wishing to see Jesus and the intermediary role of two Bethsaida disciples seem to be clues that should not be discounted too quickly.

With the death of Livia, a new dimension was added to the dying grain myth. Livia was now taking the role of the daughter figure Kore—as was not unusual in the telling of the ancient myth. No longer was rebirth considered automatic and immutable. The seed of grain had fallen into the earth and died. Just as the followers of Jesus looked in hope for his resurrection, so the adherents of the cult of Livia looked forward to her deification—a process that was not complete until the rule of Claudius in 41 CE. Although she had frequently been identified with Ceres while alive, Livia's death by no means led to an automatic rebirth. Yet it was a grass roots movement in the provinces which led to her exaltation. Her death led to the bearing of much fruit.

---

65. Spaeth (1996) 98.

66. The decision was perhaps a response to Livia's recovery from serious illness in 22 CE. Tacitus *Annals* 3.68. Upon Livia's recovery, Tiberius responded in 22 C.E. by issuing a series of coins in her honor including the *Salus* dupondius which expressed appreciation at Livia's health as well as the well being of the entire empire. BMCRE (1975) 1.131, nos. 81-4; Giorgio Giacosa, *Women of the Caesars: Their Lives and Portraits on Coins,* trans. R. Ross Holloway (New York: Arte e Moneta Publishers, 1983).

Chapter 18

The Destruction of Bethsaida

The question of the destruction of Bethsaida has been one that has led to many long discussions and formal papers and articles for members of the Bethsaida Excavations Project. It provides a good example of the way the scholarly enterprise works. Hypotheses are proposed, debated, and criticized while new hypotheses emerge. The difficulty on this particular question is related in part to the fact that over many centuries of time settlements go through periods of expansion and contraction, and, in many cases, periods of settlement, destruction, and resettlement with the cycle sometimes repeated again and again. Because of its location on a geological fault line Bethsaida finds itself in an especially precarious position for earthquakes, landslides, and shifting formations. At the same time, wars, invasions, changes in government, and economic factors also contribute to changes in a community. In the case of Bethsaida, war brought a dramatic end to the iron-age settlement with the surrounding land depopulated for several centuries. With perhaps a small settlement in the late Persian period, Bethsaida clearly developed into a substantial community throughout the Hellenistic era because of its position at the north end of the Sea of Galilee. At some point, Bethsaida's access to the lake was blocked along with its livelihood in fishing and transportation across the sea. This led to a dramatic end of the city—the primary question for this chapter.

Early discussions: Jewish Revolt 67 CE

When Bargil Pixner first surveyed the site in the 1980s and found Roman era pottery near the surface, the question of Bethsaida's destruction soon came to mind. At many surrounding towns—especially those related to early Christianity like Capernaum and Chorazin, remains from Byzantine era occupation often dominated the site. Yet when the courtyard house, later dubbed the Fisherman's House, immediately yielded Roman cooking pots, Herodian oil lamps, a coin of Philip, and a Roman toga pin, one could only think of the Q saying of woe that prophesied destruction for Bethsaida. What happened to Bethsaida? The nearby town of Gamla offered an intriguing model of what might have happened. During the Jewish revolt of 67 CE that community had been totally annihilated so that it was lost—except for the written reports of Josephus—until rediscovered by archaeologists in the 1970s.

Josephus, in fact, reports on a battle which took place near Bethsaida when Agrippa 2 sent troops to cut off the supply network between Galilee and Gamla (Josephus, *Life* 398-406).[1] The troops under the command of Sulla were thus stationed about a half a mile to the north of Bethsaida-Julias. The Galilean forces then arrived to do battle with two thousand men under the command of Jeremiah and three thousand men under the command of Josephus himself—supporting the basic veracity of this report. His description perfectly fits the topography with the battle taking place on the level ground between et-Tell and the Jordan River and troops hiding in a ravine to the west. Josephus describes the initial success of the Galilean troops until his own horse stumbled in the soft marshes so that he broke his wrist and had to be removed to Capernaum. From that point on, Josephus' demoralized troops were no match for Sulla and the battle ended.

As excavations proceeded during the late 1980s and early 1990s, it soon became obvious that there was no evidence at the top of et-Tell typical of battles: no first-century arrowheads, balustrades, or burn layers. The city itself had apparently been by-passed. Josephus, in fact nowhere suggests that the city itself was attacked and implies that the purpose for the battle was to open up the supply routes to Gamla, not to control the city itself.[2] Quite possibly the city had been deserted for the course of the war with those sympathetic to the revolt having already sought refuge at Gamla—and dying there—and those sympathetic to Rome having fled to Tiberias. Later survivors would have returned so that by 77 CE Pliny reported Julias to be a "lovely" city on the Sea of Galilee.

---

1. John T. Greene, "Bethsaida-Julias in Roman and Jewish Military Strategies, 66-73 CE," in *Bethsaida* (1995), 203-27.

2. Josephus had not even mentioned this battle in *Jewish War*. In the case of two other fortified cities of the Golan, Seleucia and Sogane surrendered without a fight (Josephus, *War* 2.574; 4.4).

Early coin evidence

When the 1994 excavation season produced four early Trajan coins (98-117 CE) in Area B, a whole new perspective emerged. Previously, only a handful of Roman era coins (second century CE and later) had appeared in Area A—and none in the residential sections of Areas B and C. So I proposed destruction by the 115 CE earthquake that had affected the entire eastern Mediterranean from Antioch to the Dead Sea.[3] It was not coincidental that geologists were engaged in field work during 1994 and 1995 that made us all aware of the subterranean forces that lay beneath et-Tell.

Dio Cassius' detailed report of the city of Antioch—where Trajan was visiting in 115 CE—presents a vivid picture of what might befall Bethsaida:

> While the emperor was tarrying in Antioch a terrible earthquake occurred; Many cities suffered injury, but Antioch was the most unfortunate of all. Since Trajan was passing the winter there and many soldiers and many civilians had flocked thither from all sides . . . there was no nation or people that went unscathed; and thus in Antioch the whole world under Roman sway suffered disaster. There had been many thunderstorms and portentous winds, but no one would ever have expected so many evils to result from them. First there came, on a sudden, a great bellowing roar, and this was followed by a tremendous quaking. The whole earth was upheaved, and buildings leaped into the air; some were carried aloft only to collapse and be broken in pieces, while others were tossed this way and that as if by the surge of the sea, and overturned, and the wreckage spread out over a great extent even of the open country. The crash of grinding and breaking timbers together with tiles and stones was most frightful. . . As for the people, many even who were outside the houses were hurt, being snatched up and tossed violently about and then dashed to the earth as if falling from a cliff; some were maimed and others were killed. Even trees in some cases leaped into the air, roots and all.[4]

The destructive nature of this earthquake is clear from reports of a tidal wave hitting Yavneh on the south coast and evidence of structural damage at sites as scattered as Caesarea, Jerash, Petra, Heshbon, Avdat, Khirbet Tannur, and Mampsis.[5] Coins from the era of Trajan (97-117 CE) were

---

3. Fred Strickert, "The Destruction of Bethsaida: The Evidence of 2 Esdras 1:11," in *Bethsaida* (1999), 347-72.

4. Dio Cassius, 68.24. 1-3.

5. Kenneth W. Russell. "The Earthquake Chronology of Palestine and Northwest Arabia from the 2nd through the Mid-8th Century AD," *Bulletin of the American Schools of Oriental Research* (1985), 37-60, especially 40-41.

found in destruction layers at Masada, Petra, and Avdat while coins of his successor are absent—the same pattern as had appeared thus far at Bethsaida. When considering the kind of calamity that might be the demise of Bethsaida's harbor, Dio Cassius' report about Antioch provided a perfect model:

> Even Mt. Casius itself was so shaken that its peaks seemed to lean over and broke off and to be falling upon the very city. Other hills also settled, and much water not previously in existence came to light, while many streams disappeared.[6]

This was a model that made sense for the evidence available in 1995. However, further excavation provided ample evidence that proved this theory wrong and pointed to several more centuries of occupation.

Coin patterns

Among the nearly five hundred et-Tell coins catalogued through the 2008 season of excavation the following pattern emerges. Bethsaida-Julias continued to flourish in the second and third centuries CE as is clear from 59 Roman era coins from this period. Then the numbers began dropping off:

Gold coin of Antonius Pius— 138 CE—discovered in 2010. Courtesy of Hanan Shafir, photographer, BEP.

- five coins in the fourth century CE
- one from the late fifth century CE
- four from the sixth century CE
- and none from the seventh century CE.

Since major earthquakes for this region have been registered over the past two millennia at a rate of about one per century, it is natural to look for other earthquakes that fit into this pattern—namely the earthquakes that occurred in 306 CE and 363 CE. We will return to these particular earthquakes shortly. However, a deeper examination of coin patterns is necessary to show that destruction evidence is a bit more complicated than may appear at first glance.

A chronological survey of coin finds for the whole of Bethsaida is not enough. The following chart presents a chronological listing of coins that is broken down by distribution according to the three major areas of et-Tell.

6. Dio Cassius, 68.25.6.

Chart: Coin Distribution at Bethsaida—1987-2008

Era	Area A	Area B	Area C	Survey
Persian- 5-4 C bce	2	2	7	
Ptolemy 3 C bce	31	6	12	3
Seleucid 2 C bce	31	41	33	5
Hasmonean 130-63 bce	19	8	5	1
Herodian 37 bce – 100 ce	18	6	0	2
Roman 2 C ce	26	4	0	
Roman 3 C ce	25	3	0	1
Roman 4 C ce	5	0	0	
Byzantine 5-6 C ce	4	0	1	

A quick glance at this chart shows how et-Tell had a modest beginning in the 4th century BCE and then grew to prominence in the Ptolemaic and Seleucid eras before declining somewhat in the Hasmonean and Herodian eras. The coin numbers are basically the same during the 2nd and 3rd centuries CE before dropping off drastically in the 4th through 6th centuries CE. The numbers are even more pronounced for the middle Roman period when focusing on Area A where most of these coins have been uncovered only recently in the section inside the city gate.

In contrast, Area B and C present a totally different picture. In Area C, no coins appear after the first century BCE until a coin of Justinian 2 (570 CE) shows up in a pit in the courtyard of the Winemaker's House. Pottery evidence appears to confirm this pattern. Something happened in the first century BCE that changed the occupation pattern of et-Tell. During the 2005 to 2007 seasons another courtyard house was excavated along the paved lane in the northern part of Area C (squares BC-25/26). The nine meter by four meter courtyard led to several rooms and, like the Winemaker's House, to a storage structure covered by flat basalt stones. Finds from the house included two Hasmonean coins and two Tyrian city coins, also a Hellenistic juglet, Eastern Sigilatta fine dinner ware, a complete spattered-wash-ware fish plate, and a complete Erotes lamp. The storage structure yielded seventeen jars and juglets. The most interesting part of the field reports is the notation that the inhabitants appear to have "left in a hurry."

The field reports also ventured to offer a possible explanation, the quick departure occurred "possibly as a result of the Hasmonean conquest." The pattern throughout the Galilee and southern Golan is that a major cultural change took place with the Hasmonean expansion. For several centuries towns like Bethsaida had been under the influence of Tyre and other Phoenician cities, and now they began shifting south under the growing impact of

Jerusalem. Likely this took place about 80 BCE when Alexander Jannaeus (103-76 BCE) ventured into the Golan, capturing the towns of Gamla and Seleucia (*Antiquities* 13. 395-7). So it is no surprise than eleven Alexander Jannaeus coins show up at Bethsaida. At the same time, there are also five coins of John Hyrcanus (130-104 BCE) who had never made it as far as Galilee or the Golan, and another eleven Bethsaida coins have been identified with the general category of "Hasmonean" (134-37 BCE).

Some have proposed that the transformation was a forced conversion. The residents of Bethsaida, for example, would have been given the choice of converting to Judaism or leaving. Josephus is quoted concerning Aristobulus 1 who ruled several decades earlier and for only a single year (104-103 BCE), "Aristobulus made war against Iturea, and added a great part of it to Judea, and compelled the inhabitants, if they would continue in that country, to be circumcised, and to live according to the Jewish laws" (*Antiquities* 13. 318). Yet Josephus' report has been widely criticized as reflecting his own ideas, partly from a similar report with Idumaea. Richard Horsley says, "It would be unrealistic to imagine that the extension of Hasmonean rule over Galilee resulted in a sudden or thorough conformation of social life in Galilee to 'the laws and customs of the Judeans.'"[7]

A more reasonable variation of this "decision to convert or leave" hypothesis is one that sees a gradual transformation. The flood of Hasmonean coins points to an economic transformation of the region. Alexander Jannaeus' program appears more concerned with the economic development of his expanding nation than with religious conformity. It may be that residents of Bethsaida who had been business agents with connections in Tyre voluntarily chose to leave. So the residential Area C, which clearly flourished in the 2nd century BCE was later abandoned. However, this scenario of exclusivity is not totally adequate. Thirty Hasmonean coins appear alongside twenty autonomous city coins during this period including several that have been dated to the years 76, 61, 54, and 41 BCE. Others are designated with a more general 1st century BCE date. Coin evidence is sometimes less than conclusive because of these general dates. At times even the specialists disagree. Bethsaida coins have been analyzed by two top Israeli numismatists. Arie Kindler identified five coins of Aristobulus 2 (67 to 63 BCE) later in the Hasmonean period, yet Don Ariel has placed these coins into a general category of "Hasmonean." If the former dating is accepted, this would argue against any drastic shift under Alexander Jannaeus.

---

7. Richard Horsley, *Galilee: History, Politics, People* (Valley Forge, PA: Trinity Press, 1995), 51.

There is another reason that casts doubt on the theory that the settlement change was the result of Hasmonean take over. The abandonment of Area C appears to have been total and final. If inhabitants left for religious or economic reasons, then why did these houses remain uninhabited? The abandoned houses were some of the largest and well constructed dwellings. Other families would have certainly moved in, especially under Philip when new residents were added to the community. Yet there is no evidence of later occupation. The northern part of the tell continued in ruins. Another possibility is that these houses were destroyed by one of the major earthquakes that frequented this area. A good candidate would be the 31 BCE earthquake that destroyed Qumran and affected many other communities.

Earthquake destruction in Winemaker's house

My earlier analysis of the Winemaker's House continues to support such an earthquake scenario: roofing stones were discovered collapsed in the southwest corner of the courtyard. A lintel was positioned on ground level just inside the north courtyard doorway. Several of the walls also had a twisted appearance. Along the south wall of the kitchen were found numerous shattered, but complete, cooking vessels stacked on top of each other suggesting the collapse of shelving. This evidence points to a violent type of destruction. The discovery of a Roman key on the kitchen floor near the broken cooking vessels suggests that the occupants had to flee suddenly, unable to lock up their house for a possible return. This is fitting of earthquake destruction. Only my dates were wrong—arguing for the 115 CE earthquake. This house did have one undisturbed section, the wine cellar on the east side, where the roofing stones remained in place—leaving a sealed locus. This cellar contained four complete jars and a Hellenistic cooking pot. While I had identified the four jars with Lapp type 11 jars (100 BCE- 70 CE),[8] Sandra Fortner has found a parallel with Capernaum "large sack jars with concave rims" that date to a range of several centuries up until the end of the first century BCE.[9] Similarly I previously dated the cooking pot to the first century CE, while Sandra Fortner's identification as a Kefar Hananya Type 3A casserole provides a date of 50 BCE to 100 CE.[10] My error had been in misidentification and in opting for a date on the late end of the spectrum. Following Fortner's identification, the only range of dates that fit all five items is the second half of the first century BCE. This analysis is consistent with the 31 BCE earthquake. This appears to be the case also for nearby houses. By the time of Philip, Area C was in ruins.

Coin analysis for Area B presents a slightly different picture. The coin numbers do drop off dramatically following the Seleucid era, yet there is some evidence for continuing occupation. The courtyard-style Fisherman's House, while yielding nearly a dozen Seleucid era coins, continues with five Hasmonean coins, and then a coin of Philip from 29 CE. After that there are no more coins. Unlike Area C, however, a new two-room house appears along the old iron-age city wall with an Agrippa 1 coin (41 CE); two Agrippa 2 coins (53 CE and 84 CE), two Trajan coins (109 CE and 98-117 CE) and an Antonius Pius coin (138-161 CE). Another Trajan coin (99 CE) was found to the south of the house. Over three thousand pottery shards were uncovered including Kefar Hananya and Kefar Shikin ware from the second through fourth centuries CE. These two buildings stand in sharp contrast to the larger courtyard houses. It would seem that the two-room house began its period of occupation at about the same time that the large courtyard house was going out of use. If the Fisherman's House had also been affected by the 31 BCE earthquake, then why had there been no attempt to rebuild?

There are two possible answers to the question of a failure to rebuild in Areas B and C. The first is that many inhabitants of Bethsaida left for

---

8. Paul W. Lapp, *Palestinian Ceramic Chronology: 200 B.C.–A.D. 70* (New Haven: 1961), 149-52.

9. Sandra A. Fortner, *Die Keramik und Kleinhundevon Bethsaida-Iulias am See Gennesaret, Israel* (München: Ludwig-Maximilians Universität, 2008), 85-86, catalogue # 1075, 1088, 1103, 1104.

10. Sandra A. Fortner, (2008) catalogue # 443.

other locations. Interestingly, Josephus reports about a program by Herod of incentives of tax-relief for people to settle in Batanea and Trachonitis to the east. The current evidence for et-Tell suggests that Bethsaida may have shrunk to a rather low population when Philip began to rule. The second possible answer is that residents of Bethsaida moved to other sections of the tell. However, until other sections are excavated, this remains in the realm of speculation. The coin distribution pattern, however, does suggest that we look to the south. The high numbers of Roman era coins in Area A would suggest that the Roman city followed the southern slopes down the hill toward the lake. It is significant that evidence for a rebuilding of the city wall in the Roman era—quite possibly by Philip—occurs only from the eastern gate heading south. There is some legitimacy in critiques that have questioned the relatively small amount of evidence that Philip had added residents to the village. Yet there is no reason to question the identification of et-Tell with Bethsaida. Because of the strong Roman coin evidence in Area A it is clear that there was a resurgence of the city and that it continued to flourish during the first three centuries CE.

Geological evidence

At the foot of et-Tell on the southwest there is located a fresh water spring that likely served the community during its occupation two thousand years ago. The spring has been artificially dammed up resulting in a pool that is likely not indicative of its former appearance. However, the water does form a channel which flows into the Jordan River and thus into the lake, perhaps providing boat access from ancient times. Soil samples yield a fine clay to a depth of 1.5 meters and silty sand at two meters depth.[11]

Nearby there stands an impressive wall made up of large boulders that has yet to be excavated. The appearance suggests that this may have been a docking facility for boats coming to Bethsaida. There is a major problem, however. The elevation at the top of the wall is 204 meters below sea level, significantly higher than the remains of other harbors around the lake—Capernaum at 209.25 below sea level and Tiberias at 208.3 meters below sea level.[12] Upon initial examination, the theory of this structure as a Bethsaida harbor does not make sense. Yet when geologists dug a backhoe trench some twenty-five

---

11. John F. Shroder Jr. and Moshe Inbar, "Geologic and Geographic Background to the Bethsaida Excavations," in *Bethsaida* (1995), 65-98, especially 85.

12. Mendel Nun, *The Sea of Galilee: Water Levels, Past and Present* (Kibbutz Ein Gev, Israel: HaKibbutz Ein Gev, 1991).

meters south, they found similar fine clay sediment to a depth of 1.5 meters with bones and shells that are typical of soil samples found below lagoons, swamps, and estuaries. This was covered over by a 50 to 70 centimeter layer of fluvial gravel that would have been deposited by rushing flood waters from the Jordan River. Again the top of the black soil is measured at about five meters higher than the level of the Sea of Galilee. The difference in elevations cannot be explained by a higher sea level since this would have placed towns like Capernaum and Kursi under water—an argument that continues to be repeated by a number of critiques. However, this is counter to the geological reports. The only possible explanation is that a dramatic uplifting of land has resulted from the unstable subterranean seismic activity.

A study by another team of geologists has documented this sort of activity at a location about ten kilometers north of et-Tell. The Ateret Crusader Castle was built in 1178 CE a short distance south of the Benot Ya'akov Bridge. An uplifting of 2.1 meters has altered the castle's water system dramatically.[13] While some of the change has been attributed to a gradual upward creep, the geologists concluded that the 1202 CE earthquake was responsible for such a dramatic shift. The Bethsaida team of geologists has concluded that similar seismic activity—occurring centuries earlier—brought about the change in elevation of the wall at the base of et-Tell.[14]

These changes at et-Tell were even more earth-shattering because of the tri-partite geological conditions:

- continuous gradual shifting to the north of the eastern plate;
- periodic flooding and silting from the Jordan and Meshoshim Rivers;
- and the uplifting of land masses.

This combination of circumstances has led to several extraordinary events that have totally changed the course of Bethsaida's history. Field work in 1995 focused on two major landslides that occurred on the western side of the Jordan River gorge—Tuba 1 located seven kilometers north and Tuba 2

13. R. Ellenblum, S, Marco, A. Agnon, T. Rockwell, and A. Boas, "Crusader Castle Torn Apart by Earthquake at Dawn, 20 May, 1202," *Geology* 26 (1998), 303-6.

14. John F. Shroder Jr,. M. P. Bishop, K. J. Cornwell, and Moshe Inbar, "Catastrophic Geomorphic Processes and Bethsaida Archaeology, Israel," in *Bethsaida,* (1999), 2:115-74. Recent studies independent of the Bethsaida Excavations Project provide further support to the proposals of Shroder and his team of geologists, S. Marco, A. Heimann, A. Agnon, T. Rockwell, and U. Frieslander, *Paleoseismicity of the Jordan Fault, the Beteiha Valley.* Geological Survey of Israel, Report-ES/ 55/ 97 (Jerusalem: Geological Survey of Israel, 1997).

located six kilometers north. In both cases a similar pattern of events took place. Extensive rains and earthquakes caused these landslides which extended across the gorge to dam up the Jordan River. The Tuba 1 landslide is estimated to have occurred over eight thousand years ago and helped shape the peninsula that once was et-Tell. It is the smaller Tuba 2 landslide that affected the end of occupation at et-Tell. The size of the land mass of Tuba 2 is almost beyond comprehension—50 meters high, 200 meters wide, and 25 meters thick. The water buildup over several days led to increased pressure that eventually broke through the dam at a rate estimated at between 15,000 and 30,000 cubic meters per second. With such a great force massive debris was carried down river. Huge boulders now positioned 40 meters above the present river level confirm the force of the water breaking through the landslide.[15] On the basis of probes taken in the Beteiha plain, it has been confirmed that such debris from the landslides filled in the area at the mouth of the Jordan. Here gravel deposited from moving water now covers silt deposited from earlier quiet waters, all of which began a process that presently leaves et-Tell two and a half kilometers from the lake's edge. The current shoreline is partially the result from continuous silting typical of all river systems. However, a more dramatic seismic event that included the uplifting of land masses and the landslide of Tuba 2 with its subsequent rush of flood waters resulted in the end of access to the Sea of Galilee. The Bethsaida harbor became inoperable and a significant portion of Bethsaida's livelihood came to an end. Carbon 14 dating of the Tuba 2 landslide suggests a date between 1,600 and 1,900 years ago.

Earthquake History

With major earthquakes documented at a rate of one per century, one can easily compare listings of recorded earthquakes with coin charts and other patterns of ceramic frequency. According to a recently published catalogue of earthquakes in Israel, major earthquakes are listed in 31 BCE, 115 CE, 306 CE, and 363 CE, as well as others in following centuries.[16] Because of Bethsaida's position on this major fault line, one would expect that Bethsaida's

---

15. John F. Shroder Jr,. M. P. Bishop, K. J. Cornwell, and Moshe Inbar, "Catastrophic Geomorphic Processes and Bethsaida Archaeology, Israel," in *Bethsaida,* (1999), 2:115-74.

16. D.H.K. Amiran, E. Arieh, T. Turcotte, "Earthquakes in Israel and Adjacent Areas: Macroseismic Observations since 100 BCE," *Israel Exploration Journal* 44:3-4 (1994), 260-305. Kenneth W. Russell, "The Earthquake Chronology of Palestine and Northwest Arabia from the 2nd through the Mid-8th Century A.D.," *Bulletin of the American Schools of Oriental Research* (1985), 37-60.

demise was the result of at least one, or, more likely, the cumulative affect of several of earthquakes in antiquity. The destruction evidence in the residential Area C suggests that Bethsaida was affected by the 31 BCE earthquake. From present excavation records, less is known about possible effects of the 115 CE earthquake on this community. From the pottery record and from the sharp decrease in coins after the third century CE, the 306 CE, and 363 CE earthquakes are the likely candidates for the Tuba 1 landslide and flooding and for the destruction of Bethsaida's harbor. The major earthquake in 363 CE is well documented, with the destruction of 21 urban centers and the temple restoration project initiated by Julian in 361 CE.

Literary evidence about destruction

The earthquake of 363 CE is documented in *Harvard Syriac* 99, a Syriac manuscript, that describes the destruction taking place "at the third hour, and partly at the ninth hour of the night" on May 19 in 363 CE. The tremors were so wide spread that 21 urban centers, including Paneas, Tiberias, and Sepphoris, suffered damage and brought to an end the Jerusalem temple restoration project initiated by the Emperor Julian in 361 CE.[17] Bethsaida, however, is not specifically mentioned.[18]

In the Palestinian Talmud (5th century CE) there is a section that mentions the abundance of fish that were known to have been caught near Tzaidan (the Rabbinic name for Bethsaida) where the Jordan River empties into the lake. As Richard Freund has noted, this is a section that shows evidence of the gathering of traditions about fishing over a long period of time.[19] The final section, however, reads:

> [It is written in Ezek. 47:8] ". . . and its waters will be healed. . ." [and it is also written in Ezek. 47:11] "But its swamps and marshes will not be healed; they are to be left for salt." It is written, "And its waters will be healed," and yet you have said, "And they will not be healed?" There is a place which is called, "And they will not be healed."[20]

17. S. P. Brock, "A letter Attributed to Cyril of Jerusalem on the Building of the Temple," *Bulletin of the School of Oriental and African Studies* 40 (1977), 274-80.

18. Z. Yeivin in discussing the earthquake destruction of Chorazin mistakenly cites Eusebius' Onomastican as a source although Eusebius wrote this document in 294 CE. Z. Yeivin, "Ancient Chorazin Comes Back to Life," *BAR,* 13 (1987), 322-36.

19. Richard A. Freund, "The Search for Bethsaida in Rabbinic Literature," in *Bethsaida* (1995), 267-311, especially 286-9.

20. PT *Sheqalim* 6.2, 50a.

It would seem that this reference to Tzaidan has been added in the final redaction in the fifth century CE at a time when Bethsaida no longer was a fishing village and when the land below the tell contained only swamps and marshes.

2 Esdras 1:11 and the destruction of Bethsaida

There is one final piece of literary evidence that specifically confirms Bethsaida's destruction by earthquake.[21] In the apocryphal work 2 Esdras the fate of Bethsaida is compared to that of the cities Tyre and Sidon:

> Did I not destroy Bethsaida because of you
> and to the south burn two cities, Tyre and Sidon, with fire,
> and kill those who hated you? (2 Esdras 1:11)

While the author speaks of the burning of Tyre and Sidon, corresponding to historical fact, the Latin verb *everto* is used to describe the end of Bethsaida.[22] One might expect the verb *perdo* in speaking about destruction by war. However, the verb is *everto* which commonly refers to a natural, violent agitation of the sea or the uprooting of trees or even the ploughing up of land. What then is the significance of this reference to Bethsaida's destruction? When was it written? What does it mean?

The book 2 Esdras

2 Esdras is part of the pseudepigrapha which means that it is connected with a famous Biblical figure—in this case the scribe Ezra who helped rally the returning exiles in the fifth century BCE around the law. 2 Esdras is actually a composite work for which the core is a Jewish apocalyptic work concerned with the significance of the destruction of Jerusalem by the Romans in 70 CE. For this reason it is sometimes included in the Old Testament apocrypha although it was for the most part written at the close of the New Testament era perhaps slightly before 100 CE. This dating fits the author's own remarks setting Ezra's speech to "the thirtieth year after the destruction of the city" (2 Esdras 3:1). This work survives in one form under the title "Fourth Ezra" and contains 2 Esdras chapters 3-14.

---

21. Fred Strickert, "The Destruction of Bethsaida: The Evidence of 2 Esdras 1:11," in *Bethsaida:* (1997), 2:249-74.

22. *Nonne propter vos Bethsaidam civitatem everti, et ad meridianum duas civitates, Tyrum et Sydonem, igne cremavi, et eos qui adversum vos fuerunt male interfeci?*

Fourth Ezra, however, was not included in the Septuagint—the Greek translation of the Old Testament—and its place in the apocrypha came about because of Christian additions appended at the beginning and end of the document so that the present 2 Esdras is structured as follows:

> 5th Ezra = 2 Esdras 1-2
> 4th Ezra = 2 Esdras 3-14
> 6th Ezra = 2 Esdras 15-16

Although this document was included in many manuscripts of the Vulgate of the Middle Ages, it was not accepted as either Canonical or Deutero-canonical by the Council of Trent in 1563. The Clementine revision of the Vulgate in 1592 incorporated Deuterocanonical works within the Old Testament, but placed 1-2 Esdras along with the Prayer of Manasseh as a supplement following the New Testament. Therefore, 2 Esdras often occurs in the apocrypha of Protestant Bibles, although it is not usually included in either the Orthodox or Roman Catholic Bibles.

The Christian edition known as 2 Esdras 1-2 or Fifth Ezra was probably written between the middle of the second century to the early third century.[23] Just as 2 Esdras 3-14 was written as a reflection on the significance of the destruction of the temple in 70 CE, so this later section seeks answers and comfort in the face of further developments during the Bar Kochba revolt in 132-135 CE. 2 Esdras 2:6 speaks of Jerusalem as destroyed and her people scattered. The revolt came about shortly after a visit to the area by the Emperor Hadrian around 129-131 CE. Two of his actions brought about the revolt. He attempted to rebuild Jerusalem as Aeolia Capitolina and to establish a pagan shrine on the site of the temple, and he issued an edict forbidding the practice of circumcision.[24] Like the Old Testament prophets (Isaiah 1:10-17; Amos 5:21-24; Jeremiah 7:1-15), the second century writer speaks out in the strongest terms against the temple:

> When you offer sacrifices to me, I will turn my eyes from you, for I did not command you to observe feast days, new moons, sabbaths and circumcisions (2 Esdras 1:31).

However, he goes beyond the concerns of these prophets and, like other Christian writers since Paul, condemns also the practice of circumcision.

---

23. Theodore A. Bergren, "A Note on 5 Ezra 1:11 and 2:8-9," *JBL* 128 (2009), 809–12.
24. Dio Cassius, 69. 12.1-2; *Vita Hadriani* 22.10.

Since Antonius Pius, who became emperor in 138 CE, lifted this ban, it is possible that 2 Esdras 1-2 was written around 135-140 CE.

According to Justin Martyr this second Jewish revolt was a time of persecution against Christians by those who recognized the messianic claims of Bar Kokhba.[25] Thus 2 Esdras 1-2 notes how his community has experienced hardship and persecution (2:23-32), yet they have endured through their confession of the Son of God (2:42-48). It shows evidence that the "separation of the church from Israel is felt so keenly in 5 Ezra that it may well have been a recent event."[26] Thus the metaphor of mother and sons occurs a number of times (2:10, 15, 17, 31) so that it is clear that Christian and Jews have shared the same mother (Jerusalem) and now a coming people inherit the privileges of Israel.

2 Esdras 1-2, therefore, opens with Ezra commissioned as a prophet to speak out against the misdeeds of the people in contrast to the gracious mighty acts of God. These deeds begin with the Exodus and include the deliverance through the sea, guidance through a pillar of fire, feeding of manna and quail, and providing water from a rock. In addition God shows his strong arm destroying "many kings because of them" and culminating in the destruction of Tyre, Sidon, and Bethsaida. According to this author, Israel's rejection of the Lord, however, leads to their own house becoming desolate. "I will hand over your houses to a people coming from far away, and those who have not known me will believe me" (1:35). Following this prophetic indictment of God's people, assurance of redemption is offered for the new people (2:10-48).

2 Esdras 1:11 and manuscript history

The use of 2 Esdras 1-2 as a source for reconstructing the history of the destruction of Bethsaida is complicated by the fact that there are two manuscript recensions for these two chapters. In the case of 2 Esdras 1:11, there is extensive variation between the two recensions as can be seen as follows:

> Recension # 1—I destroyed all nations before them, and scattered in the east the peoples of two provinces, Tyre and Sidon; I killed all their enemies.
>
> Recension # 2—Did I not destroy the city of Bethsaida because of you, and to the south burn two cities, Tyre and Sidon, with fire, and kill those who hated you?

---

25. Justin Martyr, *First Apology* 33.6.

26. G.N. Stanton, "5 Ezra and Matthean Christianity in the Second Century," *JTS* 28 (1977), 71.

As can be seen, only the second recension mentions the destruction of Beth-saida. This is significant since this reading cannot be accepted as very helpful if it is merely a medieval scribal addition.

The manuscript history of 2 Esdras 1-2 is quite complicated with nine Latin manuscripts surviving from the ninth to 13th centuries. The two earliest, which are often referred to as the French family of manuscripts, are reflected in the first recension and the rest, referred to as the Spanish family of manuscripts, are reflected in the second recension. Since the French text was used in the 1592 Clementine revision of the Vulgate, it has generally been used uncritically in modern translations. Only in the New Revised Standard Version is the Spanish text even reflected in a series of footnotes. Nevertheless there is a long history of scholarship which challenges the preference for the French text and which today is calling for a critical edition of 2 Esdras 1-2 which takes seriously the Spanish text. Although it is impossible to treat this complicated argument in detail here, the work of Theodore Bergren gives the most thorough analysis of these issues.[27]

It is becoming apparent that variations between the two recensions is not simply the matter of scribal error and a few intentional changes here and there.[28] Rather the changes originate at the time of translation from Greek to Latin. It perhaps can be said that the Spanish recension reflects a fairly literal translation while the French recension adapts the text for Western Christendom. As an example, 2 Esdras 1:38-40 includes a long list of Old Testament figures who will lead a return to Palestine from the east. While the Spanish recension lists in a haphazard order a number of prophets, apocalyptic figures, and twelve angels, the French recension includes only the twelve minor prophets in the exact order of the Septuagint. In other words, while the text originally spoke of a return to the land from Mesopotamia, the medieval translator has shifted the meaning to speak of the movement of Christianity from Palestine to Europe.

A similar thing has happened in 2 Esdras 1:11. The French recension offers the perspective of a European writer who understands Tyre and Sidon as "provinces" located "in the east." The Spanish recension correctly understands Tyre and Sidon as "cities" and, writing from a Syrian perspective, speaks of them "to the south." It is not difficult to understand how a medieval scribe would also have omitted reference to Bethsaida since its destruction

---

27. Theodore A. Bergren, *Fifth Ezra: the Text, Origin, and Early History.* Septuagint and Cognate Studies 25 (Atlanta: Scholars Press, 1990); Bergren, *JBL* (2009), 809.

28. Robert A. Kraft, "Towards Assessing the Latin Text of '5 Ezra': the 'Christian' Connection," *Harvard Theological Review* 79 (1986), 158-69.

seems out of place in a book which fits more with the Old Testament. The opposite argument is less convincing that a medieval writer wanted to include Bethsaida because of familiarity with the woe saying of Jesus. Why then would they not have also mentioned Capernaum and Chorazin? The Spanish recension of 2 Esdras 1:11 is to be preferred. In other words, this reference to Bethsaida's destruction by earthquake was probably written shortly around the time of the event itself.

The significance of Bethsaida's destruction in 2 Esdras

Earthquakes are commonly mentioned in Apocalyptic Literature (Mark 13:8; 2 Apocalypse of Baruch 27:7) among the final cosmic signs. In the earlier-written portion of 2 Esdras, such earthquakes will precede the great return of God's people to the land (2 Esdras 6:14; 9:3). Along with earthquakes, this writing looks forward to another mighty act of God which will alter the courses of rivers making possible such a return. This belief is built upon the ancient intervention of God to bring about safe passage such as the stopping of the Red Sea at the time of the Exodus and the stopping of the Jordan River at the time of Joshua. It also includes a tradition that after King Shalmaneser of Assyria took the exiles "across the river" into another land (2 Esdras 13:40), the people resolved to keep the laws of God and therefore chose to travel even further to the north away from possible corruption and assimilation. Therefore, God performed a "sign" by stopping the channels of the Euphrates so that they could cross over to safety (2 Esdras 13:41-45). The descendants of these exiles remained faithful until the last times when God would bring about a new Exodus from the north.[29] How would this take place?

> The Most High will stop the channels of the river again, so that they may be able to cross over (2 Esdras 13:47).

Just as in the first Exodus God dried up the Red Sea and the Jordan River, so God would bring about a latter day return by diverting the waters again.

The later writer of 2 Esdras 1:11 was very much aware of the traditions in 2 Esdras 13. The destruction of Bethsaida, along with landslides which blocked the Jordan, was understood then as that final sign. It is important to note that this reference to Bethsaida comes at the end of a brief summary of defeats brought about by the hand of God (verses 4-11). Then the author

---

29. Theodore A. Bergren, "The 'People Coming from the East' in 5 Ezra 1:38," *JBL*, 108 (1989), 675-83.

continues describing in detail the various mighty acts throughout the Exodus period (verses 12-23). Most significantly, the reference to Bethsaida's destruction in verse 11 is followed directly (in the Spanish recension there is no verse 12) by a report of the passage through the sea:

> Didn't I lead you across the sea, and make walls on the right and the left? I gave you Moses and Aaron as leaders. I gave you light in a pillar of fire. These are my great wonders that I have done for you, but you have forgotten me, says the Lord (vs. 13-14).

The expression "on account of you" in verse 11 and "for you" in verse 14 link the Exodus and destruction of Bethsaida together as great wonders of God.

2 Esdras 1-2 and Matthew

The reference to the mighty acts of God in 2 Esdras 1-2 is reminiscent of the words of Jesus speaking woe to Bethsaida and other cities because they did not respond to the deeds that Jesus worked in those communities. The parallel is even more closely drawn because the Bethsaida miracles portray Jesus as the new Moses who crosses the sea (walks on water) and feeds the multitude in the wilderness with bread from heaven in a new Passover meal.

It is clear that 2 Esdras is dependent upon the Matthean version of the Q saying (Mt 11:20-24). In verse 11, only three of the six cities are mentioned, Bethsaida, Tyre, and Sidon. However, in 2 Esdras 2:9 the description of Sodom and Gomorrah "whose land descends to hell" reflects knowledge of the Matthean version since this description was connected with the woe against Capernaum and only indirectly with Gomorrah. The connection is not made in the Lukan version which is likely closer to Q. However, 2 Esdras 2:9 replaces the word of woe against Capernaum with a condemnation of Assur (Syria), the context in which 2 Esdras was writing. For 2 Esdras 1-2, the condemnation of Syria and the destruction of Tyre and Sidon to the south prepare for the community to return to the land by way of Bethsaida.

G.N. Stanton has demonstrated a very close connection between the writer of 2 Esdras 1-2 and the Gospel of Matthew, even to such a degree that the second century writer shows no knowledge of other New Testament works.[30] Of special concern to 2 Esdras 1-2 is the section of Matthew 21-25 where the focus is on the kingdom of God "taken away from you and given to a people that produces the fruits of the Kingdom" (Mt 21:43). The events of the Bar Kochba revolt therefore have been interpreted in terms of the

---

30. Stanton, 67-83.

"people to come" (2 Esdras 1:35, 38) who will take the place of Jacob and Judah (1:24) and inherit the "kingdom of Jerusalem" (2:10). Knowledge of the long series of earthquakes and landslides along the Jordan Valley fault line—and especially those that had affected Bethsaida—would have shaped the thinking of the 2 Esdras 1-2 writer.

The abandonment of Bethsaida

It is not uncommon for cities destroyed by earthquake or war to be rebuilt and reinhabited. However, this pattern does not follow for fourth-century Bethsaida. After three thousand years of occupation, with stages of building and rebuilding, et-Tell was abandoned because the geographical and geological changes rendered it no longer economically feasible. Bethsaida's history had been connected to its access to the sea as a center for the fishing industry and as a stopping off point for travelers heading north and south. With its harbor destroyed, both means of livelihood had come to an end and et-Tell was abandoned.

Such theories of the abandonment of the Tell should not automatically lead to the assumption that all activity in the area around Bethsaida came to an abrupt end. It is reasonable to assume that some inhabitants moved to other fishing villages—especially where the shoreline moved south—while others decided to rebuild at another location. General surveys of the region have noted evidence of a dozen Jewish communities within five miles of Bethsaida.[31] Especially significant is the small community at Khirbet ed-Dikke in the general vicinity where an east-west road crossed the Jordan within several kilometers to the north. The presence of a synagogue there, excavated in 1905-7, suggests the need for further exploration.[32] Some of the references to Tzaidan in Rabbinic literature may apply to this wider area of communities. Especially interesting is the passage datable to the time of Rabbi Judah ha-Nasi which speaks of a debate about work and the Sabbath. At the end it is stated that "the incident took place on the highway of Tzaidan and it was completely inhabited by Israel."[33] The reference to the highway of Tzaidan seems more fitting to this location slightly to the north.

---

31. Dan Urman, "Jews in the Golan," in *Ancient Synagogues: Historical Analysis and Archaeological Discovery, vol. 2,* edited by Urman and Paul V.M.Flesher (Leiden: E.J. Brill, 1995), 382.

32. Heinrich Kohl and Carl Watzinger, *Antike Synagoguen in Galilaea* (Leipzig: J.C.Hinrichs, 1916), 112-24.

33. PT *Abodah Zarah* 5:5, 44d.

Bethsaida and pilgrims

While some in the Jewish community may have relocated to the north, others built villages closer to the sea, perhaps wanting to preserve the memory of Bethsaida as a fishing village. Today the remains of villages el-Araj[34] and Mesadiyeh are located on the Beteiha plain close to the water's edge. With the coming of pilgrims, such fishing villages would have offered a confusing picture, and the site of et-Tell receded in importance.

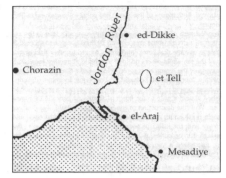

Later sites near Bethsaida

Et-Tell after the earthquake

The sharp decrease in coins after the 3rd century provides a strong reason to accept the 363 CE earthquake date for the city's end. Still a handful of coins remain during the following centuries. Quite possibly a few individuals continued to live there. With the beginning of the age of pilgrimage, others may have come to see the biblical sites. Some intrigued by the Q woe saying may have wanted to experience the ruins as prophesied. Others may have wanted to come close to former homes of apostles. Such is the case in 725 CE for Willibald, later the first bishop of Eichstätt in Bavaria

> From there [Capernaum], they went to Bethsaida, the city of Peter and Andrew; there is now a church there in the place where originally their house stood.[35]

References like this leave more questions than answers. Was there in fact a church built on this site? Or was Willibald confused with another location as Capernaum or Tabgha? However, four 8th century CE coins would argue that such a visit should not be disregarded out of hand.

Still others arrived as scavengers trying to salvage something from the once prosperous town. This included dressed stones and decorated architectural fragments that could be used in other building projects at sites like

---

34. Rami Arav, "Et-Tell and el-Araj," *IEJ* 38, 3 (1988), 187-8.

35. John Wilkinson, *Jerusalem Pilgrims Before the Crusades*, 128.

Pilgrim's jar

el-Araj. Thus it should not be surprising that a Justinian 2 coin from 570 CE appears in a large pit in the courtyard of the Winemaker's House in Area C.

Bethsaida in later years

One area that needs further study is the history of et-Tell during the Islamic era. After a period of five hundred years when coins finds are absent, a few coins do appear during the Crusader years. However, during the Mamluk era from the 13th through 15th centuries, no less than twenty Mamluk coins have been uncovered from all areas of the tell. Decorated pottery and glassware suggest an occupation during this era. The discovery of a Mamluk military drum probably means that et-Tell

Bedouin coins and jewelry

served as a military outpost.[36] Again there is a decline to only a single coin (Suleiman 1—1520 CE) during the first two hundred years of Ottoman rule.

Then the site (primarily in Area A) was utilized as cemetery for Bedouins from the lower Golan with eighty Ottoman coins turning up from the time of Mahmud 2 (1808-1839) through the rule of Abdul Hamid 2 prior to the beginning of World War 1. Several coins point to renewed interest from European explorers, especially during the 18th century, prior to the visit of Edward Robinson in 1838 CE.

From 1947 until 1967, et-Tell became a Syrian military base. The installation of concrete bunkers and communication trenches provide a modern destruction that encroached upon ancient buildings throughout the tell that once were Bethsaida.

36. Rami Arav, "A Mamluk Drum from Bethsaida," *IEJ* 43 (1993), 241–45.

Index of Ancient Sources

Index of Persons

Index of Places

(Map pages in italics)